Graf von Anderson's College German Grammar and Culture

Graf von Anderson's College German Grammar and Culture is a beginners' textbook (CEFR A1-B2, ACTFL novice low – intermediate low) for the German language for college students and for those engaged in self-study with popular software programs and apps.

In addition to illuminating profiles of key places and individuals who helped shape German history from Roman times to the present day, the textbook also includes important cultural briefings. Chapter by chapter the book delineates the scope of the German language, beginning with "ich", and moving on to subjects and verbs. Later chapters introduce cases, indirect and direct objects, prepositions, tenses, moods, and adjectives. Each chapter includes challenging exercises, and an answer key is provided. The rich cultural component in each chapter includes a travel guide, a historical snapshot, several musical selections, and a German text to read.

This book is a straightforward and thorough introduction to the basic structures of German grammar and provides an overview of selected highlights of German culture to engage and enthuse.

Christian Anderson is Assistant Professor of German at Cal Poly in San Luis Obispo, USA, where he coordinates the German program. Professor Anderson engages in a broad program of phenomenological research focused primarily on cultural production in German-speaking Europe.

Graf von Anderson's College German Grammar and Culture

Christian Anderson

Routledge
Taylor & Francis Group

LONDON AND NEW YORK

First published 2021
by Routledge
2 Park Square, Milton Park, Abingdon, Oxon OX14 4RN

and by Routledge
52 Vanderbilt Avenue, New York, NY 10017

Routledge is an imprint of the Taylor & Francis Group, an informa business

© 2021 Christian Anderson

British Library Cataloguing-in-Publication Data
A catalogue record for this book is available from the British Library

Library of Congress Cataloging-in-Publication Data
A catalog record for this book has been requested

ISBN: 978-0-367-54413-3 (hbk)
ISBN: 978-0-367-54411-9 (pbk)
ISBN: 978-1-003-08917-9 (ebk)

Typeset in Times New Roman
by Apex CoVantage, LLC

Meiner geliebten Mica, die sich sehr gut um mich kümmert und mich glücklich macht, ist dieses Buch gewidmet.

Weiterhin bedanke ich mich bei Gottfried, Louisa, und Andreas von Goßler, die mir in den letzten zwei Jahrzehnten mit Freundlichkeit manches von dem Wahren Schönen Guten gezeigt haben.

Contents

Introduction

There are many ways to learn the German language, and perhaps someday "the best one" will be discovered – it will undoubtedly involve cool lights and electronic dance music (EDM). If you are already using this method, then you will not need this book.

If, however, you are suffering through a college language class in which, perhaps unexpectedly, the very subject matter of the course – the language itself – is off limits for classroom discussion, then you might find this straightforward and thorough introduction to the basic structures of German grammar profoundly useful, and maybe even stimulating, like a good textbook for symbolic logic or game theory.

Graf von Anderson's College German also provides an essential overview of selected highlights of German culture, defined broadly and within the context of college and university humanities and liberal arts traditions. In addition to illuminating profiles of key places and of individuals who helped shape German history from Roman times to the present day, the book presents short guides to astonishing recordings of German classical music from Hildegard von Bingen to Karlheinz Stockhausen and shares a fantastic series of specially selected and pedagogically translated dual-language (German-English) textual excerpts from literary masterworks like *Faust* and *Also sprach Zarathustra*.

Read this book from cover to cover if you are an absolute beginner. Or, if you have already learned some German: *Starten Sie mit Kapitel Eins*. Of course, you could skip around, but you might miss something. By moving through this book slowly and methodically, you will learn basic German. You will also gain valuable insights into the sublime beauty of German grammar, which will help you improve your thinking and writing, both in German and in English.

The first chapter clearly delineates the boundaries of the domain that the German language covers, beginning with *ich* and moving into the several classes of *nicht ich* that constitute the "outside world". The second chapter showcases subjects and verbs. Later chapters introduce the dreaded cases (you will learn to recognize and enjoy direct and indirect objects), prepositions, tenses and moods, various clauses, and, finally, adjectives. Each chapter includes several challenging exercises, for which an answer key is provided. A three-page Executive Summary is found at the end of the book.

The exercises are intended to reinforce and expand the material in the various chapters. Sufficient time spent puzzling over the problems should be followed by a period of reflection on the solutions offered in the answer key. Students who carefully read each chapter, sometimes repeatedly, and then diligently work through the problem sets before comparing their answers with those in the key make the most of what this volume has to offer.

Vocabulary lists are not a feature of this book. The best way to expand vocabulary always has been and remains READING. Read something in German every day, and you will learn new words every day. Find a German band and listen to their music, or find some German friends and see what they have to say about the world. If they are really your friends, they will be patient as you try to tell them what you think – *auf Deutsch*. Older editions of American textbooks can be purchased for under ten dollars; you could buy one of those for extra exposure to vocabulary and for additional exercises, just be certain to ignore the grammar explanations. There is not another product in the English-speaking world that comes close to this book's exposition of German grammar.

The abundant cultural readings – each chapter includes a travel guide, an historical essay, musical selections, and a dual-language text – will help you refresh your mind and hopefully will inspire you to take your German studies to the next level. The photographs that punctuate the various chapters and sections of the book capture a series of moments in the autumn of 2007 in and around Berlin. Students in the past have attempted to recreate these images while visiting Berlin, capturing the flux of the great metropolis over the last dozen years.

Capturing the flux – that's the Graf von Anderson Advantage!
Vorwärts!

Christian Graf von Anderson, PhD
Assistant Professor of German
Cal Poly, San Luis Obispo

1   Basic structures of reality

ich / nicht ich

This chapter begins with the fundamental distinction between self and other developed by the German philosopher Johann Gottlieb Fichte in 1794.

This basic distinction, a sort of first principle, is made in the following manner:

> Point at yourself and say *ich*.
> Then, point at anything else and say *nicht ich*.

Remember that unlike the English "I", *ich* is not capitalized, unless it stands at the beginning of a sentence. *Nicht* means "not" – you should think of it like the negation sign in symbolic logic.

Point at yourself once again and say *ich*, and then point at the wall and say *nicht ich*. Then point at yourself again and say *ich*. Then point at the ceiling, the floor, and the window, saying *nicht ich* each time. For extra practice, you could wander around your dorm, neighborhood, or even New York City, pointing at yourself and saying *ich* and then pointing at objects and at other people while saying *nicht ich*.

Congratulations. You are essentially fluent.

ich / nicht ich 2.0

The next step is to name all of the *nicht ich* things – this is called "vocabulary" in English and *Wortschatz* (literally: word treasure) in German. Many students find the acquisition and expansion of *Wortschatz* difficult, as there are, indeed, many, many words to learn.

Let's begin with the rest of the basic pronouns. So far, we have learned that *ich* means "I". Now, let's learn the German words for we, you, he, she, it, and they, and then we can learn the nouns in the next section.

Moving beyond the simple *ich / nicht ich* dichotomy, we discover a world with SIX MAJOR CATEGORIES OF BEING, three singular and three plural.

	Singular	*Plural*
1st person	ich	wir
2nd person	du	ihr
3rd person	er, sie, es	sie

Compare these pronouns to English:

	Singular	Plural
1st person	I	we
2nd person	you	you
3rd person	he, she, it	they

Note that the second person has a singular form and a plural form. The pronoun *du* looks and sounds very much like "you", as in "Hey, you!" The pronoun *ihr* is the plural of *du*, and it rhymes with *wir*, which is the plural of *ich*. Perhaps you have heard someone say, "Hey, y'all!" or even "Hey, youse guys!" That's *ihr:* "you, plural".

Notice also that the third person singular has three genders: *er*, *sie*, and *es*. There is only one third person plural, *sie*.

Students often ask at this point, with a mixture of disbelief and anxiety, how *sie* can possibly mean "she" and also "they". You will simply have to have faith that it works.

Why? Because *Sie* also means "you". German, like many other languages, but unlike modern English, has a form of the second person used to maintain appropriate social distance with those with whom one is not on familiar terms. This formal *Sie* is always capitalized, and, like the English "you", it is used in the singular and plural.

Here's the complete table:

	Singular	Plural
1st person	I = ich	we = wir
2nd person	you = du or Sie	you = ihr or Sie
3rd person	he, she, it = er, sie, es	they = sie

Undoubtedly, you will need to re-read this section several times as you begin your German studies. Perhaps read the following explanations now, and then re-read from the beginning before moving on from the pronouns to the nouns.

The FIRST PERSON exists in German exactly as it exists in English.

Singular	Ich bin allein.	I am alone.
Plural	Wir sind allein.	We are alone.

The FAMILIAR SECOND PESON exists in a singular and a plural form, unlike standard English.

Singular	Du bist mein Freund.	You are my friend.
Plural	Ihr seid meine Freunde.	You are my friends.

If you are having trouble with *du* and *ihr*, think of it this way: Imagine your two best friends, and then point to them, one at a time, and each time say: *Du bist mein Freund.* I see good old Bob and I say: *Bob, du bist mein Freund!* And then I see dear old Fred. *Fred, du bist mein Freund!* Back to Bob: *Du bist mein Freund!* And then back to Fred again: *Du bist mein Freund.* Now point at them both simultaneously, maybe using two hands, or maybe moving your pointer finger rapidly from Fred to Bob and then back again: *Bob und Fred, ihr seid meine Freunde!*

You can and must use the FAMILIAR SECOND PERSON with your family, friends, and classmates. As a general rule, you should use *du* and *ihr* when speaking with other college students. In some workplaces, the members of a team or department will use *du* and *ihr* with each other, but will use the formal second person with colleagues from other departments and teams, and almost certainly with those from other firms.

The FORMAL SECOND PERSON is very much like standard English.

Singular	Sie sind ein Baron.	You are a baron.
Plural	Sie sind Barone.	You are barons.

The FORMAL SECOND PERSON is used with EVERYONE outside of family members, friends, fellow students, and in some cases, colleagues. The postman, the police officer, the supermarket cashier, your professors (unless they are trying to be young and hip), random panhandlers, and the neighbors should each be addressed with *Sie* until and unless other arrangements are made.

You will notice that the FORMAL SECOND PERSON is the same for singular and plural, just like the English "you". This second person *Sie* is always capitalized, regardless of its location in the sentence.

The THIRD PERSON exists in three singular forms, *er*, *sie*, and *es*, and one plural form, *sie*.

Singular	Er ist mein Bruder.	He is my brother.
	Sie ist meine Schwester.	She is my sister.
	Es ist mein Kind.	It is my child.
Plural	Sie sind meine Brüder.	They are my brothers.
	Sie sind meine Schwestern.	They are my sisters.
	Sie sind meine Kinder.	They are my children.

German pronouns exist in three genders: masculine *er*, feminine *sie*, and neuter *es*.

The plural pronoun *sie* is used for all third person plurals regardless of gender. This *sie* is only capitalized at the beginning of a sentence.

Naming the *nicht ich*s: nouns

Just like the pronouns, each German noun is assigned one of three genders and a plural form. To learn a German noun involves learning three parts: the word, its gender, and the plural form.

Here are three nouns to begin with:

der Mann, die Männer	the man, the men
die Frau, die Frauen	the woman, the women
das Kind, die Kinder	the child, the children

Notice that each noun has a definite article,[1] *der*, *die*, or *das*, that shows its gender, as well as a plural form. Each of the plurals uses the same definite article, *die*.

Let's take a closer look at the German word for "man".

der Mann

The German word for "man" is clearly *Mann*, and the gender of this noun is clearly masculine, as indicated by the definite article *der*, which means "the".

Singular	der Mann	the man
Plural	die Männer	the men

The pronoun used to replace and refer to *Mann* is *er*, which is probably unsurprising, since it strongly resembles the masculine definite article *der*.

Der Mann ist mein Vater.	The man is my father.
Er ist mein Vater.	He is my father.

The pronoun for *Männer* is *sie*, which is probably unsurprising, since it strongly resembles the plural definite article *die*.

Die Männer sind meine Brüder.	The men are my brothers.
Sie sind meine Brüder.	They are my brothers.

Note that ALL GERMAN NOUNS ARE CAPITALIZED. This makes it easy to find them in a sentence.

The German word for "woman" follows a pattern very much like that of *Mann*.

die Frau

The German word for "woman" is *Frau*, and the gender of this noun is feminine, as indicated by the definite article *die*, which means "the".

Singular	die Frau	the woman
Plural	die Frauen	the women

The pronoun for *Frau* is *sie*, which is probably unsurprising, since it strongly resembles the definite article *die*.

Die Frau ist meine Mutter.	The woman is my mother.
Sie ist meine Mutter.	She is my mother.

The pronoun for *Frauen* is *sie*, which is also unsurprising, since it strongly resembles the plural definite article *die*.

Die Frauen sind meine Schwestern.	The women are my sisters.
Sie sind meine Schwestern.	They are my sisters.

The German word for "child" follows a pattern just like *Mann* and *Frau*.

das Kind

The word for "child" is *Kind*, and the gender is neuter, as indicated by the definite article *das*, which means "the".

Singular	das Kind	the child
Plural	die Kinder	the children

The pronoun for *Kind* is *es*, which by now simply must be unsurprising, since it strongly resembles the definite article *das*. If you don't see this resemblance, try harder.

Das Kind ist mein Sohn.	The child is my son.
Es ist mein Sohn.	It is my son.

The pronoun for *Kinder* is *sie*, which is unsurprising, since it strongly resembles the plural definite article *die*.

Die Kinder sind meine Neffen.	The children are my nephews.
Sie sind meine Neffen.	They are my nephews.

Now, take a look at these exciting nouns:

der Körper, die Körper	the body, the bodies
die Seele, die Seelen	the soul, the souls
das Gehirn, die Gehirne	the brain, the brains

Obviously, the genders of German nouns are not always as intuitive as *der Mann, die Frau*, and *das Kind*. Grammatical gender is not the same as physical gender, and indeed, as time moves forward, human gender concepts increasingly are being called into question. For now, in order to learn and use the German language, you need to accept that nouns have genders. For example: tables are masculine; lamps are feminine; and windows are neuter.

der Tisch, die Tische	the table, the tables
die Lampe, die Lampen	the lamp, the lamps
das Fenster, die Fenster	the window, the windows

If this section has taught you anything, it should be this: in order to really know a German noun, you need to learn its gender and its plural form! The best place to find this information is in a reputable German dictionary. Graf von Anderson endorses the online dictionary created and maintained by students at the *Technische Universität München:* www.leo.org.

Here is one final chart that should make the relationship between the nouns and pronouns very clear.

der Tisch: er	die Tische: sie
die Lampe: sie	die Lampen: sie
das Fenster: es	die Fenster: sie

Perhaps the article/pronoun relationship could not be more clearly stated: *der/er, die/sie, das/es.*

Total clarity – that's the Graf von Anderson Advantage!

Übungen (exercises)

A   Walk around your home, campus, or city pointing at yourself while saying *ich* and pointing at surrounding objects while saying *nicht ich*.

B   Look up the following words and make a list with the definite article and the plural.

emperor, empress, king, queen, prince, princess, duke, duchess, count, countess, baron, baroness, knight, dragon, butterfly, unicorn, frog, mushroom, castle, tower, forest, witch, wizard, magic, cloud, thunder, lightning, mountain, valley, field, house, room, fire, fireplace, bed, wine, beer, pizza, delivery

C   Replace each noun in the sentences below with the appropriate pronoun.

Der Mann ist groß.	Die Seele ist unsterblich.	Der Körper ist stark.
Die Frau ist intelligent.	Die Seelen sind unsterblich.	Die Körper sind stark.
Das Kind ist klein.	Das Gehirn ist grau.	Die Tafel ist schwarz.
Die Männer sind nett.	Die Gehirne sind grau.	Das Fenster ist durchsichtig.
Die Frauen sind stark.	Der Tisch ist braun.	Die Tafeln sind weiß.
Die Kinder sind schön.	Die Tische sind braun.	Die Fenster sind schmutzig.

D   Circle each of the nouns in the modern German selection from Walther von der Vogelweide at the end of the chapter. Look these words up in the dictionary and make a list, including the article and the singular and plural forms for each one.

Travel: Amsterdam, Utrecht, Cologne, and Frankfurt

Learning German is a worthwhile activity for many reasons. Perhaps the greatest one of all is that the concept of linguistic and cultural immersion justifies extended periods of international travel. Who would say no to a summer, a semester, or even an academic year abroad? Who wouldn't like to work in the European Union or in Switzerland for a few years (or even longer) after graduation?

Amsterdam is an outstanding place to begin your journey. The ease of navigating to and from the Netherlands through Schiphol Airport makes the city an ideal starting point for a trip through western Europe. Amsterdam is also one of Europe's most beautiful, unique, and tolerant cities. The Rijksmuseum, the Concertgebouw, and Vondelpark are only three of the hundreds of attractions that draw nearly five million tourists to the city each year. In addition to the mind-expanding modern dance performances at the Muziektheater, Graf von Anderson enthusiastically endorses the wildly extensive breakfast buffet served daily in the Winter Garden at the Grand Hotel Krasnapolsky.

As you might be able to tell, Dutch and *Deutsch* are related languages with many common words and structures, but speaking German in the Netherlands is not polite – would you speak French in Italy? Just speak English, unless *je spreekt toevallig Nederlands*.

From Amsterdam, it is a short train ride to vibrant and historic Utrecht, although the temptation to explore the great Flemish cities of Ghent, Antwerp, and Bruges, or the European

Union capital city of Brussels, not to mention the less touristy, tri-national Liege-Aachen-Maastricht region, will be hard to resist. Save those trips for another time, perhaps in conjunction with visits to London, Paris, and Madrid. In Utrecht, be sure to visit the *Duitse Huis*, a complex of historic buildings dating back to 1348 that once belonged to the Teutonic Knights. If you are in luck, your visit will coincide with the Festival Oude Muziek or the Netherlands Film Festival.

Cologne, which is *Köln* in German, is easily accessible by train from Utrecht, following the course of the Rhine through Arnhem and Duisburg. Cologne is a remarkable city with one of the most impressive gothic cathedrals in the world, the *Kölner Dom*. Graf von Anderson highly recommends attending an organ concert in the cathedral, especially during the summer, when the coolness in the cathedral allows one to become absorbed in the stained-glass windows as one merges with the music. Visiting the *Römisch-Germanisches Museum*, an archaeological museum with a fascinating collection of artifacts from the Roman settlement of *Colonia Claudia Ara Agrippinensium*, out of which the modern city of Cologne emerged, is essential. Be sure to spend some time with the Dionysus mosaic before checking out the enormous *Reiterstatuen* on the ends of the nearby *Hohenzollernbrücke*. Cologne is famous for its vibrant student life – over 70,000 students live in the city! Graf von Anderson spent a memorable summer in Cologne, where he learned to grill various forms of meat and drank *Kölsch* in harmony with thousands of other students nearly every evening in the lovely parklands near the main university. If you are lucky enough to spend *Rosenmontag* in Cologne, just smile and shout *Kölle alaaf!* and you will certainly enjoy yourself.

The train ride to Frankfurt from Cologne is quite lovely, with many vineyards and a few ruined castles, as well as the beautiful cities of Bonn, Koblenz, and Mainz along the way. Frankfurt is famous for its New York City–like skyscrapers, called *Wolkenkratzer* (literally "cloud-scrapers"), which has earned it the nickname *Mainhattan*. Frankfurt is also sometimes called *Bankfurt* and even *Krankfurt*, since it is the home of the German financial industry. Deutsche Bank, Deutsche Börse (the German stock exchange), and hundreds of other companies are headquartered in Frankfurt. The *Historisches Museum Frankfurt* has a fascinating model of the city before it was destroyed during the Second World War, and the Städel Museum is a world-class gallery with important works from artists ranging from Botticelli to Max Beckmann. Graf von Anderson recommends walking from the *Römer* in the center of the old city to the *Alte Oper*, enjoying a stroll along the *Zeil*, one of the most interesting pedestrian shopping streets in all of Europe, as one heads toward the lovely *Opernplatz*. The *Wochenmarkt* on Wednesdays and Saturdays in the charming Bornheim neighborhood is also not to be missed. The nearby Taunus hills are accessible by S-Bahn, and the *Meisterturm* on the *Kapellenberg* just northwest of Hofheim is an excellent destination, combining a long, scenic hike with the possibility of fantastic food and drink at the rustic *Waldgaststätte Meisterturm*.

German history from ancient times to the middle ages

A healthy state of curiosity sometimes leads us to ponder the historical mist surrounding the ancient Germanic tribes, or to gaze with wonder at the sunlight-through-stained-glass reality that gave form to the medieval castles and cathedrals that punctuate the magical landscape of Europe and provide settings for the myths of the Grail, the Nibelungen, and Kaiser Barbarossa (1122–1190), who, according to legend, still slumbers in a cave in the Kyffhäuser hills. German history inspires us and activates our sense of wonder.

Julius Caesar wrote briefly about Germanic tribes in his account of the Gallic Wars in 53 BCE, as did the Roman historian Tacitus in the year 98 CE. The *wilde Germanen* described by Caesar and Tacitus delivered the Roman Empire one of its greatest defeats in the Battle of Teutoburg Forest in the year 9 CE. This battle marked the final Roman attempt to conquer the Germanic territories on the eastern side of the Rhine. In German, the battle is often referred to as the *Hermannsschlacht*, in honor of Arminius,[2] the leader of the anti-Roman forces. One result of this battle was the eventual construction of the *Limes Germanicus*, a series of fortifications separating the Roman Empire from the unconquered, pre-agricultural Germanic tribes and their lands. Portions of the Limes, which extended from the Rhine at the North Sea all the way to Regensburg on the Danube and beyond, have been excavated and reconstructed.[3] It is interesting to note that southern Germany, including much of modern-day Bavaria, was part of the Roman Empire, while most of northern Germany was not. The Roman ruins in Trier are certainly worth a visit, as is Rome itself.

The period during which barbarian invasions hastened the end of the Roman Empire and set the stage for the creation of the medieval world is called the *Völkerwanderung*, or Migration Period (roughly 375–600 CE). During this time, Germanic tribes invaded former Roman territories, while simultaneously the Huns invaded former Germanic territories from the east, eventually reaching Orleans, far west of the Rhine. The names of the ancient Germanic tribes live on in the modern place-names of Friesland, Bayern, and Sachsen, among others. Coinciding with the waning of the *Völkerwanderung*, Saint Boniface (675–754 CE), patron saint of Germany, brought Christianity to the pagan people of the Frankish kingdom, serving as bishop of Mainz and later of Utrecht. Boniface's disciple, Saint Sturm, founded the well-preserved Abbey at Fulda in 744 CE.

As conditions gradually stabilized, a new political order emerged, which eventually took the name Holy Roman Empire, or *Heiliges Römisches Reich der deutschen Nation*. The first *Kaiser* (emperor) was crowned in 800 CE in Rome. His court was based in the city of Aachen near the border with modern Belgium, and his name was *Karl der Große*, although he is better known in English-speaking countries by his French name, *Charlemagne*. The period between the coronation of Charlemagne and the conquest of Europe by Napoleon Bonaparte lasted just over a thousand years – this was the era of the First Reich.[4]

Germanic culture flourished in the period between 1190 and 1250, which saw the creation of the great epics of Middle High German literature – *Parzival*, the mystical story of the knights of the Grail; *Tristan*, the greatest love story ever told; and the *Nibelungenlied*, a complicated, bloody tale set in the Burgundian Kingdom at the time of the invasion of Attila the Hun. This period also corresponds to the lifetime of the Hohenstaufen[5] Kaiser Friedrich II, perhaps the most remarkable figure of the Middle Ages. Called *Stupor Mundi* (wonder of the world) by his contemporaries, Friedrich lived most of his life in Sicily, where he ruled an empire that – at least in name – extended from the North Sea to Jerusalem. Friedrich spoke six languages, supported the arts and sciences, and was a force for social justice in his time. Friedrich II also wrote the first scientific treatise on the art of falconry. You can visit his grave beneath the beautiful cathedral in Palermo.

It is important to remember that the Holy Roman Empire was more of a social network than anything resembling a modern nation-state. Although the Kaiser, alongside the Pope in Rome, sat at the top of the representational structure of power, everyday political power was broadly diffused, exercised locally by whichever *Graf* (count), *Freiherr* (baron), or *Ritter* (knight) rode forth from the closest castle, and by their overlords, the *Kurfürsten* (electoral princes), who assembled, usually in Frankfurt, to elect the Kaiser.

The Teutonic Knights, the Free Imperial Cities, and later the Hanseatic League were all similar, insofar as their vassalage extended directly to the Kaiser (or to the Pope, in the case of the Prince Bishoprics), without intermediate levels of control. The great cathedrals still stand in the leading cities of the time – Aachen, Münster, Cologne, Mainz, Worms, Speyer, Trier, Strasbourg, Freiburg, Regensburg, Magdeburg – providing mesmerizing windows into the past.

Text and translation: Walther von der Vogelweide

Mittelhochdeutsch (Middle High German), the language in which *Parzival*, *Tristan*, and the *Niebelungenlied* were written, is quite different from contemporary German. Take a look at the following short poem of joyful gratitude by Walther von der Vogelweide (1169–1230), the greatest of the medieval German poets. Can you see similarities between the three languages?

Ich hân mîn lêhen	Das Reichslehen	The Imperial Fiefdom
Ich hân mîn lêhen, al die werlt! ich hân mîn lêhen!	Ich habe ein Lehen, alle Welt, ich habe ein Lehen!	I have a fief, all the world, I have a fief!
nû enfürhte ich niht den hornunc an die zêhen	Nun fürchte ich nicht den Hornung an den Zehen,	Now I no longer fear February at my toes,
und wil alle bœse hêrren deste minre vlêhen.	und werde alle kargen Herren desto minder flehen.	and will beg all meager lords so much the less.
der edel künec, der milte künec hât mich berâten,	Der edle König, der milde König hat mich versorgt,	The noble king, the kind king has taken care of me,
daz ich den sumer luft und in dem winter hitze hân.	dass ich im Sommer Luft und im Winter Hitze habe.	that I have air in summer and heat in winter.
mîn' nâhgebûren dunke ich verre baz getân:	Meinen Nachbarn sehen mich jetzt	My neighbors see me now so much better:
sie sehent mich niht mêr an in butzen wîs', alsô sie tâten.	um so viel lieber an: sie sehen mich nicht mehr an, als wäre ich ein Buhmann, wie sie es früher taten.	They no longer see me as a whipping boy, like they once did.
ich bin ze lange arm gewesen ân' mînen danc.	Ich bin zu lange ohne mein Verschulden arm gewesen.	I've been poor for too long through no fault of my own.
ich was sô volle scheltens, daz mîn âtem stanc:	Ich war so voller Schelte, dass mein Atem stank.	I was so full of scolding that my breath stank.
daz hât der künec gemachet reine und dar zuo mînen sanc.	Den hat der König rein gemacht und dazu auch meinen Sang.	The king made that pure and my song along with it.

German music: medieval and Renaissance

The German musical tradition is rich and vast, and surely someday soon, creative ethnomusicologists, perhaps aided by supercomputers with strong artificial intelligence, will release simulations of the music of the German tribes at the time of the Romans and even earlier. For now, the German musical tradition begins with Hildegard von Bingen (1098–1179), a Benedictine abbess and mystical visionary, as well as the composer of several works of medieval music.

As was common at the time, these works were composed in Latin, rather than Middle High German. The sounds of Gregorian Chant transport the listener to a contemplative frame of mind that is seldom encountered in the modern world. The songs of Oswald von Wolkenstein (1376–1445) capture the spirit of the knightly, medieval world before its transformation into the modern world of states and capital. The music of French composer Josquin des Prez (1450–1521) is central to the Franco-Flemish School and rewards meditative listening.

Graf von Anderson endorses the following recordings:

Emma Kirkby, *A Feather on the Breath of God*
Sinfonye, *O noblissima viriditas: The Complete Hildegard von Bingen (3 volumes)*
Anonymous 4, *The Origin of Fire. Music and Visions of Hildegard von Bingen*
Sequentia, *Canticles of Ecstasy*
Emily Van Evera, *Vision: The Music of Hildegard von Bingen*
Philip Picket, *Knightly Passions: The Songs of Oswald von Wolkenstein*
Daniel Reuss, Capella Amsterdam, *Josquin des Prez: Miserere mei Deus. Sacred Motets*

The Emma Kirkby and Sinfonye recordings are amazing, and although the Emily van Evera album might have shocked the medieval mind with its electronic dance music interpretation, it is highly listenable. The songs of Oswald von Wolkenstein are fun to sing while walking briskly through the halls or rambling through the meadows and the woods.

Recommended films

Spartacus (Stanley Kubrick, 1960)
Kampf um Rom I and *Kampf um Rom II: Der Verrat* (Robert Siodmak, 1968 and 1969)
Die Nibelungen: Siegfried and *Die Nibelungen: Kriemhilds Rache* (Fritz Lang, 1924)
The Adventures of Robin Hood (Michael Curtiz and William Keighley, 1938)
Till Eulenspiegel (Rainer Simon, 1975)

Notes

1 Definite article = "the" as opposed to the indefinite article, "a". Much more on this topic will follow!
2 Arminius is the Latin form of Hermann. If you say the names in quick succession, you might hear the similarity.
3 Can be visited while hiking the beautiful wooded trails in the Taunus Hills, a short and inexpensive S-Bahn ride away from Frankfurt.
4 The Second Reich began in the 19th century under Kaiser Wilhelm and Bismarck. The dismal Third Reich lasted twelve years.
5 Hohenstaufen refers to his family name. Several hundred years later another Friedrich II captured the popular imagination, but this Friedrich II was not a Kaiser, but rather the *König von Preußen* (King of Prussia). He was the greatest of the Hohenzollern, *Friedrich der Große* (Frederick the Great).

2   Simple sentences

Subjects and verbs

If you had an excellent German dictionary close at hand, you could now point at every recognizable object in the universe and say the German word that names it. The words that name objects are called "nouns". After you have looked up the nouns and learned their genders, you would be able to refer to each object with the appropriate pronoun.

The next step is to use VERBS in order to describe what the nouns and pronouns are doing. "Verbs" are words that indicate actions. The combination of a SUBJECT (always either a noun or a pronoun) and a verb creates a simple, single-clause sentence.

Every sentence needs a subject!

The subject always appears in the sentence, either as a noun or as a pronoun. The subject is, to put it plainly although unpoetically, the thing that is doing the verb. If that description bothers you, think of the subject as the noun or pronoun that performs the action described by the verb. If that description makes your eyes glaze over, re-read the unpoetic description and then skip ahead to these examples:

Der Professor schreibt ein Buch.	**The professor** writes a book.
Er schreibt ein Buch.	**He** writes a book.

In the first of the two sentences above, the subject is *der Professor*, which can be replaced by the pronoun *er*, which is the subject of the second sentence. *Er* refers to *der Professor*. This is not rocket science.

The verb is *schreibt*, which describes what the subject is doing, which is, in each sentence, writing.

The remainder of the sentence is the direct object *ein Buch*. We will revisit direct objects in Chapter 3. For now, remain focused on the subject and the verb in each of the examples that follow.

Die Professorin besucht die Stadt Bozen.	**The professor** visits the city of Bolzano.
Sie besucht die Stadt Bozen.	**She** visits the city of Bolzano.

In the first of the two sentences above, *die Professorin* is the subject. In German, many titles (like professor, for example) exist in masculine and feminine forms. Since *Professorin* is a feminine noun, the pronoun *sie* is used to replace and refer to it.

The verb is *besucht* – it describes what the subject is doing, which is, in this case, visiting.

The remainder of the sentence is the direct object *die Stadt Bozen*. We will spend a great deal of time with direct objects in Chapter 3. For now, focus once again on the subject and the verb.

Das Kind hat eine Tante in Zürich.	**The child** has an aunt in Zürich.
Es hat eine Tante in Zürich.	**It** has an aunt in Zürich.

In the first of the two sentences above, *das Kind* is the subject. Since the noun *Kind* is neuter, the correct pronoun is *es*. Perhaps it feels awkward to refer to the child as "it"? Don't worry – *es* refers to the gender of the noun, not to the child itself. German speakers use *es* to refer to *das Kind*, but they could also use *er* to refer to *der Junge* (the boy) or *sie* to refer to *die kleine Marlene* (little Marlene, who identifies as female).

The verb is *hat*, which means "to have" and which vaguely resembles the English word "has".

The remainder of the sentence is the direct object *eine Tante in Zürich*. As mentioned, we will return to direct objects in Chapter 3. For now, focus yet again on the subject and the verb.

Die Blumenkinder tanzen unter dem Regenbogen.	**The flower children** dance under the rainbow.
Sie tanzen unter dem Regenbogen.	**They** dance under the rainbow.

In the first of the two sentences above, *die Blumenkinder* is the subject. Since *Blumenkinder* is plural, the pronoun is *sie*.

The verb is *tanzen*, which means "to dance" and which somewhat resembles the English word "dance".

The remainder of the sentence is the prepositional phrase *unter dem Regenbogen*. If you just can't wait, skip ahead to Chapter 4 right now. Otherwise, continue to focus on the subject and the verb for the remainder of this chapter.

Obviously, the subject will not always be in the third person. Remember the first and second person?

Ich wohne in Meran.	**I** live in Merano.
Wir wohnen in Meran.	**We** live in Merano.
Du wohnst in Meran. (familiar, singular)	**You** live in Merano.
Ihr wohnt in Meran. (familiar, plural, as in y'all)	**You** live in Merano.
Sie wohnen in Meran. (formal, singular and plural)	**You** live in Merano.

The subjects in the sentences above are the first and second person pronouns.
The verb in each sentence is a form of *wohnen* (to live in a place, to dwell).
The remainder of the sentence is the prepositional phrase *in Meran*.

Every subject needs a verb, and these verbs must be conjugated!

Imagine your professor standing in front of a large lecture hall. As the silence grows and all eyes focus heavily upon him, he exclaims:

Ich bin der Professor!	I am the professor!

The subject is clearly *ich* and the verb is *bin*, which is a form of the verb *sein* (to be). The remainder of the sentence is the predicate noun *der Professor*. We will learn more about predicates in Chapter 3.

Since *sein* is the most important verb in German, we begin by learning to conjugate it.

	Singular	*Plural*
1st person	ich bin	wir sind
2nd person	du bist	ihr seid
	Sie sind	Sie sind
3rd person	er ist	sie sind
	sie ist	sie sind
	es ist	sie sind

Hopefully you can see that a verb must be conjugated to agree with the subject.

Imagine now that the professor has grown tired of being alone on the stage. He finds an intelligent person in the hallway, grants them a PhD and a full professorship, and then brings them onto the stage. Now they exclaim, together:

Wir sind die Professoren!	We are the professors!

Hopefully the idea of conjugating a verb has not discouraged you from further study. Assuming that it has not done so, let's go through a few more *Gedankenexperimente* (thought experiments).

Imagine that the person from the hallway feels unprepared to be a professor. He throws away his newly acquired PhD and storms off, back into the hallway, exclaiming to the original professor:

Sie sind der Professor!	You are the professor!

Of course, if they were good friends or family members, or had otherwise previously established a *du* relationship, the person from the hallway also could have exclaimed:

Du bist der Professor!	You are the professor!

At this point, the professor could accept his fate, or he could abdicate, leaving his teaching responsibilities to his students and shouting as he leaves the room:

Sie sind die Professoren!	You are the professors!

Do you see that he is using the formal second person? Of course, if the professor were supercool and progressive, he might use the familiar form with his students. In this case he would shout:

Ihr seid die Professoren!	You are the professors!

Pause for a moment to reflect upon the relative complexity of the second person in German. Make certain that you understand what *du*, *ihr*, and *Sie* have in common and also what sets them apart from each other.

Meanwhile, a group of anarchist art students has assembled, and they are radically turning everything they can think of into a professor:

Der Tisch ist der Professor!	The table is the professor!
Die Kreide ist der Professor!	The chalk is the professor!
Das Lineal ist der Professor!	The ruler is the professor!
Die Fenster sind die Professoren!	The windows are the professors!

Perhaps matters have become absurd. In any case, one sees that subjects and verbs must always agree.

One should also see that a simplified chart is possible for *sein* and for all other verbs.

	Singular	*Plural*
1st person	ich bin	wir sind
2nd person	du bist	ihr seid
3rd person	er/sie/es ist	sie sind

Since the formal *Sie* is always conjugated in the same form as the plural *sie*, we need not include it in the chart. Likewise, since *er*, *sie*, and *es* share a conjugation, they can appear together on one line, and sometimes only *er* will appear on charts to save ink.

Since students often like shortcuts, one might be delighted to discover that the *wir* and plural *sie* conjugations are always the same.

Now, behold the verb *heißen*,[1] which means "to be called [a name]". In order to introduce yourself, you could use either this verb, or the verb *sein*.

	Singular	*Plural*
1st person	ich heiße	wir heißen
2nd person	du heißt	ihr heißt
3rd person	er/sie/es heißt	sie heißen

When I introduce myself, I say:

Ich heiße Graf von Anderson.	I am called Graf von Anderson.

Or I might use *sein* rather than *heißen*:

Ich bin Graf von Anderson.	I am Graf von Anderson.

In either case, *ich* is the subject and the verb must be conjugated accordingly.

Of course, if I find learning new languages uncomfortable, I could directly translate from English and say:

Mein Name ist Graf von Anderson	My name is Graf von Anderson.

That's fine, although most Germans would use the expression *ich heiße*, as shown above. Essentially, all three of these sentences express the same idea. Notice that the subject, *mein Name*, determines the conjugation of the verb, *ist*.

Let's focus on the first two sentences for a few moments. If I were to have a sudden memory lapse, you could remind me of my name with a formal:

Sie heißen Graf von Anderson!	You are called Graf von Anderson!
Sie sind Graf von Anderson!	You are Graf von Anderson!

Or, if we had already established a familiar relationship, you could use *du* rather than *Sie*:

Du heißt Graf von Anderson!	You are called Graf von Anderson!
Du bist Graf von Anderson!	You are Graf von Anderson!

Likewise, if you were to brag about me to a friend, you could say:

Mein Professor heißt Graf von Anderson!	My professor is called Graf von Anderson!
Mein Professor ist Graf von Anderson!	My professor is Graf von Anderson!

Imagine how you would form sentences if you and I were to merge cybernetically into one being:

Wir heißen Graf von Anderson!	We are called Graf von Anderson!
Wir sind Graf von Anderson!	We are Graf von Anderson!

Or if I, through a misconception of mitosis, were to split into two identical human beings and you needed to remind us of our name:

Sie heißen Graf von Anderson!	You are called Graf von Anderson!
Sie sind Graf von Anderson!	You are Graf von Anderson!

Of course, if we already had a *du* relationship before I split into two, then you would say:

Ihr heißt Graf von Anderson!	You are called Graf von Anderson!
Ihr seid Graf von Anderson!	You are Graf von Anderson!

At that point, you would have two professors to brag about:

Meine Professoren heißen Graf von Anderson!	My professors are called Graf von Anderson!
Meine Professoren sind Graf von Anderson!	My professors are Graf von Anderson!

Someday, all of the professors will be Graf von Anderson. Until then, just remember that everyone is doing the best they can.

Verb conjugation essentials: infinitives, stems, and endings in the present tense

The verb in its most abstract form is called THE INFINITIVE. The infinitive in English usually includes the word "to". Since you are learning German, the verb "to learn" will be of vital interest.

The INFINITIVE FORM of the verb "to learn" is *lernen*.

The infinitive form of the verb is listed in the dictionary. If you were to look up *lernen*, you would see that it means "to learn", and also that it means "to study", in the sense of the mental effort one expends in order to learn something.

Ich lerne Deutsch.	I am learning German.
Ich lerne für die Prüfung.	I am studying for the exam.

A conjugated verb consists of a STEM and an ENDING. For the vast majority of German verbs, the stem is found by removing the "en" from the infinitive. The stem of the verb *lernen* is *lern*.

Look at these simple steps for finding the stem:

1. Find the infinitive ⟹	lernen
2. Remove the "en" from the infinitive ⟹	lern – en
3. Rejoice! The stem has been discovered ⟹	lern

Once the stem has been located, one simply adds the appropriate ending, and the verb is conjugated.

	Singular	*Plural*
1st person	ich lerne	wir lernen
2nd person	du lernst	ihr lernt
3rd person	er/sie/es lernt	sie lernen

You have probably already noticed that the endings of regular verbs follow a pattern. You can detect the basic pattern in the chart above and see it even more clearly in the chart below, where the stem is represented by a "–".

	Singular	*Plural*
1st person	ich –e	wir –en
2nd person	du –(e)st	ihr –(e)t
3rd person	er/sie/es –(e)t	sie –en

The "(e)s" are there to remind you that sometimes an "e" is added, usually when the addition of an "st" or "t" to the stem would be unpronounceable.

Let's look at the verb *arbeiten* (to work) to make this clear.

	Singular	*Plural*
1st person	ich arbeite	wir arbeiten
2nd person	du arbeitest	ihr arbeitet
3rd person	er/sie/es arbeitet	sie arbeiten

The stem of *arbeiten* is clearly and obviously *arbeit*. Adding a "t" to *arbeit* would result in *arbeitt*, which would be quite difficult to pronounce in a way that made the presence of the final "t" audible. Adding an "et" produces the magnificent word *arbeitet*, which simply rolls off the tongue.

Another verb that students should learn is *lesen* (to read).

	Singular	*Plural*
1st person	ich lese	wir lesen
2nd person	du liest	ihr lest
3rd person	er/sie/es liest	sie lesen

Since the stem already ends in "s", there is no need to add another "s" when forming the *du* conjugation. But take a closer look at the stem for the *du* and *er/sie/es* forms – it seems to have changed, from the predictable *les* (formed by removing the "en" from *lesen*) to the unexpected *lies* – how did that occur?

Lesen is one of many STEM-CHANGING VERBS. The stem changes in the *du* and *er/sie/es* forms from *les* to *lies*, which makes *lesen* an "e" to "ie" stem-changing verb.

Stem-changing verbs come in the following types. Notice that the stem only changes in the *du* and *er/sie/es* conjugations.

a to ä		
halten (to stop, to hold)		
	ich halte	wir halten
	du hältst	ihr haltet
	er hält	sie halten

au to äu		
laufen (to walk, to run)		
	ich laufe	wir laufen
	du läufst	ihr lauft
	er läuft	sie laufen

Now is a good time to mention that the letters crowned with umlauts are more or less equivalent to the same letter followed by an "e". For example, "ä" = "ae", "ö" = "oe", and "ü" = "ue".

If you needed to write *läuft* without using an umlaut (as part of a URL, for example) you would simply write *laeuft* and move on with your life. If you see how unattractive *laeuft* is, then you understand why the umlauts are likely to remain part of the German alphabet for a long time to come.

Continuing with the varieties of stem-changing verbs, we now come to:

e to i		
nehmen (to take)		
	ich nehme	wir nehmen
	du nimmst	ihr nehmt
	er nimmt	sie nehmen

e to ie		
sehen (to see)		
	ich sehe	wir sehen
	du siehst	ihr seht
	er sieht	sie sehen

The most effective way to learn a verb is to look it up in a dictionary like www.leo.org and to copy out a chart like the ones above. Naturally there are several tenses in German, but for now you should limit your focus to the present tense, which will be listed under *Indikativ: Präsens*.

Soon you will be able to conjugate verbs without looking them up – through the magic of human cognition. Stay tuned!

The verb goes in second place and the subject must touch the verb

The prime directive of German grammar, the concept of SECOND PLACE, will be extraordinarily useful to you, since it is the most important structural feature of German sentence formation.

Observe the simple sentences below. The subjects are bolded and the verbs are underlined.

Ich <u>bin</u> der Weltmeister.	**I** <u>am</u> the world champion.
Du <u>bist</u> sehr schön.	**You** <u>are</u> very beautiful.
Tahiti <u>ist</u> eine Insel.	**Tahiti** <u>is</u> an island.

In each sentence, the verb is in second place and the subject is touching it. We could also place the subject in third place, as in the examples below.

Der Weltmeister <u>bin</u> **ich**.	**I** <u>am</u> the world champion.
Sehr schön <u>bist</u> **du**.	**You** <u>are</u> very beautiful.
Eine Insel <u>ist</u> **Tahiti**.	**Tahiti** <u>is</u> an island.

In English, "The world champion am I" sounds ridiculous. This is not the case with the German, *Der Weltmeister bin ich*. Likewise, "very beautiful are you" and "an island is Tahiti" sound strange in English, unless the person saying them lives in a swamp and is over eight hundred years old. "Strange, the equivalent German sentences do not sound." These sentences have the same meanings, regardless of whether the subject is in first place (immediately before the verb) or in third place (immediately after the verb).

The important point is that the verb must be in second place in each of these sentences and that the subject must touch the verb. It might help if you imagine that the verb is the power source and that the subject cannot do anything unless it is plugged into the verb.

Die Sonne.	The sun.
Die Sonne <u>scheint</u>.	The sun shines (is shining, does shine).
Die Sonne <u>scheint</u> nicht.	The sun is not shining (does not shine, shines not).
Die Sonne <u>sieht</u> alles auf der Erde.	The sun sees everything on Earth.
Die Sonne <u>sieht</u> nachts woanders hin.	The sun looks somewhere else at night.

Going forward, you can point at the sun and tell the people you encounter that it is shining, or, if it is not shining, you can tell them that.

If you find the idea that the sun has vision ridiculous, then you see the importance of the subject-verb relationship. You might want to say:

Die Sonne <u>scheint</u>, aber **sie** <u>sieht</u> nicht.	The sun shines, but it does not see.

The jury is still out on that one. Notice, however, that the sentence above is formed from two clauses connected with *aber* (but). Notice also that each clause has a subject and a verb, that the subject is touching the verb, and that the verb is in second place within the clause (*aber* is counted as space zero, after which the order restarts).

Die Sonne	<u>scheint</u>	
1. (subject)	2. (verb)	
Sie	<u>sieht</u>	nicht.
1. (subject)	2. (verb)	3.

Let's agree to focus on sentences with only one clause for the time being (the grammar involved with clauses becomes more complex and will be impossible to comprehend without mastering simple one-clause grammar first). We will return to multiple clause sentences in Chapter 6.

Using an approved method, let's take an indirect look at the sun:

Die Sonne <u>ist</u> der am besten erforschte Stern.	**The sun** <u>is</u> the most well-researched star.
Der am besten erforschte Stern <u>ist</u> **die Sonne**.	**The sun** <u>is</u> the most well-researched star.

Observant students might look at the second sentence above and complain that the verb does not appear to be in second place. Expand your mind and see that the entire predicate *der am besten erforschte Stern* is in first place, followed by the verb, *ist*, which is then followed by the subject, *die Sonne*.

Die Sonne	<u>ist</u>	der am besten erforschte Stern.
1. (subject)	2. (verb)	3. (predicate)
Der am besten erforschte Stern	<u>ist</u>	**die Sonne**.
1. (predicate)	2. (verb)	3. (subject)

This logic will hold for all kinds of parallel structures:

Mein Freund <u>hat</u> einen Audi.	**My friend** <u>has</u> an Audi.
Einen Audi <u>hat</u> **mein Freund**.	**My friend** <u>has</u> an Audi.

Mein Freund is the subject, and *hat* is the verb. *Einen Audi* is the direct object – much more about those in the next chapter (and no, there is no way to misread the sentence in such a way that the Audi would have your friend). For now, focus again on the subject and the verb, noting that in each sentence, the verb is in second place and the subject is touching it.

Look at this sentence, which has a subject, a verb, a direct object and an indirect object:

Eine Mutter <u>kauft</u> ihrer Tochter einen Audi.   **A mother** <u>buys</u> her daughter an Audi.

The subject is clearly *eine Mutter*. She is the one who is doing the verb, which is *kaufen* (to buy). What is she buying? *Einen Audi* (an Audi). And for whom is she buying an Audi? *Ihrer Tochter* (for her daughter).

This sentence can be written three different ways:

Eine Mutter <u>kauft</u> ihrer Tochter einen Audi.
Ihrer Tochter <u>kauft</u> **eine Mutter** einen Audi.
Einen Audi <u>kauft</u> **eine Mutter** ihrer Tochter.

In each sentence, the verb is in second place and the subject is touching the verb. In each sentence, the mother is buying an Audi for her daughter.

The flexibility of forming equivalent sentences in multiple ways is one of the great strengths and sublime beauties of the German language.

Some verbs have prefixes, and some of these are separable prefixes

German verbs often have prefixes, just like English verbs. If you are unsure about this, just consider the verbs "to stand" and "to understand". "Under" is a prefix that radically changes the meaning of "stand". Do you stand? Do you understand?

The same is true in German:

---

stehen (to stand)		*verstehen (to understand)*	
ich stehe	wir stehen	ich verstehe	wir verstehen
du stehst	ihr steht	du verstehst	ihr versteht
er steht	sie stehen	er versteht	sie verstehen

The verbs for "to look for" and "to visit" are also similar:

---

suchen (to look for)		*besuchen (to visit)*	
ich suche	wir suchen	ich besuche	wir besuchen
du suchst	ihr sucht	du besuchst	ihr besucht
er sucht	sie suchen	er besucht	sie besuchen

You can see how the difference in prefix changes the meaning of the verb:

Der Student **sucht** einen Freund.   The student **is looking for** a friend.
Der Student **besucht** einen Freund.   The student **visits** a friend.

Here are a few further examples of inseparable prefix verbs:

---

leben (to live) and **erleben** (to experience)
Der Student **lebt** in Berlin.   The student **lives** in Berlin.
Er **erlebt** etwas Neues.   He **experiences** something new.

---

horchen (to listen to) and **gehorchen** (to obey)

Die Studentin **horcht** dem Schrei des Schmetterlings.	The student **listens** to the scream of the butterfly.
Sie **gehorcht** dem Polizisten.	She **obeys** the policeman.

mieten (to rent out) and **vermieten** (to rent)

Der Mieter **mietet** ein Zimmer.	The tenant **rents** a room.
Der Vermieter **vermietet** eine Wohnung.	The landlord **rents out** an apartment.

Students often want to know the magic formula by which the prefixes change the meanings of the verbs. There are some patterns, but nearly as many exceptions. Perhaps after you have learned several hundred verbs you will be able to justify spending your time thinking about this topic. Until then, just learn the meanings of the verbs as you encounter them.

Some of the German prefixes separate from the stem of the verb when they are conjugated.

Take a look at the verbs *stehen*, which hopefully you remember, and *aufstehen*, which means "to stand (or get) up".

stehen (to stand)		*aufstehen (to stand/get up)*	
ich stehe	wir stehen	ich stehe auf	wir stehen auf
du stehst	ihr steht	du stehst auf	ihr steht auf
er steht	sie stehen	er steht auf	sie stehen auf

When separable prefix verbs are conjugated, the prefix goes all the way to the end of the sentence.

Ich **stehe** normalerweise montags bis freitags gegen 7.00 Uhr **auf**.	I normally **get up** Monday through Friday around 7:00.

I can rewrite the sentence in several ways, so long as the verb remains in second place, the subject remains touching the verb, and the prefix remains at the very end of the sentence.

Normalerweise **stehe** ich montags bis freitags gegen 7.00 Uhr **auf**.	Normally, I **get up** Monday through Friday around 7:00.

Do you see that there is not a comma between the verb and the subject? Hold that idea close to your heart. Commas are used in German to separate clauses and adjectives, and that's it! Placing a comma after *normalerweise* in the example above is incorrect and, if repeated, quickly becomes an irritating mistake.

Montags bis freitags **stehe** ich normalerweise gegen 7.00 Uhr **auf**.	Monday through Friday, I **get up** normally around 7:00.

This one sounds a little odd in English, but is perfectly fine in German:

Gegen 7.00 Uhr **stehe** ich I montags bis freitags normalerweise **auf**.	Around 7:00 I normally **get up** Monday through Friday.

Spend a moment or two pondering the combinations of the various sentence elements in the four variations above.

The same pattern is exhibited by the verbs *schreiben* and *aufschreiben*.

schreiben (to write)		*aufschreiben (to write down)*	
ich schreibe	wir schreiben	ich schreibe auf	wir schreiben auf
du schreibst	ihr schreibt	du schreibst auf	ihr schreibt auf
er schreibt	sie schreiben	er schreibt auf	sie schreiben auf

Just look at these two in action:

Die Studentin **schreibt** einen Aufsatz.	The student **writes** an essay.
Sie **schreibt** die Adresse **auf**.	She **writes down** the address.

Notice once again that the verb is in second place, that the subject touches the verb, and that the separated prefix goes to the very end of the sentence.

Here are a few further examples of separable prefix verbs:

wachen (to watch, to guard) and **aufwachen** (to wake up)

Der Engel **wacht** über den Studenten.	The angel **watches** over the student.
Der Student **wacht** in der Bibliotek **auf**.	The student **wakes up** in the library.

bringen (to bring) and **mitbringen** (to bring along)

Der Student **bringt** seine Freundin zum Bahnhof.	The student **brings** his girlfriend to the train station.
Er **bringt** sein Mittagessen **mit**.	He **brings along** his lunch.

machen (to do, to make) and **zumachen** (to shut)

Der Student **macht** seine Hausaufgaben.	The student **does** his homework.
Er **macht** die Tür **zu**.	He **shuts** the door.

The placement of verbs in second place, with the separable prefix at the very end of the sentence will be a recurring structure and should never be forgotten or ignored. Placing the verb elsewhere simply is not allowed![2]

Questions

The German word for "question" is *Frage*. If you have a question, you can say, *Ich habe eine Frage!* Hopefully someone will know the answer.

There are two types of questions:

1. yes/no questions, which are called *geschlossene Fragen* or "closed questions"
2. open-ended questions, called *offene Fragen* or "open questions"

Yes/no questions are formed by placing the verb at the beginning of the sentence:

Bist du Bobfried[3] Schmidt?	Are you Bobfried Schmidt?

Notice that the subject is touching the verb!
We can rewrite the sentences from the last section into questions with relative ease:

Sucht der Student einen Freund?	Is the student looking for a friend?
Besucht der Student einen Freund?	Is the student visiting a friend?
Schreibt der Student einen Aufsatz?	Is the student writing an essay?
Schreibt der Student seine Adresse auf?	Is the student writing down his address?

Notice that the separated prefix remains at the very end of the sentence!

Wacht der Engel über den Studenten?	Does the angel watch over the student?
Wacht der Student in der Bibliothek auf?	Does the student wake up in the library?
Bringt der Student seine Freundin zum Bahnhof?	Is the student bringing his girlfriend to the train station?
Bringt er sein Mittagessen mit?	Does he bring along his lunch?
Macht der Student seine Hausaufgaben?	Is the student doing his homework?
Macht er die Tür zu?	Does he shut the door?

Open-ended questions are formed with question words:

Was?	What?
Was ist das?	What is that?
Was willst du von mir?	What do you want from me?

Wer?	Who?
Wer bist du?	Who are you?
Wer ist diese Person?	Who is this person?

Wann?	When?
Wann kommt die Pizza endlich an?	When does the pizza finally arrive?
Wann gehen wir?	When do we go?

Wo?	Where?
Wo wohnst du?	Where do you live?
Wo ist das Bier?	Where is the beer?

Wie?	How?
Wie geht's?	How goes it?
Wie ist das Wetter heute?	How is the weather today?

Wieso?	Why?
Wieso ist der Himmel blau?	Why is the sky blue?
Wieso fragst du?	Why do you ask?

Warum?	Why?
Warum regnet es so oft in Hamburg?	Why does it rain so often in Hamburg?
Warum fragst du?	Why do you ask?
Warum? Darum.	Why? Because.

The question word goes first and is followed by the verb, which is unsurprisingly in second place and which is followed directly by the subject, which touches the verb as you have come to expect.

Separable-prefix verbs leave their prefixes at the end of the sentence.

Wann stehst du normalerweise auf?	When do you normally get up?

Once you understand how questions are formed, which is to say, now, you should be able to turn any German sentence into at least two questions. Take for example this sentence from a recent letter from my aunt in Antwerp:

Der Cousin des Gärtners ist einer der besten Pizzabäcker Europas.	The gardener's cousin is one of the best pizza bakers in Europe.

You could easily ask a yes/no question:

Ist der Cousin des Gärtners einer der besten Pizzabäcker Europas?	Is the gardener's cousin one of the best pizza bakers in Europe?

Notice that all you needed to do was remove the verb from second place and set it at the beginning of the sentence. All of the other words remained right where they were! Imagine the power of this knowledge: going forward, you can simply repeat everything that anyone says to you in German in the form of a yes/no question. In the words of several geniuses, "Fake it 'til you make it!"

You could also ask a few open-ended questions:

Wer ist einer der besten Pizzabäcker Europas?	Who is one of the best pizza bakers in Europe?
Wer ist der Cousin des Gärtners?	Who is the gardener's cousin?
Wie ist der Cousin des Gärtners?	What is the gardener's cousin like? "How" is he? Supply a description of the phenomenon!

We don't really know much about the gardener's cousin, but one answer to the last question would be:

Er ist einer der besten Pizzabäcker Europas.	

Beyond that, we just don't know:

Wie ist er?	What is he like?
Vielleicht ist er klein.	Perhaps he is small.
Vielleicht ist er blond.	Perhaps he is blonde.
Hat er rote Haare?	Does he have red hair?
Wir wissen es nicht.	We don't know.
Ist er nett?	Is he nice?
Oder ist er ziemlich schwierig?	Or is he rather difficult?
Wir wissen es einfach nicht.	We simply do not know.

Germans use *wie* in many cases where an American might want to use *was*, so get comfortable with *wie*, even if it might be tempting to ask:

Was ist der Cousin des Gärtners?	What is the gardener's cousin?

But the likely answer would be something along the lines of:

Der Cousin des Gärtners ist ein Mensch.	The gardener's cousin is a human being.

Perhaps German seems a little bit more literal than English. That's not a bad insight to keep in mind as you move forward. But don't forget the famous pub in the Grafenhafen historic district:

Was ist der Cousin des Gärtners?	What is the Gardener's Cousin?
Der Cousin des Gärtners ist eine berühmte Kneipe in Grafenhafen.	The Gardener's Cousin is a famous pub in Grafenhafen.

We could also ask about the location of the gardener's cousin, about the person, especially if he also delivers the pizzas, or about the pub, if we are ready for a decent pint:

Wo ist der Cousin des Gärtners?	Where is the gardener's cousin?

You will certainly find it useful to note that "who" is *wer*, and "where" is *wo*, which is to say that *wer* is "who" and *wo* is "where". That should keep you busy for a while.

Basic answers: *ja und nein* and *richtig und falsch*

Now that you can form basic questions, it makes sense to learn how to give basic answers.
    The most basic answers are *ja* and *nein*, roughly (or exactly), "yes" and "no".
    Perhaps someone will ask you if you are a count.

Sind Sie ein Graf?

If you are a count, then you would answer:

Ja.

If you are not a count, then you would answer.

Nein.

The *ja*/*nein* concept is strikingly similar to the English yes/no concept.

Another pair of words that work like *ja* and *nein* are *richtig* and *falsch*; they correspond to "right" and "wrong" and to "true" and "false".

For example, people often claim that Cal Poly is the best university in the whole world.

Cal Poly ist die beste Universität der ganzen Welt!

If you know this to be true, then you can exclaim with Mustang Pride:

Richtig!

But perhaps you were not able to fully hear what they said. Listen again:

Cal Poly ist **nicht** die beste Universität der ganzen Welt!

Now you might want to bellow, or chuckle dismissively:

Falsch!

Making statements and having your friends decide if they are *richtig oder falsch* is one way to have fun while learning German. Luckily, there are also other ways.

Imperative forms

The last topic for this chapter is the imperative, which describes the grammar for commands like "Get out of my room!" as well as for polite suggestions like "Let's go to the cinema!"

There are four types of imperatives: *du*-commands, *ihr*-commands, *Sie*-commands, and *wir*–polite suggestions.

Each type of imperative is formed very much like a yes/no question: the verb goes first.

Let's start with the *Sie*-commands.

Imagine encountering a group of strangers speaking German. You might be excited, forget the rule about "stranger danger" and say to them:

| Sie sprechen Deutsch. | You are speaking German. |

That was obviously not a command, but rather a simple sentence about reality as you perceive it. Recall your earlier attempt or intention to share with those surrounding you a report that the sun is shining.

But now imagine that you encounter an unruly group of reprehensible people who speak English when they should be speaking German, perhaps in your language class or in the German-speaking pub on your college campus. You would now create a command by inverting the subject and the verb:

Sprechen Sie Deutsch!	Speak German!

Notice the similarity to the question form.

Sprechen Sie Deutsch?	Do you speak German?

The only difference is the punctuation mark at the end.

Now, let's take a look at the *ihr*-commands.

Imagine that you are the cool teacher that uses the familiar forms *du* and *ihr* with your students. You encounter a group of them speaking English when they should be speaking German, so you say, with mild horror and honest disgust:

Ihr sprecht Englisch.	You are speaking English.

Again, that was obviously not a command. But now, before they can burst into tears of dishonor, you command them:

Sprecht Deutsch!	Speak German!

Notice that the *ihr*-command differs from the *Sie*-command. Although the verb is conjugated just like it would be in a simple, present-tense sentence, there is no *ihr*. That is the difference: the *ihr*-command drops the subject and just conjugates the verb. This is a rare occurrence in German, since there almost always will be a subject and a verb in every sentence.

Now let's learn some *du*-commands. Like the *ihr* form, we will drop the *du*, but unlike the *ihr* form, the verb will be conjugated slightly differently than it would in the present indicative tense (the one and only tense we have learned so far). Pay attention to the situation below:

The professor sees a group of A-plus students speaking German, but one D-triple-minus student insists on speaking English. The professor says:

Du sprichst Englisch!	You are speaking English!

The poor student doesn't understand (not doing enough homework probably), so the professor becomes enraged and starts shouting:

Sprich Deutsch! Sprich Deutsch! Sprich Deutsch!	Speak German! Speak German! Speak German!

Obviously, something has changed: the "st" has been dropped from the *du* form. Rather than *sprichst*, we conjugate the *du*-command into *sprich*. But the story isn't over yet.

The *du*-commands for "a" to "ä" and "au" to "äu" stem-changing verbs undergo another change.

Imagine encouraging your running partner, who runs very slowly. With a strong hint of disapproval, you might say:

Du läufst ziemlich langsam.	You run rather slowly.

Perhaps your running partner does not take the initiative to run faster after this subtle hint. At this point, you have no alternative but to shout repeatedly, with fury:

Lauf schneller! Lauf schneller!	Run faster! Run faster!

You will notice that the "au" to "äu" stem-change has been undone for the *du*-command. This works the same way with the "a" to "ä" stem-changing verbs.

Many of the *du*-commands add an "e" to the end of the verb. Sometimes this is optional, as with *laufe!*, which is just as correct as *lauf!*, and sometimes this is required, as with *arbeite! – arbeit!* is incorrect.

Finally, the imperative form for *wir* allows us to make polite suggestions. These are easy, just like the *Sie*-commands.

Imagine that you enjoy narrating every single thing that you and your group of friends are doing.

For example, imagine that you are going to the cinema. You would narrate, almost certainly to their profound irritation:

Wir gehen ins Kino!	We are going to the movies!

Now imagine that you are all sitting around the living room in various postures of relaxation and boredom, and you would like it if everyone got off of the sofas and went to the movies. You could say:

Gehen wir ins Kino!	Let's go to the movies!

Just like the *Sie*-commands, the *wir*–polite suggestions are formed in the same manner as a yes/no question. The only difference is the punctuation at the end.

Imagine yourself riding along with your friends in the back of a Mercedes S-Class, presumably on the way to the cinema, when you suddenly realize that you are driving out of the city into the deserted countryside, where everything is dark and all is silent. You might ask:

Gehen wir ins Kino?	Are we going to the movies?

Let's look at the separable-prefix verb *aufstehen*, which you will remember means "to get up", as in: "out of bed".

Imagine that your friend who always seems to be in bed suddenly starts getting out of bed. You could say:

He! Du stehst endlich auf!	Hey! You are finally getting up!

But maybe that was only a fantasy. You want to encourage the friend to get up, so you shout in German:

He! Steh endlich auf!	Hey! Get up finally!

Maybe upon closer inspection you realize that your friend is not in bed alone, and you decide to give the loving couple (or are there three of them in there? Would that be a throuple?) some motivation to get out of bed.

You could tell them:

He! Steht endlich auf!	Hey! Get up finally!

It is unlikely that you will be commanding strangers, singular or plural, to get up out of bed, but maybe you will encounter one (or more) on your sofa some morning after you go to bed without locking the door to your apartment.

You could say to them (singular or plural):

Hallo! Stehen Sie bitte auf!	Hello! Get up please!

Finally, maybe there will be a Sunday afternoon where you and your special someone finally need to get the day started.

You could say, with inspirational intonation:

Stehen wir endlich auf!	Let's finally get up!

It is more likely, however, that you would phrase the intention as a question, since no one likes to be rushed out of bed on the weekend.

Stehen wir endlich auf?	Do we (shall we) finally get up?

Here are some further examples so that you can see how the imperative forms work:

Sie-command	*du-command*	*ihr-command*	*English*
Schreiben Sie!	Schreib!	Schreibt!	Write!
Lesen Sie ein Buch!	Lies ein Buch!	Lest ein Buch!	Read a book!
Halten Sie!	Halt!	Haltet!	Stop!
Bleiben Sie stehen!	Bleib stehen!	Bleibt stehen!	Stand still!
Gehen Sie weg!	Geh weg!	Geht weg!	Go away!
Kaufen Sie mir ein Bier!	Kauf mir ein Bier!	Kauft mir ein Bier!	Buy me a beer!
Geben Sie mir Ihren Geldbeutel!	Gib mir deinen Geldbeutel!	Gebt mir eure Geldbeutel!	Give me your wallet(s)!
Sagen Sie mir etwas Nettes!	Sag mir etwas Nettes!	Sagt mir etwas Nettes!	Say something nice to me!
Haben Sie ein bisschen Geduld!	Hab ein bisschen Geduld!	Habt ein bisschen Geduld!	Have a little patience!
Essen Sie jeden Tag einen Apfel!	Iss jeden Tag einen Apfel!	Esst jeden Tag einen Apfel!	Eat an apple every day!
Trinken Sie nicht zu viel Bier!	Trink nicht zu viel Bier!	Trinkt nicht zu viel Bier!	Don't drink too much beer!
Vergessen Sie mich nicht!	Vergiss mich nicht!	Vergesst mich nicht!	Don't forget me!

Of course, if you live on California's Central Coast, you should also learn the following commands:

Nehmen Sie immer einen Kapuzenpullover mit!	Nimm immer einen Kapuzenpullover mit!	Nehmt immer einen Kapuzenpullover mit!	Always take a hoody with you!

Staying warm and avoiding surprises when the evening air gets cold – that's the Graf von Anderson Advantage!

Übungen

A   Learning the present-tense conjugations and imperative forms of the following frequently encountered verbs is an ideal way to become acquainted with the German language. The free online dictionary www.leo.org is the best first stop for this task.

For verb tables, click on the table icon next to the verb on Leo. You will want to find the *Präsens* column in the *Indikativ* part of the chart – this is the simple present tense. For the commands, look for the table labeled *Imperativ*.

The three most important verbs are *sein* (to be), *haben* (to have), and *werden* (to become). Start by looking these up. Depending on how you learn, you might want to copy out the charts for each of them by hand, creating something like this:

sein (to be)	
ich bin	wir sind
du bist	ihr seid
er/sie/es ist	sie sind

You might also write out the imperative forms:

Seien Sie!
Sei!
Seid!
Seien wir!

Do the same for *haben* and *werden*:

haben (to have)		*werden (to become)*	
ich habe	wir haben	ich werde	wir werden
du hast	ihr habt	du wirst	ihr werdet
er/sie/es hat	sie haben	er/sie/es wird	sie werden

Again, with the imperative forms:

Haben Sie!	Werden Sie!
Hab!	Werde!
Habt!	Werdet!
Haben wir!	Werden Wir!

Another option would be to write simple sentences.

---

sein (to be)

Ich bin sehr intelligent.	Wir sind nette Leute.
Du bist mein Freund.	Ihr seid meine Freunde.
Er ist mein Bruder.	Sie sind meine Schwestern.

Seien Sie nicht böse!	Don't be angry!
Sei cool!	Be cool!
Seid nicht unfreundlich!	Don't be unfriendly!
Seien wir tolerant!	Let's be tolerant!

Of course, you might begin by copying charts and then progress to writing sentences after you have learned a little bit more.

Learning the following verbs will keep you busy for a while, but if you make a solid, consistent effort to learn them over the next weeks or months, your German will take off at some point, leaving you *leicht erstaunt* or maybe even totally amazed.

anbieten	*denken*	*fragen*	*küssen*	*schaffen*	*tragen*
anfangen	dichten	fühlen	lassen	scheinen	treffen
ankommen	drücken	führen	laufen	schlagen	tun
ansehen	durchfallen	geben	leben	schließen	verbinden
arbeiten	entwickeln	gehen	legen	schreiben	vergehen
aufmachen	erhalten	gehören	lernen	sehen	vergessen
aussehen	erinnern	gewinnen	lesen	setzen	vergleichen
bedeuten	erkennen	glauben	lieben	sitzen	verlieren
beginnen	erklären	halten	liegen	spielen	verstehen
bekommen	erreichen	handeln	machen	sprechen	versuchen
bestehen	erscheinen	heißen	meinen	springen	vorstellen
bezahlen	erwarten	helfen	mögen	starten	warten
bieten	erzählen	hören	nehmen	stehen	werfen
bilden	fahren	interessieren	nennen	stellen	wissen
bleiben	fallen	kennen	öffnen	stoßen	wohnen
brauchen	fehlen	kicken	ordnen	studieren	zählen
bringen	finden	kommen	reden	suchen	zeigen
darstellen	folgen	kosten	sagen	tanzen	ziehen

B Rewrite the following sentences, paying special attention to the conjugations of the verbs, changing *ich* to *du*, then changing *du* to *ihr*, then changing *ihr* to *er*, before finally changing *er* to the plural *sie*.

Ich studiere Philosophie und Betriebswirtschaftslehre (BWL).
Ich helfe dem alten Mann.
Ich brauche einen Kaffee.
Ich bekomme eine E-Mail.
Ich trage jeden Tag Jeans und ein T-Shirt.
Ich denke immer positiv.

Ich erzähle gern alte Geschichten.
Ich höre gern klassische Musik.
Ich weiß, wie schön die Welt ist.
Ich kenne Angela, und ich kenne Berlin.
Ich erscheine jeden Tag auf dem Campus.
Ich bestehe alle Prüfungen.
Ich vergesse nie.
Ich mag Käse.
Ich will nach Amsterdam fliegen.
Ich komme aus Hamburg.
Ich tanze unter den Sternen.
Ich renne durch den Wald.
Ich sitze in der Kneipe.
Ich spreche Deutsch und Englisch.
Ich wohne in Bonn.
Ich mache immer das Fenster auf.
Ich werfe meinem Sohn den Ball zu.
Ich singe gern.

C   Take the *du* version of each sentence above and turn it into a yes/no question.

D   Use the question word *wer* to make an open-ended question out of the *er* versions of sentences above. Could you make a second question with *was, wie, wo,* or *wann*? Don't worry if there are questions you want to ask but cannot yet form. Chapter 3 will teach you what you are looking for.

E   Translate everything into English, every single exercise. If you write something in German, you should know what it means.

Travel: Würzburg, Rothenburg, Nuremberg, Regensburg, and Munich

From Frankfurt, take a scenic train ride to medieval Rothenburg ab der Tauber, stopping in Würzburg along the way to enjoy the lovely *Altstadt* and to walk across the *alte Main-brücke* to explore the *Festung Marienberg* high on a hilltop above the town. The Marien-berg fortress was the residence of the prince-bishops of Würzburg for nearly half a millennium. If you are interested in splendid Baroque palaces, you will find the *Würz-burger Residenz*, located in the town itself, of the highest quality and finest style. The memorial to Walther von der Vogelweide, who is said to be buried in Rothenburg, is worth seeking out as well.

Stepping into Rothenburg ob der Tauber is like stepping back in time to the Middle Ages. Wandering through the town in whatever direction it takes you will ensure that you see everything that looks interesting; after an hour or so of astonished wandering, consider taking a guided tour. Be sure to visit the *Handwerkerhaus*, a museum that shows the everyday life of medieval craftsmen and their families by recreating the rooms in which they lived and worked. Certainly, the *Stadtkirche St. Jakob*, with its historically important Holy Blood altarpiece carved by Tilman Riemenschneider, is an essential sight. If you are in luck, your visit will coincide with an organ concert.

Nuremberg, which is *Nürnberg* in German, has many highlights and one of the truly great Christmas markets in the world. The *Nürnberger Burg* is one of Europe's most formidable medieval fortresses and deserves a lengthy visit. The 15th-century stained-glass windows in the St. Lawrence church also deserve attention. The exciting culinary scene in Nuremberg is also worth exploring, perhaps with a legendary *Nürnberger Rostbratwürstchen*, or maybe with one of the many organic or vegan delights that also await the city's sophisticated residents and visitors.

The enchanting medieval city of Regensburg is entered by crossing an impressive medieval stone bridge, the *Steinerne Brücke*, over the Danube River. The Danube is called *die Donau* in German, and it is the principle river in southern Germanic Europe, much like the Rhine in the west and the Elbe in the east. Over twenty thousand students are enrolled at the highly respected university in Regensburg, which opened its doors in 1966. The torture chamber in the basement of the *Altes Rathaus* is considerably older, as is *der Hutkönig* – a custom hat shop in business for over a century across from the Gothic *Regensburger Dom*. While visiting the cathedral, perhaps you will attend a mass during which the legendary *Regensburger Domspatzen*, one of Europe's most enchanting children's choirs, will sing the liturgy. Remember to be respectful of those who worship in the church – the religious traditions you will observe there have been taking place since before the cathedral was founded in 1275.

The Benedictine monks who live and work in nearby *Kloster Weltenburg an der Donau* carry on a monastic tradition that has flourished there since roughly 700 CE, making *Kloster Weltenburg* one of the oldest monasteries in Germany. Built on a site that previously had been a Roman fortress, *Kloster Weltenburg* has been producing beer since at least 1050. *Weltenburger Kloster Barock Dunkel* won "best dark beer" in 2004, 2008, and 2012 at the World Beer Cup and is one of Graf von Anderson's enduring favorites. A visit to the monastery is a highlight of any trip to Germany.

Two other places near Regensburg are absolutely essential to visit: Walhalla and the *Befreiungshalle*. Created by Bavarian king Ludwig I in 1842, Walhalla is dedicated to the common heritage of the German people. Over one hundred marble busts honor German heroes, including Arminius, hero of the *Hermannsschlacht*; Alarich, king of the Visigoths; and Hermann von Salza, fourth grand master of the Teutonic Knights, as well as mathematicians and scientists like Kepler and Leibniz, and musicians and poets like Bach, Mozart, Beethoven, Goethe, and Schiller, among a wide variety of others. In recent years busts of Albert Einstein, Carl Friedrich Gauss, Konrad Adenauer, Heinrich Heine, and Sophie Scholl have been added to the collection.

The nearby *Befreiungshalle* was created, also by Ludwig I, to commemorate the victory of united Germanic forces over the armies of Napoleon in the *Befreiungskriege* (Wars of Liberation). Thirty-four marble statues of beautiful, winged *Siegesgöttinnen* (Goddesses of Victory) lightly touch hands as they form a ring around the domed hall, and a powerful inscription in the center of the marble floor reads:

MOECHTEN DIE TEUTSCHEN NIE VERGESSEN WAS DEN BEFREIUNGSKAMPF NOTHWENDIG MACHTE UND WODURCH SIE GESIEGT.	MAY THE GERMANS NEVER FORGET WHAT MADE THE FIGHT FOR LIBERATION NECESSARY AND THE MEANS BY WHICH THEY WON.

Arriving in Munich, which is *München* in German, one steps into the capital of Bavaria, which is *Bayern* in German, and simultaneously into a world-class, cosmopolitan city that is also one of the most well-loved places on earth. Standing inside of the iconic *Frauenkirche*, the Cathedral of Munich, one can find the *Teufelstritt*, a spot marked by the devil's footprint, from which none of the windows in the cathedral are visible, leaving one to ponder the origin of the abundant light that illuminates the building. Nearby *Marienplatz* is the central square of the city, and the imposing neo-gothic *Neues Rathaus* provides a fabulous background for the various street performances and markets, including an outstanding Christmas market, that take place there.

Munich is a food and beer paradise, as well as one of the truly great places in the world for making merry. Start with a plate of *Weißwürste mit Brezel und süßem Senf*, and drink whichever local beer you want – you can trust the *Wirt* to offer only the finest selection. The *Englischer Garten* in summertime is sublime, and on a rainy day the art collections in the *Alte Pinakothek* (look for Dürer's famous self-portrait from 1500), the *Neue Pinakothek* (Carl Spitzweg's *Der arme Poet* is there – consider it a warning if you are not studying math and science along with languages and cultures), and the *Städtische Galerie im Lenbachhaus* (home of outstanding works by Paul Klee and Wassily Kandinsky, among others) will transport you to the heights of beauty and sublimity of the aesthetic realm.

River surfing on the Eisbach looks like fun, and a visit to the nearby *Starnberger See* showcases the Alpine elements of Munich's charm. If you are fortunate enough to have friends in Munich, you should spend as much time with them as they will allow.

German history from the Renaissance to the Baroque

One of the grand narratives of history involves the peaking of the Middle Ages during the Renaissance, which broke open the static medieval metaphysical mindset through the rediscovery of the praxis of philosophy in a broad and holistic sense. The most famous Europeans of the Renaissance were the Italians Leonardo da Vinci (1452–1519), famous for painting the *Mona Lisa* and the *Last Supper*, as well as for designing flying machines centuries before they came into existence, and Michelangelo (1475–1564), famous for the sculpture of *David*, which expresses an ideal of human form, and for the paintings on the ceiling of the Sistine Chapel.

In Mainz, the German Johannes Gutenberg (1400–1468), through refinements in the production and use of mechanical moveable type, ushered in a revolution in printed communication that set the modern world into motion. By dramatically increasing the ease of producing printed texts, Gutenberg's printing press expanded the exchange of ideas and knowledge, leading to increases in literacy that opened the world of ideas to the masses. The information age of which we are all a part begins with Gutenberg.

Foremost among the important Germans active during the Renaissance was the brilliant artist Albrecht Dürer (1471–1528), whose engravings, especially *Ritter, Tod und Teufel*, capture the existential realities of the era while simultaneously displaying the technical achievements for which the Renaissance is famous. Dürer's portrait of Kaiser Maximillian and his paintings of Innsbruck provide valuable windows into the past.

The paintings of Lucas Cranach the Elder (1472–1553) and his son Lucas Cranach the Younger (1515–1586) are also high points of the German Renaissance. Cranach the Elder's paintings of scenes from classical mythology are captivating, notably his *Venus mit Amor als Honigdieb*. Among the many outstanding portraits of leading figures of the era, Cranach the Elder's portrait of his friend Martin Luther is worth a moment of your time – find it on the internet.

The Renaissance was followed by the Protestant Reformation, which is commonly traced back to Martin Luther (1484–1546), who nailed his 95 Theses onto the door of the church in

Wittenberg in 1517, and his refusal to renounce his writings at the Diet of Worms in 1521. The Reformation grew from the cultural soil that had created Renaissance humanism, first in Italy with Petrarch (1304–1374) and later in the Netherlands with Erasmus of Rotterdam (1466–1536), known in his time as the "Prince of the Humanists". The emergence of the modern German language can be traced back to the publication of Martin Luther's translation of the New Testament in 1522 and of the complete Bible in 1534.

The Reformation led to a series of bloody conflicts, beginning with the Knights Rebellion of 1512 and continuing with the German Peasant's War (1524–1525), which was the largest and most serious uprising of the common people against the ruling class until the revolutions of the 18th century. The violence grew much greater in the devastatingly destructive Thirty Years' War (1618–1648), which reduced the population of Germanic Europe by nearly a third. Fictionalized accounts of the horrors of the war are depicted in Hans Jakob Christoffel von Grimmelshausen's (1622–1676) literary masterpiece *Der abenteuerliche Simplicissimus Teutsch*. The Peace of Westphalia ended the war and established the principle of national sovereignty in Europe – including the right of sovereign rulers to determine the religions tolerated in their realms. Westphalian sovereignty is the basis for the system of nations and international relations that exists today. The map of Europe in 1648 is a good starting point for understanding modern European history.

The Baroque style emerged as an attempt to fight the Reformation with an architectural affirmation of awe-inspiring grandeur that would draw minds and spirits to the Catholic Church. The ceiling of the dome of *San Carlo alle Quattro Fontane* in Rome illustrates the phenomenon quite well. As the Baroque style spread throughout Europe, it was adapted to express the aesthetics of absolutism, functioning as an assertion of state power against the individual. The great Baroque palaces in Ludwigsburg, Mannheim, and Würzburg, as well as the recently reconstructed *Berliner Stadtschloss*, remain powerful symbols of the apparently limitless aspirations of worldly power.

Text and translation: Martin Luther

The translation of the New Testament by Martin Luther in 1522 paved the way for the modern German language. Luther's sermons, hymns, and various other writings and sayings remain interesting and insightful today.

Wer sich die Musik erkiest, hat ein himmlisch Werk gewonnen; denn ihr erster Ursprung ist von dem Himmel selbst genommen, weil die lieben Engelein selber Musikanten sein.	Whoever gives himself over to music, has won a heavenly work; since music's first origin is taken from heaven itself, because the dear little angels themselves are musicians.
Des Menschen Herz ist gleich wie Quecksilber, das jetzt da, bald anderswo ist, heut also, morgen anders gesinnt.	The heart of man is the same as mercury, that is now here, soon elsewhere, feels one way today, tomorrow another way.
Wie man nicht wehren kann, daß einem die Vögel über den Kopf herfliegen, aber wohl, daß sie auf dem Kopfe nisten, so kann man auch bösen Gedanken nicht wehren, aber wohl, daß sie in uns einwurzeln.	As one cannot defend against the birds flying up over one's head, but certainly against them nesting on one's head, so one cannot defend against evil thoughts, but certainly against them taking root in us.
Der Wein ist stark, der König ist stärker, die Weiber noch stärker, die Wahrheit am allerstärksten.	The wine is strong, the king is stronger, the women even stronger, the truth is most powerful of all.
Hier stehe ich. Ich kann nicht anders. Gott helfe mir. Amen.	Here I stand. I cannot do otherwise. God help me. Amen.

German music: Baroque

The transition from the late Renaissance to the Baroque period is best exemplified in the music of Italian composer Claudio Monteverdi (1567–1643), whose vocal music surely stands as one of the highlights of Western culture. Outstanding German contributions to the Baroque were made by Johann Jakob Froberger (1616–1667); Johann Pachelbel (1653–1706), whose Canon in D remains a standard part of the contemporary repertoire; and Dietrich Buxtehude (1637–1707).

The incomparable Johann Sebastian Bach (1685–1750) and Georg Friedrich Händel (1685–1759) created music that stands at the apex of human achievement. Bach came from a musical family in Saxony and spent the majority of his career in Leipzig. Händel was born in Halle in the Duchy of Magdeburg but spent the majority of his career in London – this is why we know him as "Handel", without the "ä".

The music of Georg Philipp Telemann (1681–1767) is often overlooked and contains many gems.

Graf von Anderson endorses the following recordings:

René Jacobs, Concerto Vocale, *Monteverdi: Un concert spirituel. Motets*

Gustav Leonhardt, *Froberger: Harpsichord Works*

London Baroque, *Pachelbel: Canon & Gigue*; *Chamber Works*

Freiburger Barockorchester, *J.S. Bach: Brandenburg Concertos*

Glenn Gould, *Bach: Goldberg Variations*

Vittorio Ghielmi, *Bach: Die Kunst der Fuge*

Christopher Herrick, *Bach: Toccatas and Fugues*

Bach Ensemble, Joshua Rifkin, *Bach: 6 Favourite Cantatas*

René Jacobs, *J.S. Bach: Christmas Oratorio*

Swedish Chamber Orchestra, Alexei Ogrintchouk, *Bach: Oboe Concertos*

Emmanuel Pahud, *Bach: Complete Flute Sonatas*

Pierre Fournier, *Bach: 6 Cello Suites*

Hillary Hahn, *Bach: Violin Sonatas Nos. 1 & 2*; *Partita No. 1*

Concerto Köln, *Händel: Water Music*

Nikolaus Harnoncourt, *Handel: Messiah*

Lumiere String Quartet, *Hooked on Handel*

Menuhin Festival Orchestra, *Handel Sarabande*

Chandos Baroque Players, *Telemann: Chamber Music*

Florilegium, *Telemann: Paris Quartets (3 volumes)*

Ton Koopman, Amsterdam Baroque Soloists, *Telemann: Chamber Music*

Ensemble Luxurians, Margaret Hunter, *Telemann: Trio Sonatas for Recorder*

Fabio Biondi, *Telemann: 12 Fantasias for Solo Violin*

Gottfried von der Goltz, *Telemann: Frankfurt Violin Sonatas*

The Monteverdi recording is especially satisfying if set on a timer to begin playing one hour before waking up in the morning. The third movement of the Third Brandenburg Concerto is consistently uplifting. Telemann's chamber music is perfect for contemplative listening and is also conducive to meditative tasks like painting, cooking, reading, studying, and writing.

Recommended films

The Last Valley (James Clavell, 1971)
Ludwig – Requiem für einen jungfräulichen König (Hans-Jürgen Syberberg, 1972)
Ludwig (Luchino Visconti, 1973)
Angst essen Seele auf (Rainer Werner Fassbinder, 1974)
Rollerball (Norman Jewison, 1975)
Keep Surfing (Bjoern Richie Lob, 2009)

Notes

1 Don't let the *ß* (*Eszett*, sometimes also called *scharfes S*) slow you down. It is essentially a doubled "s", as in the Swiss German spelling of *heissen*. There are many videos on the German alphabet on the internet. Now might be a good time to watch one of them.
2 Unless you are asking a yes/no question, giving a command or making a polite suggestion (see later sections of this chapter), or constructing a subordinate clause (see Chapter 6).
3 The popularity of the name "Bobfried" can only increase.

3 *Der-* and *ein*-words and three cases

Nominative, accusative, and dative

German nouns and pronouns exist in cases, and learning how the cases work is essential if you are ever to understand German or produce German that others will understand.

Take a look at the way we express "I", "me", and "mine" in English and in German:

Ich bin ein sehr begabter Student.	**I** am an extremely gifted student.
Viele Leute mögen **mich**.	Many people like **me**.
Der Kellner bringt **mir** ein Bier.	The waiter brings **me** a beer.
Mein Wagen ist grün.	**My** car is green.

Focus on the first person above: "I" corresponds to *ich*, "me" corresponds to *mich* in the second sentence and to *mir* in the third sentence, and "my" corresponds to *mein*. The main difference between English and German is that German recognizes a distinction between *mich* and *mir* that English does not recognize. English uses "me" for *mich* and "me" for *mir*. Let's look into the difference with a triangle to shape our thoughts.

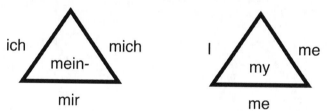

You could call this first person triangle the *ich*-triangle. When something belongs to the *ich*-triangle, which is to say, when something belongs to "me", I call it "my" something, whatever it might be. The dash following *mein-* and the other possessive articles reminds you that they will generally be followed by a noun.

Grammatically, the *ich* side is called "nominative", the *mich* side is called "accusative", and the *mir* side is called "dative". The rest of the chapter will help you understand those concepts. The possessive articles exist in each of the cases, as the rest of this chapter will make clear.

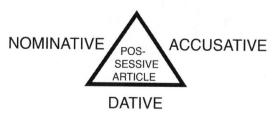

Now that we have taken a look at the *ich*-triangle, let's have a look at the *du*-triangle:

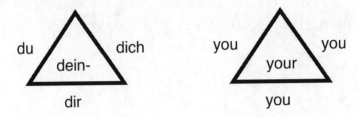

Hopefully, you can see that German is slightly more complex than English when it comes to the familiar second person singular pronouns and possessive articles. The English version of this triangle would consist of "you-you-you" rather than *du-dich-dir*. Notice that *dein* means "your", just like *mein* means "my".

Take a look at the third person masculine singular, the *er*-triangle:

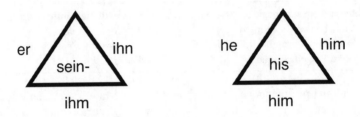

Each of the third person singular pronouns has a triangle. To complete the concept, the definite and indefinite articles belong on these triangles as well.

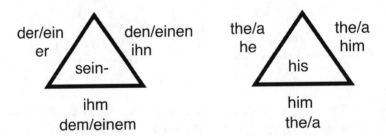

Recall the basic categories of existence outlined in Chapter 1. Each basic category of existence has three modes of being and a possessive article that are easily mapped onto triangles: *ich-mich-mir/mein-*; *du-dich-dir/dein-*; *er-ihn-ihm (der-den-dem/ein-einen-einem)* / *sein-*; and so on.

Obviously, you will need to know these categories in order to construct or understand even the simplest German sentences, so do whatever it takes to internalize them. This chapter will show you what it takes. Later in the chapter (and in the Executive Summary) the complete set of triangles will be presented.

First small step: *der*-words

You have learned already that each German noun has a definite article (*der/die/das*) that indicates its gender in the singular. All of the plurals, regardless of their gender, use the definite article *die*.

Der Mann ist mein Vater.	**The man** is my father.

In the sentence above, *der* means "the". But what if I want to say something other than "the man", for example, "which man?", "this man", or "that man"?

German has several words that follow the pattern of *der* – these are the *der*-words. Take a look at three common *der*-words.

Welcher Mann ist dein Vater?	**Which man** is your father?
Dieser Mann ist mein Vater.	**This man** is my father.
Jener Mann ist mein Vater.	**That man** is my father.

Notice that the endings of *welcher*, *dieser*, and *jener* are "er", just like *der*. Let's look at a feminine noun.

Die Frau ist meine Mutter.	**The woman** is my mother.
Welche Frau ist deine Mutter?	**Which woman** is your mother?
Diese Frau ist meine Mutter.	**This woman** is my mother.
Jene Frau ist meine Mutter.	**That woman** is my mother.

Notice that these words end with "e", just like *die*. Now let's look at a neuter noun.

Das Kind ist mein Sohn.	**The child** is my son.
Welches Kind ist dein Sohn?	**Which child** is your son?
Dieses Kind ist mein Sohn.	**This child** is my son.
Jenes Kind ist mein Sohn.	**That child** is my son.

Hopefully, you see that *welches*, *dieses*, and *jenes* end in "s" just like *das*. Let's observe a plural noun as well.

Die Autos sind neu.	**The cars** are new.
Welche Autos sind neu?	**Which cars** are new?
Diese Autos sind neu.	**These cars** are new.
Jene Autos sind neu.	**Those cars** are new.

Of course, these *der*-words end in "e", just like *die*. Perhaps you are wondering why we call them *der*-words? Because *der-die-das*-words is rather unwieldy. The point is that these words follow the ending pattern of the definite article: *der-die-das, welcher-welche-welches, dieser-diese-dieses*. If you don't see the pattern, keep reading and hopefully it will become clear as the chapter progresses. Certainly, as you work through the exercises the pattern will emerge for you.

Keep in mind that although you might encounter *jen-* in writing, it is rarely spoken. *Dies-* is commonly used for both "this" and "that". (It just works somehow.) In addition to *welch-, dies-,* and *jen-,* there are also a few more *der-*words.

Jeder Porsche ist schön.	**Every Porsche** is beautiful.
Jede Person ist wichtig.	**Every person** is important.
Manches Brot ist dunkel, aber nicht **jedes Brot** ist dunkel.	**Some bread** is dark, but not **every bread** is dark.
Manche Autos sind neu.	**Some cars** are new.
Aller Anfang ist schwer.	**All beginning** is difficult.
Nicht **alle Autos** sind rot.	Not **all cars** are red.
Solche Augen lügen nicht.	**Such eyes** do not lie.

Can you see that *Porsche* is masculine, *Person* is feminine, *Brot* is neuter, and *Autos* is plural? If not, perhaps you should re-read the first two chapters.

Jed- is only used in the singular; for the plural, use *alle*. *Solch-* is generally used in the plural or as part of the more complex expression *solch ein*; the expressions *so ein* and *solch ein* require knowledge of *ein*-words and adjective endings to fully understand, so stay tuned for that!

Here is a table of the *der*-words:

the	der Mann	die Frau	das Kind	die Autos
this/these	dieser Mann	diese Frau	dieses Kind	diese Autos
which?	welcher Mann?	welche Frau?	welches Kind?	welche Autos?
that/those	jener Mann	jene Frau	jenes Kind	jene Autos
some	mancher Mann	manche Frau	manches Kind	manche Autos
all	aller Mann	alle Frau	alles Kind	alle Autos
each/every	jeder Mann	jede Frau	jedes Kind	n/a
such	solcher Mann	solche Frau	solches Kind	solche Autos

Some of these combinations occur only rarely. The point at this moment is to see how the endings of these *der*-words follow the pattern of the definite article.

Second small step: *ein*-words

Sometimes, we don't want to say "the man", or even "this man" or "that man", but rather "a man".

Behold the indefinite article, *ein*.

Ein Mann spielt Gitarre.	**A man** plays guitar.
Ein Elefant spricht Deutsch.	**An elephant** is speaking German.

Ein is the indefinite article. It exists for feminine and neuter nouns as well.

Eine Frau singt.	**A woman** is singing.
Ein Kind spricht Deutsch.	**A child** speaks German.

Notice that there is not an indefinite article for plural nouns! If this is unclear to you, try to imagine "a children" or "a cars" – see how it just doesn't work?

In this case, we just use the noun without an article.

Kinder spielen.	**Children** are playing.
Frauen sprechen.	**Women** are speaking.
Männer singen.	**Men** are singing.

Ein follows this basic pattern:

der Mann (**the** man)	**ein** Mann (**a** man)
die Frau (**the** woman)	**eine** Frau (**a** woman)
das Kind (**the** child)	**ein** Kind (**a** child)
die Autos (**the** cars)	**meine** Autos (**my** cars)

Since *eine Autos* makes no sense whatsoever, we jump ahead slightly and insert one of the *ein*-words into the chart so that we can see the pattern. If you object to *meine Autos*, rest assured that you soon will be able to replace them with *deine Autos* or even *keine Autos*, especially if you think mass transit is the wave of the future.

Kein essentially means "not a" or "not any", as the examples below should make clear.

Take a look at *ein* and *kein* in action by imagining that two aliens have come to earth and disagree about what they are seeing. The use of *das* to mean "that" is something you should simply accept, as in the general question, *Was ist das?* (What is that?).

Alien 1:	Das ist **ein** Mann.	That is **a** man.
Alien 2:	Das ist **kein** Mann!	That is **not a** man!
Alien 1:	Das ist **eine** Frau.	That is **a** woman.
Alien 2:	Das ist **keine** Frau!	That is **not a** woman!
Alien 1:	Das ist **ein** Kind.	That is **a** child.
Alien 2:	Das ist **kein** Kind!	That is **not a** child!
Alien 1:	Die sind Blumen.	Those are flowers.
Alien 2:	Die sind **keine** Blumen!	Those **are not (any)** flowers!

A famous mathematician once expressed the *kein*-concept as a formula:

kein = nicht ein

As a general rule, *kein* is preferable to *nicht ein*, although *nicht ein* is certainly not "wrong".

Like *kein*, The POSSESSIVE ARTICLES are also *ein*-words. They follow the same pattern as *ein* and *kein*, although they are slightly more complicated since there are several of them.

Recall the basic structures of reality from Chapter 1:

	Singular	*Plural*
1st person	ich	wir
2nd person	du	ihr
3rd person	er, sie, es	sie

Each of these basic structures has a corresponding possessive article:

	Singular	*Plural*
1st person	mein (my)	unser (our)
2nd person	dein (your)	euer (your)

Each of these possessive articles will always be followed by a noun. If you have trouble with this concept, say the word "my" and wait a moment. Do you hear the universe asking you, "Your what?" Possessive articles require nouns.

The third person chart looks like this:

	Singular	*Plural*
3rd person masculine	sein (his)	ihr (their)
3rd person feminine	ihr (her)	ihr (their)
3rd person neuter	sein (its)	ihr (their)

In order to see clearly how these possessive articles work, let us imagine that everyone in the world has a beautiful dragon, which you will recall from your homework in Chapter 1 is *der Drache*.

1st person	**Mein** Drache ist schön!	**My** dragon is beautiful!
	Unser Drache ist schön!	**Our** dragon is beautiful!
2nd person	**Dein** Drache ist schön!	**Your** dragon is beautiful!
	Euer Drache ist schön!	**Your** dragon is beautiful!
3rd person	**Sein** Drache ist schön!	**His** dragon is beautiful!
	Ihr Drache ist schön!	**Her** dragon is beautiful!
	Sein Drache ist schön!	**Its** dragon is beautiful!
	Ihr Drache ist schön!	**Their** dragon is beautiful!

Now imagine that everyone has a beautiful cat, which you probably already know is *die Katze*.

1st person	**Meine** Katze ist schön!	**My** cat is beautiful!
	Unsre Katze ist schön!	**Our** cat is beautiful!
2nd person	**Deine** Katze ist schön!	**Your** cat is beautiful!
	Eure Katze ist schön!	**Your** cat is beautiful!
3rd person	**Seine** Katze ist schön!	**His** cat is beautiful!
	Ihre Katze ist schön!	**Her** cat is beautiful!
	Seine Katze ist schön!	**Its** cat is beautiful!
	Ihre Katze ist schön!	**Their** cat is beautiful!

Hopefully you can see that *meine*, *deine*, and *seine* look very much like *eine*. Can you also see that *ihre*, *eure*, and *unsre* end in "e", just like *eine* does? Do you see how the masculine forms *mein*, *dein*, *sein*, *ihr*, *unser*, and *euer* do not add an ending, just like *ein* does not add an ending?

Keep these patterns in mind as we move forward.

Notice also that *unsere* and *euere* can be spelled *unsre* and *eure*, since *euere* and *unsere* can appear to be a little unwieldy.[1] The choice is yours, although for the remainder of this book, we will always spell in the most efficient fashion.

Now imagine that everyone also has a beautiful unicorn, which you undoubtedly recall is *das Einhorn*.

1st person	**Mein** Einhorn ist schön!	**My** unicorn is beautiful!
	Unser Einhorn ist schön!	**Our** unicorn is beautiful!
2nd person	**Dein** Einhorn ist schön!	**Your** unicorn is beautiful!
	Euer Einhorn ist schön!	**Your** unicorn is beautiful!
3rd person	**Sein** Einhorn ist schön!	**His** unicorn is beautiful!
	Ihr Einhorn ist schön!	**Her** unicorn is beautiful!
	Sein Einhorn ist schön!	**Its** unicorn is beautiful!
	Ihr Einhorn ist schön!	**Their** unicorn is beautiful!

You have already noticed that both masculine and neuter nouns use *ein*, and now you see that quite logically they also use *mein*, *dein*, *sein*, etc.

Of course, plural nouns also work with the possessive articles. Imagine that everyone receives two beautiful new cars from the Social Democrats.

1st person	**Meine** Autos sind schön!	**My** cars are beautiful!
	Unsre Autos sind schön!	**Our** cars are beautiful!
2nd person	**Deine** Autos sind schön!	**Your** cars are beautiful!
	Eure Autos sind schön!	**Your** cars are beautiful!
3rd person	**Seine** Autos sind schön!	**His** cars are beautiful!
	Ihre Autos sind schön!	**Her** cars are beautiful!
	Seine Autos sind schön!	**Its** cars are beautiful!
	Ihre Autos sind schön!	**Their** cars are beautiful!

To put this concept into another perspective, look at all of the new things my wealthy best friend has.

der Mercedes	Sein Mercedes ist neu.	His Mercedes is new.
die Geige	Seine Geige ist alt.	His violin is old.
das Hemd	Sein Hemd ist teuer.	His shirt is expensive.
die Apfelbäume	Seine Apfelbäume sind gut gepflegt.	His apple trees are well tended.

In each sentence, *sein-* refers to my friend, and the ending is selected according to the gender of each noun that he possesses. After some practice, you will see that this is mind-numbingly easy.

The question word *wessen* is useful here. It means "whose".

Wessen Buch ist das?	**Whose** book is that?
Das ist **mein** Buch!	That is **my** book!

Likewise, the dative verb *gehören* is useful here. It means "to belong to".

Wem gehört das Buch?	To whom does the book belong?
Das ist **mein** Buch!	That is **my** book!

But in order to understand *wem*, we need to move into the next section.

And now a bigger step: the nominative, accusative, and dative cases

Take a deep breath. Mastering the cases is the key to speaking German in a way that will earn you the respect of native German speakers. Without the cases, you will always sound terrible to German ears. Additionally, you will not understand most of what you read or hear. The cases are the key.

The most straightforward explanation of the cases is derived from the following example:

Der Mann gibt dem Professor den Schnaps.	The man gives the professor the schnapps.

The sentence has three masculine nouns: *der Mann, der Professor*, and *der Schnaps*. The verb is *geben* (to give).

Der Mann is the SUBJECT. He is giving the schnapps to the professor. Neither the schnapps nor the professor is doing anything in this sentence – they are OBJECTS. Objects lack agency: only the subject has agency; only the subject can do anything. In life, you want to be a subject, not an object.

The SUBJECT of a sentence is ALWAYS in the NOMINATIVE CASE.

But what about *der Professor* and *der Schnaps*, you ask? Why did *der Professor* change to *dem Professor?* And why did *der Schnaps* change to *den Schnaps?* Perhaps most importantly: can one still drink *den Schnaps?* Actually, one can only drink *den Schnaps*. Why? Keep reading!

In order to show which noun is playing which role, the articles change – this is the magic of the cases!

Imagine the simple sentence:

Der Mann gibt.	The man gives.

Hopefully you have no trouble seeing that the subject is *der Mann* and the verb is *gibt*. But a loud voice inside your head should be screaming: *Was gibt er?*

Why? Because giving requires something to give, like a present, a chance, or even a damn. The thing being given is called a DIRECT OBJECT.

DIRECT OBJECTS are ALWAYS in the ACCUSATIVE CASE.

Der Mann gibt **den Schnaps**.	The man gives **the schnapps**.

In the ACCUSATIVE CASE, masculine singular nouns undergo a change: *der* changes to *den* and *ein* changes to *einen*. Can you keep your eye on *der Ball* in the sentences below?

Der Ball ist rund.	**The ball** is round.
Der Mann kickt **den Ball**.	The man kicks **the ball**.

The answer of course is "no". In German you can only keep your eye on *den Ball*.

In the ACCUSATIVE CASE, the feminine, neuter, and plural forms remain the same as in the nominative case.

Die Blume ist blau.	**The flower** is blue.
Der Mann pflückt **die Blume**.	The man picks **the flower**.
Das Bier ist kalt.	**The beer** is cold.
Der Mann trinkt **das Bier**.	The man drinks **the beer**.
Die Erdbeeren sind süß.	**The strawberries** are sweet.
Der Mann isst **die Erdbeeren**.	The man eats **the strawberries**.

The examples above should convince you that only masculine singular nouns change in the accusative case. In the accusative case, *die Blume, das Bier*, and *die Erdbeeren* remain exactly as they were in the nominative case.

The pronouns behave exactly like the nouns they represent; only the masculine singular undergoes a change:

Der Mann kickt **den Ball**.	The man kicks **the ball**.
Der Mann kickt **ihn**.	The man kicks **it**.

Der Mann pflückt **die Blume**.	The man picks **the flower**.
Der Mann pflückt **sie**.	The man picks **it**.

Der Mann trinkt **das Bier**.	The man drinks **the beer**.
Der Mann trinkt **es**.	The man drinks **it**.

Der Mann isst **die Erdbeeren**.	The man eats **the strawberries**.
Der Mann isst **sie**.	The man eats **them**.

Hopefully the idea of a direct object is now clear to you.

Let's return once again to the man and the schnapps:

Der Mann gibt den Schnaps.	The man gives the schnapps.

Quite possibly another question is shouting itself through your head: *Wem?* "To whom" does the man give the schnapps?

Giving requires not only a direct object (something to give) but also an indirect object (someone to give to).

Der Mann gibt **dem Professor** den Schnaps.	The man gives **the professor** the schnapps.

Der Professor has changed to *dem Professor* – what the hell is going on?

The DATIVE CASE is for INDIRECT OBJECTS. In the example sentence, *dem Professor* is the indirect object. He neither gives nor is being given, but rather, is being given to.

In the DATIVE CASE, all nouns undergo a change. Look at the chart below.

Nominative	Dative
der Professor / ein Professor	dem Professor / einem Professor
die Professorin / eine Professorin	der Professorin / einer Professorin
das Kind / ein Kind	dem Kind / einem Kind
die Kinder / meine Kinder	den Kinder**n** / meinen Kinder**n**

Notice that the plural nouns add an "n" in the dative case (unless they end in "s" or "n"). Once again, we've used *mein-* to indicate the pattern for the plural *ein-*words. If you don't want the children, feel free to change it to *dein-* or *kein-*. If you don't understand why it cannot be *ein-*, recall that "a children" does not make sense. To illustrate the pattern, we substitute one of the other *ein-*words.

Now you can see that the man can give the schnapps to anyone he wants!

Der Mann gibt **dem Professor** den Schnaps.	The man gives **the professor** the schnapps.
Der Mann gibt **ihm** den Schnaps.	The man gives **him** the schnapps.
Der Mann gibt **der Professorin** den Schnaps.	The man gives **the professor** the schnapps.
Der Mann gibt **ihr** den Schnaps.	The man gives **her** the schnapps.
Der Mann gibt **dem Kind** den Schnaps.	The man gives **the child** the schnapps.
Der Mann gibt **ihm** den Schnaps.	The man gives **him/her/it/"them"**[2] the schnapps.
Der Mann gibt **den Kindern** den Schnaps.	The man gives **the children** the schnapps.
Der Mann gibt **ihnen** den Schnaps.	The man gives **them** the schnapps.

Notice that extra "n" on the end of *Kinder*. Dative plural nouns need this ending! Also, be aware that giving schnapps to children is illegal in most jurisdictions and is probably morally wrong everywhere.

The exciting part of the three cases is, of course, that a sentence can be written several ways without changing its meaning:

Der Mann gibt dem Professor den Schnaps.	The man gives the professor the schnapps.
Den Schnaps gibt der Mann dem Professor.	The man gives the professor the schnapps.
Dem Professor gibt der Mann den Schnaps.	The man gives the professor the schnapps.

In each variation, the verb is firmly in second place, and the subject is adjacent to the verb. The cases allow us to see, regardless of the order of the nouns, that the man is the subject, the schnapps is the direct object, and the professor is the indirect object.

The sentences above allow us to precisely answer a few questions.

Wer gibt dem Professor den Schnaps?	**Who** gives the professor the schnapps?

The best answer is clearly *der Mann*.

Der Mann gibt dem Professor den Schnaps.	**The man** gives the professor the schnapps.

Perhaps you have noticed that *wer* and *der* are similar. That's because *wer* always asks for the subject of a sentence. The answer to *wer* will always be the subject of the sentence, and hence, it will always be in the nominative case.

Wer hat einen grünen Porsche?	Who has a green Porsche?
Graf von Anderson hat einen grünen Porsche.	Graf von Anderson has a green Porsche.
Wer?	Who?
Der Graf!	The count!

The NOMINATIVE CASE is called *der Wer-Fall* in German. Hopefully, you were able to deduce that *der Fall* means "the case".

As you've already seen, another question we might ask is:

Was gibt der Mann dem Professor?	**What** does the man give to the professor?

The best answer to this question would clearly be *den Schnaps*.

Den Schnaps gibt der Mann dem Professor.	The man gives the professor **the schnapps**.

Notice that the meaning of the sentence has not changed! By placing *den Schnaps* right at the beginning of the sentence, we are able to answer the question more immediately than if we had placed it all the way at the end. We even could have answered the question without completing the sentence. This flexibility is one of the elegant features that the German cases make possible.

Imagine for a moment that the man sees the schnapps in his liquor cabinet:

Der Mann sieht den Schnaps.	The man sees the schnapps.
Den Schnaps sieht der Mann.	The man sees the schnapps.

Once again, the man is the subject, so he must be in the nominative case, and the schnapps is the direct object, so it must be in the accusative case.

You could easily form a question if you did not quite understand what the man said he saw:

Was sieht der Mann?	**What** does the man see?

And the answer would be: *den Schnaps*.

Now imagine that the man sees the professor, perhaps in the library or on the street rather than in the liquor cabinet.

Der Mann sieht den Professor.	The man sees the professor.
Den Professor sieht der Mann.	The man sees the professor.

How do we ask whom he saw? The question word *was* worked just fine for the schnapps, but the professor is a person, not a thing, so we would ask:

Wen sieht der Mann?	**Whom** does the man see?

The answer is of course *den Professor*.

Perhaps you notice that *wen* looks very much like *den*. The ACCUSATIVE CASE is called *der Wen-Fall* in German. Direct objects will always be in the accusative case.

Was hat Graf von Anderson?	What does Graf von Anderson have?
Einen Porsche hat er.	He has a Porsche.
Was?	What?
Einen Porsche!	A Porsche!

Wen liebt Graf von Anderson?	Whom does Graf von Anderson love?
Die Gräfin liebt er.	He loves the countess.
Wen?	Whom?
Die Gräfin!	The countess!

Going back to the schnapps, another question we might ask is:

Wem gibt der Mann den Schnaps?	**To whom** does the man give the schnapps?

The best answer is of course *dem Professor*.

Dem Professor gibt der Mann den Schnaps.	The man gives **the professor** the schnapps.

The DATIVE CASE is called *der Wem-Fall* in German. Indirect objects will always be in the dative case.

Wem schenkt Graf von Anderson ein Landhaus?	To whom does Graf von Anderson give a cottage?
Einem Künstler schenkt er es.	He gives it to an artist.
Wem?	To whom?
Einem Künstler!	To an artist!

Take a look at the professor as he moves through the three cases:

Nominative:	**Der Professor** spricht Deutsch.	**The professor** speaks German.
Accusative:	Der Mann kickt **den Professor**.	The man kicks **the professor**.
Dative:	Der Mann schenkt **dem Professor** Blumen.	The man gives **the professor** flowers.

As you can see, only *der Professor* can do anything! Likewise, only *den Professor* can have anything done to him, whether it is being kicked or seen. Finally, it is only to *dem Professor* that we can give anything.

Thinking of each noun and pronoun as a three-sided figure will help you. Take a look at these amazing diagrams of the third person singular,[3] one of which you will recall from the beginning of this chapter:

Before we rewrite the classic sentence with the man, the professor, and the schnapps with pronouns, take a look at the order of the words:

Der Mann	gibt	dem Professor	den Schnaps.
1.	2.	3.	4.

When the subject is in the first place, the indirect object should come before the direct object. We do this in English as well.

> The man gives the professor the schnapps.

It would be awkward to reverse the order of "professor" and "schnapps".

Starting with this basic sentence, we can replace *der Mann* with *er*, and the order of the words remains the same.

| Er gibt dem Professor den Schnaps. | He gives the professor the schnapps. |

When we replace the direct object, *den Schnaps*, with a pronoun, the order of the words changes.

| Er gibt ihn dem Professor. | He gives it to the professor. |

Again, assuming that the subject is in the first place, the general rule is that pronouns come before nouns. We would construct the English sentence exactly the same way.

If we had replaced the indirect object, *dem Professor*, then we would have written, also exactly as in English:

| Er gibt ihm den Schnaps. | He gives him the schnapps. |

Finally, if both the direct object and the indirect object are pronouns, then the order is reversed, again, just like in English!

| Er gibt ihn ihm. | He gives it to him. |

In short, if the direct object and indirect object are both nouns, the indirect object comes first. If they are both pronouns, the direct object comes first. If one is a pronoun and the other is a noun, then the pronoun comes first.

Obviously, if the sentence begins with either the direct object or the indirect object, then the rules of subject-verb placement make further rules unnecessary:

> Dem Professor gibt der Mann den Schnapps.
> Ihm gibt er ihn.

> Den Schnaps gibt der Mann dem Professor.
> Ihn gibt er ihm.

If you don't understand, try to change the order of the pronouns in third and fourth place. You cannot, because the subject has to touch the verb!

Why not read through this section once more before moving on to take a closer look at each of the three cases in the following sections? To test yourself, you could change each occurrence of *Professor* to some form of *ich*. Can you get the man to give you the schnapps?

Learning to get the schnapps from the man – that's the Graf von Anderson Advantage!

A closer look at the nominative case

The nominative case is for the subject of a sentence. Whatever is doing the verb will be in the nominative case. Feel free to review the epic tale of the man and the schnapps above if this is unclear.

The nominative case is also used for **predicate nouns**. Take a look at the example below.

Mein Vater ist **der Mann**!	My father is **the man**!

The subject of the sentence is *mein Vater*, which is in the nominative case, as all subjects always are.

Der Mann is in the nominative case because it is a predicate of *mein Vater*. Think of a predicate as anything that is stated to be equivalent to the subject, as illustrated below by the equals sign.

mein Vater = der Mann

∴ der Mann is a predicate of mein Vater

The verbs *sein* (to be) and *werden* (to become) require predicates.

Ich bin **ein Kind**.	Ich = ein Kind (now)
Ich werde **ein Mann**.	Ich = ein Mann (over time)

Imagine *Kindergartenkind Nr. 1* talking with *Kindergartenkind Nr. 2*:

K1: Ich bin!	K1: I am!
K2: Was? Was bist du?	K2: What? What are you?
K1: Ein Drache! Ich bin ein Drache!	K1: A dragon! I am a dragon!

Do you see that *ich bin* is not complete until a predicate is added? *Ich bin* requires a predicate to finish the thought.

ich = ein Drache

∴ ein Drache is a predicate of ich

Ein Drache is a predicate of *ich*, and is therefore in the nominative case.

Since every sentence has a subject, every sentence will have at least one noun or pronoun in the nominative case. If there are two nominatives, then one of them is a predicate of the other.

A closer look at the accusative case

The accusative case is for direct objects. Whatever is being acted upon is the direct object. In the example below, *den Ball* is the direct object since it is being kicked.

Der Mann kickt **den Ball**.	The man kicks **the ball**.

Not every direct object is as obvious as *den Ball*, but when in doubt, you can always ask yourself: is this like the ball, when it is being tossed, kicked, purchased, stored, sold, used, or thrown away?

Imagine *Student Nr. 1* talking with *Student Nr. 2*:

S1: Ich habe!	S1: I have!
S2: Was hast du?	S2: What do you have?
S1: Einen Hund habe ich!	S1: I have a dog!

As you can see above, the verb *haben* (to have) requires a direct object, just like *sein* and *werden* require predicates. Whatever is "being had" will always be in the accusative case.

The expression *es gibt* deserves special attention. *Es gibt* means "there is", but is constructed more like "it gives", as if the UNIVERSAL "IT" that provides all of the elements of reality that exist at each and every moment were constantly handing them out.

Was gibt es in dem Klassenzimmer?	**What** is there in the classroom?
Es gibt **einen Professor**.	There is **a professor**.
Es gibt **eine Lampe**.	There is **a lamp**.
Es gibt **ein Fenster**.	There is **a window**.
Es gibt **keine Studenten**.	There are **no students**.

Whatever follows *es gibt* will be in the accusative case. The subject of the sentence is *es* and the verb is *geben* (to give). Once again, imagine *es* as the all-powerful universal force, and make yourself believe that everything that exists is only there on account of the universe constantly giving it out.

Gibt es Fragen?	Are there questions?
Nein, es gibt keine Fragen!	No, there are not any questions!

Keine Fragen – that's the Graf von Anderson Advantage!

A closer look at the dative case

The dative case is for indirect objects. Imagine that I alter the earlier example to include a few more indirect objects.

Der Mann gibt **mir** den Schnaps.	The man gives **me** the schnapps.
Der Mann gibt **dir** den Schnaps.	The man gives **you** the schnapps.
Der Mann gibt **meinem Sohn** den Schnaps.	The man gives **my son** the schnapps.
Der Mann gibt **dieser Frau** den Schnaps.	The man gives **this woman** the schnapps.
Der Mann gibt **unsren Freunden** den Schnaps.	The man gives **our friends** the schnapps.

You could take every noun in the dictionary and turn it into the indirect object in the sentence above just by putting it in the dative case. Wow.

The common expression *wie geht's?* requires an indirect object, although sometimes it is only implied. Let's take a closer look.

Like the *es* in *es gibt*, *wie geht's?* assumes the existence of an all-powerful universal *es* that is constantly going. *Geht's* is a contraction of *geht es*.

Wie geht es?	How goes it?
Wie geht's?	How's it going?

Of course, when we ask *wie geht's?* we don't want to know about everything in the universe, but rather just a small part of it. We specify that small part by using the dative case.

Wie geht es **dir**?	How goes it **for you**?
Es geht **mir** gut.	It goes well **for me**.
Wie geht es **unsrem König**?	How goes it **for our king**?
Es geht **ihm** sehr gut!	It goes very well **for him**.
Wie geht es **dieser Königin**?	How goes it for **this queen**?
Ihr geht es wunderbar!	It goes wonderfully **for her**.

You can ask how it is going for any noun in the dictionary just by combining *wie geht's* with the dative form of that noun. What a fabulous world!

Dative verbs require an indirect object, just like other verbs require a predicate or a direct object. You probably recall the example of the verb *gehören* (to belong to) from earlier in the chapter:

Wem gehört das Buch?	**To whom** does the book belong?
Das Buch gehört **mir**.	The book belongs **to me**.

Take a look at a few more exciting examples:

Die Schüler folgen **der Lehrerin**.	The pupils follow **the teacher**.
Der Lehrer hilft **den Schülern**.	The teacher helps **the pupils**.
Die Eltern danken **den Lehrern**.	The parents thank **the teachers**.
Die Stadt gefällt **ihnen**.	The city pleases **them**.[4]
Ich glaube **dir** nicht!	I don't believe **you**!

The verbs *fragen* (to ask) and *antworten* (to answer) deserve a special comment, since *fragen* requires a direct object and *antworten* requires an indirect object. You can think about it, or just accept it.

Wen fragst du?	**Whom** are you asking?
Ich frage **dich**.	I ask **you**.
Wem antwortest du?	**Whom** are you answering?
Ich antworte **dir**.	I answer **you**.

When you spend time learning verbs, consider always whether they work with a direct object, an indirect object, or both. Look at the verb *erzählen* (to tell a story).

Ich erzähle.	I tell.
Was erzähst du?	**What** do you tell?
Ich erzähle **eine Geschichte**.	I tell **a story**.
Wem erzählst du eine Geschichte?	**To whom** do you tell a story?
Ich erzähle **meinen Freunden** eine Geschichte.	I tell **my friends** a story.

Erzählen requires both types of object, since the concept of "telling" requires both "something to tell" and "someone to tell it to".

Expanded tables and triangles

At this point, an expanded version of the tables and triangles presented at the beginning of the chapter will be useful.

First person

	Singular	Plural
Nominative	ich	wir
Accusative	mich	uns
Dative	mir	uns
Possessive article	mein	unser

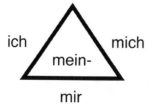

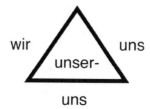

Second person (familiar)

	Singular	Plural
Nominative	du	ihr
Accusative	dich	euch
Dative	dir	euch
Possessive article	dein	euer

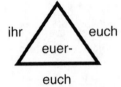

Third person (pronouns)

	Singular (masculine)	Singular (feminine)	Singular (neuter)	Plural
Nominative	er	sie	es	sie
Accusative	ihn	sie	es	sie
Dative	ihm	ihr	ihm	ihnen
Possessive article	sein	ihr	sein	ihr

Third person (definite/indefinite articles)

	Singular (masculine)	Singular (feminine)	Singular (neuter)	Plural
Nominative	der/ein	die/eine	das/ein	die/meine
Accusative	den/einen	die/eine	das/ein	die/deine
Dative	dem/einem	der/einer	dem/einem	den (+n)/ seinen (+n)
Possessive article	sein	ihr	sein	ihr

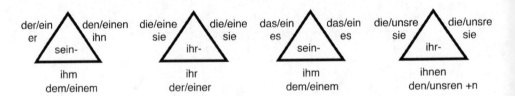

For the last time: the pattern of the plural indefinite article can be illustrated by any of the possessive articles or by the negative indefinite article, *kein-*. I have used *mein-*, *dein-*, and *sein-* in the chart above since they contain "ein". I have used *unser-* on the triangle because our future on this planet will require solidarity and cooperation.

At this point it might be useful to recall that the formal second person follows the pattern of the third person plural.

Second person (formal)

	Singular	*Plural*
Nominative	Sie	Sie
Accusative	Sie	Sie
Dative	Ihnen	Ihnen
Possessive article	Ihr	Ihr

The only difference between the third person plural and formal second person is the capitalization. As you know from Chapter 1, the singular and plural forms are identical, so there is only one triangle.

Masculine N-nouns

You might be quite pleased to have a *Graf* (count) as the author of your college German language and culture text. Please try to hold onto that positive feeling as the concept of masculine N-nouns (also known, quite slanderously, as "weak nouns") is presented.

Behold the count as he moves through the cases:

Nominative:	Der Graf fliegt nach Tahiti.	Der Graf is the subject.
	Der beste Professor ist der Graf.	Der Graf is the predicate.
Accusative:	Den Grafen haben wir als Professor.	Den Grafen is the direct object.
	Es gibt in dem Klassenzimmer einen Grafen.	Einen Grafen is the direct object.
Dative:	Wir kaufen dem Grafen eine Flasche Rotwein.	Dem Grafen is the indirect object.
	Wie geht es unsrem Grafen?	Unsrem Grafen is the indirect object.

You should see that *Graf* only exists in the nominative case, which is to say, *Graf* can only be a subject or a predicate. In every other case, the form *Grafen* is used, along with the appropriate article. Why this is called a weak form will always puzzle me; it takes strength to be unusual.

Here are some further examples of masculine N-nouns:

Nominative	*Accusative*	*Dative*
der/ein Herr	den/einen Herrn	dem/einem Herrn
der/ein Student	den/einen Studenten	dem/einem Studenten
der/ein Junge	den/einen Jungen	dem/einem Jungen
der/ ein Drache	den/einen Drachen	dem/ einem Drachen
der/ein Philosoph	den/einen Philosophen	dem/einem Philosophen

Let's follow the philosopher through the cases:

Nominative (subject)	Ein Philosoph ist sehr intelligent.	A philosopher is very intelligent.
Nominative (predicate)	Aristoteles ist ein Philosoph.	Aristotle is a philosopher.
Accusative (direct object)	Wir besuchen einen Philosophen.	We visit a philosopher.
Dative (indirect object)	Wir folgen einem Philosophen.	We follow a philosopher.

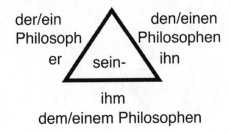

Essentially, masculine N-nouns require an "n" or an "en" ending in every case other than nominative. In other respects, they behave just like other masculine singular nouns.

Reflexive verbs

By now, unless you are truly and hopelessly lost, you understand the concepts of "subject", "direct object", and "indirect object". Think of reflexive verbs as a real test of your understanding. These verbs play an important role in the German language: German uses reflexive verbs with far greater frequency than English.

Imagine that a man is washing his dog, his car, his cat, or even his spaceships.

Ein Mann wäscht seinen Hund.	A man washes his dog.
Ein Mann wäscht seine Katze.	A man washes his cat.
Ein Mann wäscht sein Auto.	A man washes his car.
Ein Mann wäscht seine Raumschiffe.	A man washes his spaceships.

You should be able to clearly see that the man is the subject and that his dog, car, cat, and spaceships are the direct objects. If you can't see that, then you should go back and review the earlier sections of this chapter.

Now imagine that the man washes himself, perhaps after a long day of athletic practice or manual labor on behalf of the enlightened aristocracy.

Ein Mann wäscht **sich**.	A man washes **himself**.

This time, the man himself is not only the subject, but also the direct object! *Sich* is a reflexive pronoun – it means "himself", "herself", "itself", and "themselves".

Eine Frau wäscht **sich**.	A woman washes **herself**.
Ein Auto wäscht **sich** nicht.	A car does not wash **itself**.
Unsre Kinder waschen **sich**.	Our children wash **themselves**.

In each of the above examples, *sich* refers back to the subject. This reference back to the subject is what makes the verb "reflexive" – the subject does the verb to itself.

Notice that each of the examples above is in the third person. If "the third person" means nothing to you, then you absolutely need to re-read Chapters 1 and 2.

What about the first person and second person? Rather than *sich*, we use the accusative pronouns:

Ich wasche **mich**.	I wash **myself**.
Wir waschen **uns**.	We wash **ourselves**.
Du wäschst **dich**.	You wash **yourself**.
Ihr wascht **euch**.	You wash **yourselves**.

The logic here is simple: *mich*, *uns*, *dich*, and *euch* are unambiguous in a way that *ihn*, *sie*, *es*, and *sie* are not. Think about it.

Before moving on to several examples of reflexive verbs, let's go one step further with *sich waschen*, which obviously means "to wash oneself".

In English we commonly say "I wash my hands", especially if we narrate the small events of our daily lives, perhaps in front of a webcam, or maybe in an epic internal monologue.

In German, we would use *sich waschen* in the following manner:

Ich wasche mir die Hände.	I wash my hands.

It looks like "I wash myself the hands", but indeed this is how the thought "I wash my hands" is expressed in the Teutonic tongue. *Ich wasche meine Hände* sounds stilted and is uncommon outside of metaphorical use.

Notice that we used the dative pronoun, rather than the accusative! Compare:

Ich wasche **mich**.	I wash myself.
Ich wasche **mir** die Hände.	I wash my hands.

In the first example, *mich* is the direct object. In the second example, *die Hände* is the direct object, so we use the dative pronoun *mir* to show reflexivity. In the examples, *mich* and *mir* refer back to the subject, *ich*. Hopefully you can see this referring back to the subject as a reflexive action.

Observe this phenomenon in the *du* form:

Du wäschst **dich**.	You wash yourself.
Du wäscht **dir** die Hände.	You wash your hands.

In the first example, *dich* is the direct object. In the second, *die Hände* is the direct object, so the dative pronoun is used to show reflexivity. In the examples, *dich* and *dir* refer back to the subject, *du*.

Take a look at the *wir* and *ihr* forms:

Wir waschen **uns**.	We wash ourselves.
Wir waschen **uns** die Hände.	We wash our hands.
Ihr wascht **euch**.	You wash yourselves.
Ihr wascht **euch** die Hände.	You wash your hands.

You will notice that the reflexive pronouns *uns* and *euch* are both accusative and dative. Perhaps this will make it less surprising that *sich* is both accusative and dative as well.

Er wäscht **sich**.	He washes himself.
Er wäscht **sich** die Hände.	He washes his hands.
Sie wäscht **sich**.	She washes herself.
Sie wäscht **sich** die Hände.	She washes her hands.
Es wäscht **sich**.	It washes itself.
Es wäscht **sich** die Hände.	It washes its hands.
Sie waschen **sich**.	They wash themselves.
Sie waschen **sich** die Hände.	They wash their hands.

The distinction between direct object and indirect object reflexive pronouns clearly does not play a role anywhere except in the *ich* and *du* forms.

Now that the basic concept is clear, let's look at some of the reflexive verbs in action.

sich anziehen	Ich ziehe **mich** an.	I get dressed.
	Ich ziehe **mir** einen Hoodie an.	I put on a hoodie.
sich duschen	Ich dusche **mich**.	I take a shower.
sich putzen[5]	Ich putze **mir** die Zähne.	I brush my teeth.
sich kämmen	Ich kämme **mir** die Haare.	I comb my hair.
sich bürsten	Ich bürste **mir** die Haare.	I brush my hair.
sich rasieren	Ich rasiere **mich**.	I shave myself.
	Ich rasiere **mir** die Beine.	I shave my legs.
sich amusieren	Ich amüsiere **mich**.	I amuse myself.

Quite a few other reflexive verbs exist, many of which require **prepositional phrases**. We will learn about these in the next chapter. Here are a couple of examples.

sich erinnern	Ich erinnere mich **an dich**.	I remember **you**.
sich freuen	Ich freue mich **darauf**.	I'm looking forward **to it**.

We're all looking forward to it – that's the Graf von Anderson Advantage!

Übungen

A   Rewrite the following sentences as questions using the correct form of *welch* and answer the questions using the correct form of *dies*. Translate.

Das Einhorn ist weiß.	Die Frau ist reich.	Der Hund ist groß.
Der Drache ist grün.	Der Mann ist intelligent.	Die Katze ist klein.
Die Zauberin ist attraktiv.	Das Kind ist nett.	Das Raumschiff ist schön.

B   Transform the noun in each sentence above into a plural and combine with the correct form of *all*. Don't forget to re-conjugate the verb! Translate.

C   Rewrite each of the sentences in A and B using each of the possessive adjectives. Translate.

D   Rewrite each of the sentences in C into an *es gibt* statement using the correct form of *ein*. The adjectives should disappear; just use the nouns (there is a unicorn, there are unicorns, there is a dragon, there are dragons, etc.). Translate.

E   Use the singular and the plural forms of the nouns in D and the correct form of *kein* to write a sentence that begins with the phrase *in diesem Zimmer* and states either that there is not one or that there are not any of those things in this room. Translate.

F   Assume that you are talking to a friend named Lola, to whom each of the nouns in A belongs. Tell your friend that you see their nouns (I see your unicorn, I see your wife, etc.). Translate.

G   Assume that you are talking to me, telling me, rather than your friend, what you are seeing. The nouns still belong to your friend Lola, who identifies as a woman. Translate.

H   Now you are talking to Lola again. Ask her how each of her nouns is doing by using *wie geht's*. Translate.

I   Pretend that you are Lola and use pronouns to answer the questions in H. Translate.

J   You find out from a mutual friend that Lola now identifies as a man and has taken the name Lolo. That's cool, you reply. And then you ask this friend how Lolo's nouns are doing. Translate.

K   Compare your answers in G and J, reflecting on the multi-gendered character of the possessive articles; the initial selection of possessive article depends upon the gender identity of the possessor, while the ending of the possessive article depends on the gender of the noun they possess.

L   The holidays are coming! Now it is time to give. Combine the following gifts and recipients, answering the question: *wem gibst du was?* Translate.

seine Schwester: Buch	ihr (Lolas) Vater: Hut	ihr (Fritz' und Mias) Kind: Hund
seine Großeltern: Katze	unsre Brüder: Uhren	ihre (Lolas) Brüder: Batterien
mein Mann: Ring	meine Frau: Audi	unser Graf: Porsche

M   Imagine a playfully frustrating conversation with someone who becomes increasingly exasperated as they must repeat the same information, although with a different emphasis, over and over, again and again. Using your answers in L, write (and translate) a series of questions and answers as in the example below:

Ich gebe meiner Tante ein Einhorn.	I am giving my aunt a unicorn.
Was gibst du deiner Tante?	What are you giving to your aunt?
Ein Einhorn. Ein Einhorn gebe ich ihr.	A unicorn. I am giving her a unicorn.
Wem gibst du ein Einhorn?	To whom are you giving a unicorn?
Meiner Tante. Meiner Tante gebe ich es.	To my aunt. I am giving a unicorn to my aunt.
Wer gibt deiner Tante ein Einhorn?	Who is giving your aunt a unicorn?
Ich. Ich gebe es ihr.	I (am). I am giving it to her.

When you answer the question, answer it quickly, with only the requested information, and then answer with a complete sentence.

Perhaps looking at the triangles while or after completing these exercises will help you internalize the nominative, accusative, and dative cases. Essentially, for each initial sentence you should ask and answer a question for each side of the triangle.

Finally, aside from the information requested by the question, use pronouns in your answers.

N   What would you do in the following situations? In some situations, a verb will only help you if it is used reflexively. In other situations, the direct object is something or someone other than the subject. Translate the situations below and your response to each situation, and be prepared to explain to a child, which of your responses requires a reflexive verb and why:

Dein Auto ist dreckig.	Dein Körper ist dreckig.	Dein Gesicht ist dreckig.
Deine Haare sind dreckig.	Deine Zähne sind dreckig.	Du willst kein nacktes Blumenkind sein.
Dir ist kalt, aber du hast einen Pullover.	Dein Kind ist ein nacktes Blumenkind.	Deinem Kind ist kalt, aber du hast einen Pullover.

Of course you have *einen Pullover* – that's the Graf von Anderson Advantage!

Travel: Salzburg, Innsbruck, Merano, and Bolzano

Riding on the train from Munich to Salzburg, one begins to climb into the Alps, passing through the beautiful Bavarian towns of Rosenheim and Prien am Chiemsee before crossing the frontier into Austria and arriving in magical Salzburg.

Salzburg has been settled since Roman times and has been the seat of a Roman Catholic archbishop since 798 CE. Famous as the birthplace of Mozart and for providing the beautiful setting of *The Sound of Music*, Salzburg is also home to several world-class institutions of higher learning, numerous fine examples of Baroque architecture, and the annual *Salzburger Festspiele* music and drama festival. Construction of the hilltop fortress, *Festung Hohensalzburg*, which dominates the Salzburg skyline, began in 1077. The *Festung* can be reached either by taking a ride on the *Festungsbahn*, a funicular railway, or by making a steep climb that brings its own rewards.

The train ride from Salzburg to Innsbruck passes through Kufstein, famous for its medieval fortress, which, like the one in Salzburg, can be reached via funicular and which is worth exploring if you have time and interest. From Kufstein it is also possible to travel to the luxurious resort town of Kitzbühel, one of the chief centers of winter sports in all of the Alps. If you are traveling on a budget, Kitzbühel might be best saved until after you have made your fortune.

Innsbruck is the capital of the Austrian state of *Tirol* (Tyrol) and has an excellent university with roughly thirty thousand students. When you arrive in the city on the crystal-clear Inn River, already amazingly high in the Alps, you can ride three successive cable cars, always higher and higher, close to the very top of the world, where clouds and silence dominate; the city seems impossibly tiny far, far below. Innsbruck is historically important on account of its location near the Brenner Pass, connecting northern Europe to Italy and the Mediterranean world. The city is also famous for winter sports and hosts a splendid array of Christmas markets, including one in the lovely *Altstadt*, which is dominated by the *Goldenes Dachl*, a golden loggia constructed for Kaiser Maximillian I in 1500. If you spend the night at the nearby *Hotel Goldner Adler*, you will have slept in the same hotel as Kaiser Joseph II, Johann Wolfgang von Goethe (much more about him in Chapter 4), Tyrolean patriot and freedom fighter Andreas Hofer, and Graf von Anderson, among others.

Merano, called *Meran* in German, is a wealthy town in the Italian autonomous province of *Südtirol* (South Tyrol), where both German and Italian are commonly spoken. This small, elegant city surrounded by mountains was historically the capital of the *Gefürstete Grafschaft Tirol* and remains a highly desirable place to live or to visit for a spa vacation. Thoroughbred racing fans will find the *Pferderennplazt Meran* of interest, and not only gardening enthusiasts will be impressed with the thriving *Gärten von Schloss Trauttmansdorff*. Nearby *Schloss Tirol* is the ancestral home of the counts of Tyrol, and hiking there from Merano through the vineyards and hills of the surrounding countryside is an uplifting experience.

The lovely city of Bolzano, called *Bozen* in German, is the capital of South Tyrol and its largest city. The excellent *Freie Universität Bozen* serves the *Europaregion Tirol – Südtirol – Trentino*, working closely together with the universities of Innsbruck (to the north) and Trento (to the south). The various Gothic and Romanesque churches and castles in and around Bolzano make it one of the most interesting small cities in Europe. Be sure to note the statue of Walther von der Vogelweide in the main square, to explore the shops and restaurants on the medieval *Laubengasse*, and to visit the *Südtiroler Archäologiemuseum*, home of the famous mummy of Ötzi the Iceman.

The Bolzano region is known for its high-quality agricultural products, including excellent wines, delicious apples, magnificent *Südtiroler Speck*, and a local fusion of Mediterranean and Alpine cuisines that approaches the pinnacles of the culinary arts. Observing the peaks of the Dolomites as they change color at sunset is a highlight of life on earth, as is attending the annual *Südtirol JazzFestival*, with events in Bolzano and beyond.

German history in the age of Enlightenment

The rise of the scientific method and of critical philosophy shaped the intellectual contours of the modern world just as surely as the Westphalian sovereignty determined its basic political form. Modern philosophy begins with the famous assertion "I think therefore I am",[6] made by René Descartes (1596–1650) in the progressive and tolerant Netherlands in 1637, slightly over a decade before the end of the Thirty Years' War. The scientific method, as expounded by the Englishman Francis Bacon (1561–1626), remains the global standard for testing knowledge even in our own time. Bacon's German contemporary, Johannes Kepler (1571–1630), discovered the laws of planetary motion that advanced Nicolaus Copernicus's (1473–1543) heliocentric model of the solar system.

The generation of great European thinkers that followed Bacon, Kepler, and Descartes developed science and philosophy in ways that continue to shape our perception and analysis of reality. The German philosopher and mathematician Gottfried Wilhelm Leibniz (1646–1716) and the English scientist and diplomat Sir Isaac Newton (1643–1727) developed differential and integral calculus (simultaneously and independently of one another). Leibniz wrote important, influential works on an astonishing variety of philosophical, mathematical, and scientific topics. Newton completed the Copernican Revolution by developing the three Laws of Motion and the Theory of Universal Gravitation. The Dutch philosopher and precision lens-grinder Baruch Spinoza (1632–1677) created a fascinating theory of reality predicated upon the fundamental unity of God and Nature that continues to exert a profound influence on deep thinkers to this day.

The Enlightenment, known in German as the *Aufklärung*, is the cultural soil out of which modern, progressive political theory developed. In the French language, works like Voltaire's (1694–1778) *Candide*, Jean-Jacques Rousseau's (1712–1778) *Discourse on Inequality and The Social Contract*, and Diderot's (1713–1784) encyclopedia had a profound and enduring influence on European society. The contributions of the Englishman John Locke (1632–1704), both in terms of political theory and epistemology, cannot be overstated. Enlightenment intellectuals developed the foundations of the concept of social justice, in which all human beings are held to deserve life, liberty, equality, and the pursuit of happiness, that is still pursued and debated in present times.

The German philosopher Immanuel Kant (1724–1804) is a giant figure in the intellectual history of the world. Kant's famous answer to the question "What is Enlightenment?" was *sapere aude!* (dare to know!), essentially charging each individual to rise to a level of intellectual maturity by using the power of reason to think for themselves. Kant's *Critique of Pure Reason* remains the foundational work of contemporary Western philosophy, providing a model of perception and cognition that reconciles the structures of the mind with the appearances of the world. The German playwright, theorist, and critic Gotthold Ephraim Lessing's (1729–1781) play *Nathan der Weise* (*Nathan the Wise*) endures as a poignant and moving dramatization of the necessity, desirability, and essential goodness of religious tolerance.

Three major European monarchs attempted to rule their subjects based on Enlightenment principles: the Habsburg emperor Joseph II of Austria (1741–1790); the Prussian-born empress Catherine the Great of Russia (1729–1796); and the Hohenzollern king Friedrich the Great of Prussia (1712–1786). Friedrich famously exclaimed, *Räsonniert, soviel ihr wollt und worüber ihr wollt, aber gehorcht!* (Think as much as you would like and about what you would like, but obey!). He reimagined the role of monarch, defining himself, against the self-serving Machiavellian views dominant at the time, as first servant of the state and introducing religious and intellectual tolerance in the Kingdom of Prussia to an extent that was quite advanced at that time. The life of Friedrich the Great is undoubtedly worth studying, as is the rise of Prussia, which, along with Austria, dominates the history of German Europe in the 19th and 20th centuries. Friedrich's concern for the well-being of his subjects, his active friendship with Voltaire and support for the Berlin Academy, as well as his energetic patronage of and lively interest in the arts – Friedrich himself was a skilled musician and composed several flute concertos that are still played – made him *der Große* just as surely as his military conquests in Silesia. Kant and Lessing are depicted on the base of the famous equestrian statue of Friedrich on Unter den Linden in Berlin.

The French Revolution of 1789 marked a turning point in European history and created the opportunity for Napoleon Bonaparte (1769–1821) to march across the world stage. Revolutions in the British colonies in North America (1776) and in Haiti (1781) had repercussions that make them essential areas of study as well. German philosopher G.W.F. Hegel (1770–1831) saw Napoleon at the Battle of Jena (1806) and described him as *Die Weltseele zu Pferd* (the World-Soul on horseback). Hegel's *Phenomenology of the Spirit* ushered in an era of philosophical-historical discourse that reaches all the way to contemporary speculations about the Singularity. Napoleon defeated both Austria and Prussia and occupied large sections of present-day Germany for several years, bringing elements of the Enlightenment philosophy that fueled the revolution to the lands he conquered. The Holy Roman Empire was dissolved in 1806, setting the stage for the creation of the modern nation-states of Austria and Germany. The *Befreiungskriege* (Wars of Liberation, 1813–1814) saw the unification of German forces to expel Napoleon's armies from German territory and catalyzed a new form of nationalistic German consciousness that would lead to episodes of creative greatness as well as to violent, destructive tragedies in the following centuries.

Text and translation: Lessing

Gotthold Ephraim Lessing made important contributions to European Enlightenment thought, and his works deserve our attention in these volatile times. Lessing's fables are thought-provoking and powerful, as you will see from the selections below.

Die Eule und der Schatzgräber

Jener Schatzgräber war ein sehr unbilliger Mann. Er wagte sich in die Ruinen eines alten Raubschlosses und ward da gewahr, dass die Eule eine magere Maus ergriff und verzehrte.

"Schickt sich das", sprach er, "für den philosophischen Liebling Minervens?"

"Warum nicht?" versetzte die Eule. "Weil ich stille Betrachtungen liebe, kann ich deswegen von der Luft leben? Ich weiß zwar, dass ihr Menschen es von euren Gelehrten verlanget –"

Der Esel und der Wolf

Ein Esel begegnete einem hungrigen Wolfe.

"Habe Mitleid mit mir", sagte der zitternde Esel, "ich bin ein armes krankes Tier; sieh nur, was für einen Dorn ich mir in den Fuß getreten habe!"

"Wahrhaftig, du dauerst mich", versetzte der Wolf. "Und ich finde mich in meinem Gewissen verbunden, dich von deinen Schmerzen zu befreien."

Kaum ward das Wort gesagt, so ward der Esel zerrissen.

Die Ziegen

Die Ziegen baten den Zeus, auch ihnen Hörner zu geben; denn anfangs hatten die Ziegen keine Hörner.

"Überlegt es wohl, was ihr bittet", sagte Zeus. "Es ist mit dem Geschenke der Hörner ein anderes unzertrennlich verbunden, das euch so angenehm nicht sein möchte."

Doch die Ziegen beharrten auf ihrer Bitte, und Zeus sprach: "So habt denn Hörner!"

Und die Ziegen bekamen Hörner – und Bart! Denn anfangs hatten die Ziegen auch keinen Bart. O wie schmerzte sie der häßliche Bart, weit mehr, als sie die stolzen Hörner erfreuten!

The Owl and the Treasure Hunter

That treasure hunter was a very unfair man. He ventured into the ruins of an old castle and became aware that the owl had caught and eaten a meager mouse.

"Is that fitting", he said, "for the philosophical darling of Minerva?"

"Why not?" replied the owl. "Because I love silent meditations can I therefore live on air? I know of course that you humans demand that from your scholars."

The Donkey and the Wolf

A donkey encountered a hungry wolf.

"Have pity on me", said the trembling donkey, "I am a poor sick animal; Just see what a thorn I have trodden into my foot!"

"Truly, you give me pause", replied the wolf. "And I find myself by my conscience bound to free you from your pain."

Scarcely had these words been said, than the donkey was torn apart.

The Goats

The goats asked Zeus to give horns to them as well, for at first the goats had no horns.

"Think well what you're asking", Zeus said. "Another thing, which might not be so pleasing to you, is inseparably connected with the gift of horns."

But the goats persisted at their request, and Zeus said, "Ok, have horns then!"

And the goats got horns – and a beard! Because at first the goats did not have a beard either. Oh, how the ugly beard hurt them, much more than the proud horns made them happy!

German music: Classical

The two greatest composers of the Classical era were Joseph Haydn (1732–1809) and Wolfgang Amadeus Mozart (1756–1791). Along with Ludwig van Beethoven (much more about him in Chapter 4), Haydn and Mozart constitute what is known as *Wiener Klassik*, referred to as the "First Viennese School" in English, reflecting the centrality of Vienna to the development of classical music, notably through the patronage of the regional aristocracy. Haydn's

Gott erhalte Franz den Kaiser (1797) was the anthem of the Habsburg Monarchy until 1918. The same tune was used for the German national anthem, *Das Lied der Deutschen*, which can be heard after most Formula One races, in recognition of yet another win for Mercedes. Haydn's magnificent oratorio, *Die Schöpfung*, as well as his sublime string quartets and dynamic symphonies are among the highlights of Western music.

Mozart's name is synonymous with genius. *Die Zauberflöte* (*The Magic Flute*) was described by one of my students as "Enlightenment: The Musical", and I agree. Find a video of the unparalleled Diana Damrau singing the Queen of the Night Aria, *Der Hölle Rache*, and then find a way to see the entire opera, which will delight you as it elevates your consciousness. Mozart's other operas, especially *Don Giovanni, Così fan tutte*, and *Le nozze di Figaro*, are still performed regularly across the globe. Mozart's symphonies, piano concerti, and the astonishing Requiem are essential pieces of our human cultural heritage.

Graf von Anderson recommends the following recordings:

Nikolaus Harnoncourt, Wiener Symphoniker, Arnold Schonberg Chor, *Haydn: Die Schöpfung*
Emerson String Quartet, *Haydn: The Seven Last Words, Op. 51*
Alban Berg Quartet, *Haydn: String Quartets, Op. 76 Nos. 2–4*
Cuarteto Casals, *Haydn: String Quartets, Op. 33*
Medici String Quartet, *Haydn: String Quartets, Op. 64*
Jens Lindemann, Royal Philharmonic Orchestra, *Concertos of Haydn, Hummel, Hertel, and Albinoni*
Jacqueline du Pré, *Haydn: Cello Concertos*; *Boccherini: Cello Concerto*
Harnoncourt, Concentus Musicus Wien, *Haydn: Symphonies Nos. 45 & 60*
Ton Koopman, Amsterdam Baroque Orchestra, *Haydn: The Paris Symphonies*
Sir Colin Davis, Royal Concertgebouw Orchestra, *Haydn: The London Symphonies*
Sir Neville Marriner, The Academy of St. Martins in the Fields, *Mozart: Eine kleine Nachtmusik etc.*
Karl Böhm, Berliner Philharmoniker, *Mozart: Symphonies Nos. 25, 29 & 31*
Sir Simon Rattle, Berliner Philharmoniker, *Mozart: Symphonies Nos. 39, 40 & 41*
Mitsuko Uchida, Jeffrey Tate, English Chamber Orchestra, *Mozart: The Piano Concertos*
Concentus Musicus Wien, Harnoncourt, *Mozart: Clarinet Concerto, Oboe Concerto, etc.*
Ludmila Peterkova, Benewitz Quartet, *Mozart, Rejka and Kukal: Clarinet Quintets*
Jerusalem Quartet, *Mozart: String Quartets*
Cuarteto Casals, *Mozart: String Quartets Dedicated to Josef Haydn*
Karl Böhm, Philharmonia Orchestra, *Mozart: Cosi fan tutte*
Herbert von Karajan, Wiener Philharmoniker, *Mozart: Die Zauberflöte*
Wilhelm Furtwängler, Wiener Philharmoniker (1953), *Mozart: Don Giovanni*
Herbert von Karajan, Berliner Philharmoniker, *Mozart: Requiem*

Graf von Anderson found the Harnoncourt recording of *Die Schöpfung* in a record store on the Utrechtsestraat in Amsterdam over twenty years ago – it is a classic, especially satisfying when listened to on a crisp fall morning in a wooded park from the leather seats of an E30 with the sunroof open and the leaves changing color all around.

Recommended films

Nathan der Weise (Manfred Noa, 1922)
Napoléon (Abel Gance, 1927)
Der große König (Veit Harlan, 1942)
Kolberg (Veit Harlan, 1945)
Amadeus (Miloš Forman, 1984)
Vergesst Mozart (Miroslav Luther, 1985)

Notes

1 Some people claim to see an uncanny face where the "r" looks like a nose between an "e" on both sides.
2 I have included "them" in addition to "it" in the translation since we don't refer to human beings as "it" in English and since *Kind* is gender neutral.
3 The third person plural diagram appears later in the chapter, as well as in the Executive Summary.
4 In English we would say, "They like the city".
5 Used reflexively with teeth, nose, and shoes, otherwise used non-reflexively with other physical objects.
6 Commonly known in Latin, *cogito ergo sum*, it was originally written in French, *je pense, donc je suis.*

4 Prepositional phrases

Prepositions combine with nouns and pronouns in order to add information to simple sentences.

Behold this simple sentence:

Ich fliege.	I fly.

Now, become astonished as the simple sentence is enhanced with prepositional phrases:

Ich fliege am Mittwoch mit dir nach Paris.	I fly on Wednesday with you to Paris.

The prepositional phrases are: *am Mittwoch*, *mit dir*, and *nach Paris*. As you can see, prepositional phrases are composed of a preposition and a noun or pronoun.

Let's take a closer look at prepositions, starting with the basics.

Every preposition is associated with at least one case

Some prepositions work with two cases – we will explore these later. There are also genitive prepositions – we will explore those later as well, after we have learned the genitive case. There are NO NOMINATIVE PREPOSITIONS. These are, as a result, the easiest group to memorize.

We begin with the accusative prepositions and the dative prepositions, before turning to the two-way prepositions and the genitive prepositions.

Accusative prepositions

bis	until, as far as, up to
durch	through, by means of (via)
für	for
gegen	against, around (a time)
ohne	without
um	around, at (a time)

Dative prepositions

aus	out of
außer	outside of, except for
bei	at
mit	with
nach	to (long distance), after (a time)
seit	since (a time), for (a time)
von	of, from
zu	to (short distance)

To see how these prepositions work, let's look at a few examples of prepositional phrases in action.

Let's start with the accusative preposition *für*, which means for:

Bobfried bringt Wein **für den Grafen**.	Bobfried brings wine **for the count**.
Wir sind **für den Weltfrieden**.	We are **for world peace**.

As you can see, the nouns *Graf* and *Weltfrieden* are in the accusative case. If you cannot see this, then you should review Chapter 3.

Now, observe the dative preposition *mit* in action:

Bobfried trinkt Wein **mit dem Grafen**.	Bobfried drinks wine **with the count**.
Wir sind **mit dem Weltfrieden** beschäftigt.	We are occupied **with world peace**.

Hopefully, you can see that *der Graf* and *der Weltfrieden* are in their dative forms when used with the dative preposition, *mit*. If not, Chapter 3 is calling your name.

Essentially, the accusative prepositions require the noun or pronoun that accompanies them to be in the accusative case. Likewise, the dative prepositions require the noun or pronoun that accompanies them to be in the dative case. There is no other logic or rule. When you use an accusative preposition, you put the noun or pronoun that completes the prepositional phrase into the accusative case and move on with life. The same rule applies to dative prepositions, and to genitive prepositions, as you will soon see.

The easiest way to master the accusative and dative prepositions is to memorize them in action. Here are some sample sentences that might help get you started. The prepositional phrases are in bold.

Accusative prepositions

Der Graf bleibt **bis diesen Mittwoch** in der Stadt.	The count remains in the city **until this Wednesday**.
Bobfried geht **durch den Zauberwald**.	Bobfried walks **through the magic forest**.
Die Blumen sind **für meine Frau**.	The flowers are **for my wife**.
Die Wissenschaftler sind **gegen den Krieg**.	The scientists are **against the war**.
Wir treffen uns **gegen 8.00 Uhr** im Cafe Kreuzberg.[1]	We meet in Cafe Kreuzberg **around 8:00**.
Ohne Kaffee ist das Leben schwierig.	Life is difficult **without coffee**.
Der Mann geht **um die Ecke**.	The man walks **around the corner**.
Die Arbeiter wachen **um 6.00 Uhr** auf.	The workers wake up **at 6:00**.

Dative prepositions

Der Fisch springt **aus dem Wasser**.	The fish jumps **out of the water**.
Der Fahrstuhl ist **außer Betrieb**.	The elevator is **out of service**.
Die Auswahl **bei dem Bäcker** ist riesig!	The selection **at the baker's** is enormous!
Sie spielt jeden Tag **mit ihren Freunden** Fußball.	She plays soccer **with her friends** every day.
Nach meinem Studium verbringe ich ein Jahr in Rom.	**After my studies** I am spending a year in Rome.
Ich fliege **nach Deutschland**!	I am flying **to Germany**!
Ich habe Beethovens Musik **seit meiner Kindheit** geliebt.	I have loved Beethoven's music **since my childhood**.
Der Volkswagen war ein Geschenk **von meiner Frau**.	The Volkswagen was a gift **from my wife**.
Montags bis donnerstags gehe ich **zu der Universität**.	Mondays through Thursdays I go **to the university**.
Freitags fahren wir **zu dem Strand**.	On Fridays we drive **to the beach**.

Three of the sentences above might sound stiff to native German speakers. Rather than *bei dem Bäcker*, *zu der Universität*, and *zu dem Strand*, a German likely would have said *beim Bäcker*, *zur Universität*, and *zum Strand*. That's because some prepositions are commonly formed as contractions.

Let's examine some of these contractions:

fürs = für das
durchs = durch das
ums = um das
beim = bei dem
vom = von dem
zum = zu dem
zur = zu der

These contractions occur quite frequently, so you should learn to recognize them. The accusative contractions are informal, so avoid them in situations in which you want to appear polished and proper. The dative contractions should be used whenever possible – using them shows mastery and competence.

Two-way prepositions

Now that you have seen how the accusative and dative prepositions work, you will be delighted to experience the challenge of the two-way prepositions. These are prepositions that are sometimes accusative and sometimes dative.

Two-way prepositions

an	at, to
auf	onto, on, upon, at
hinter	behind
in	into, in, inside
neben	next to, beside
über	over, above, across, about (a topic)
unter	below, under, among
vor	in front of, before, (a time) ago
zwischen	between

The concept for determining whether to use the accusative or dative with these prepositions is relatively straightforward: once you've learned one of them, the others follow the same principle.

Behold the two-way preposition *in*:

Accusative:	Der Mann geht **in das Wohnzimmer**.	The man goes **into the living room**.
Dative:	Der Mann sitzt **in dem Wohnzimmer**.	The man sits **in the living room**.

Perhaps you can already see that the preposition is accusative when it describes a direction and dative when it describes a location. Luckily, there are two German question words that correspond exactly to this distinction.

Accusative:	**Wohin** geht der Mann?	**To where** is the man going?
Dative:	**Wo** sitzt der Mann?	**Where** is the man sitting?

The two-way prepositions are accusative if they answer the question *wohin?* and are dative if they answer the question *wo?*

Accusative:	**Wohin** geht der Mann?	**To where** is the man going?
	Der Mann geht **in das Wohnzimmer**.	The man goes **into the living room**.
Dative:	**Wo** sitzt der Mann?	**Where** is the man sitting?
	Der Mann sitzt **in dem Wohnzimmer**.	The man sits **in the living room**.

Take a look at the following examples:

Wohin? (Accusative)	*Wo? (Dative)*
Der Lehrer geht **an die Tafel**.	Der Lehrer steht **an der Tafel**.
The teacher goes to the board.	The teacher stands at the board.
Der Dichter schreibt **auf eine Karte**.	Ein Gedicht steht **auf der Karte**.
The poet writes onto a card.	A poem is on the card.
Der Baron läuft **hinter den Supermarkt**.	Der Baron trinkt **hinter dem Supermarkt**.
The baron walks behind the supermarket.	The baron drinks behind the supermarket.
Der Graf kommt **in das Schloss**.	Der Graf wohnt **in dem Schloss**.
The count comes into the palace.	The count lives in the palace.
Der Prinz geht **neben die Prinzessin**.	Der Prinz steht **neben der Prinzessin**.
The prince goes next to the princess.[2]	The prince stands next to the princess.
Der Kondor fliegt **über das Meer**.	Der Kondor fliegt direkt **über der Stadt**.
The condor flies across the sea.	The condor flies directly above the city.
Der Onkel kriecht **unter den Tisch**.	Der Onkel schläft **unter dem Tisch**.
The uncle crawls under the table.	The uncle sleeps under the table.
Der Neffe geht **vor das Haus**.	Der Neffe bleibt **vor dem Haus** stehen.
The nephew goes in front of the house.	The nephew stops in front of the house.
Der Anwalt geht **zwischen die Wolkenkratzer**.	Der Anwalt tanzt **zwischen den Wolkenkratzern**.
The lawyer goes between the skyscrapers.	The lawyer dances between the skyscrapers.

As with the accusative and dative prepositions, there are some common contractions to learn:

ans = an das
am = an dem
aufs = auf das
ins = in das
im = in dem

As with the earlier contractions, the accusative ones are less formal and the dative ones are essentially mandatory.

Da- and *wo-*compounds

You can add *da-* and *wo-* to most prepositions, forming magical structures that are commonly used in German.

The verb *erzählen* (to tell a story) can be used with a direct object, as in the example below:

Opa erzählt seinen Enkelkindern **eine Geschichte**.	Grandpa tells his grandchildren **a story**.

Perhaps you want to exclaim that *seinen Enkelkindern* is the indirect object. Good! If you don't want to exclaim this, you should review Chapter 3.

We can also use the verb and preposition combination *erzählen von*, replacing the direct object with a prepositional phrase.

Opa erzählt ihnen **von seiner Kindheit**.	Grandpa tells them **about his childhood**.

As you can see, *erzählen* works with either a direct object like *eine Geschichte* (a story), or *ein Ereignis* (an event), or simply *ein Ding* (a thing), or with a prepositional phrase that begins with *von*.

Erzählen von even has its own line in the online dictionary (LEO). Go look it up; we will be here when you return. See?

Now imagine that you did not understand either sentence beyond *Opa erzählt seinen Enkelkindern*. Maybe there was a loud noise, or you stopped paying attention. Who knows?

You could ask two questions to rejoin the conversation:

Was erzählt Opa seinen Enkelkindern?	**What** is Grandpa telling his grandchildren?
Wovon erzählt Opa seinen Enkelkindern?	**What** is Grandpa telling his grandchildren **about**?

Nearly all of the prepositions can combine with the prefix *wo-* in order to form a question in this manner. Combining *was* with a preposition will always be a mistake – that's what the *wo-*compounds are for.

But the story gets even more interesting! Imagine that Opa tells stories about his childhood frequently, perhaps approaching "all of the time".

Wovon erzählt Opa?	**What** is Grandpa telling stories **about**?
Er erzählt wieder **von seiner Kindheit in Wien**.	He's telling stories again **about his childhood in Vienna**.
Ach, **davon** erzählt er immer.	Oh, he's always telling stories **about that**.

Nearly all of the prepositions can combine with the prefix *da-* in order to form a "pronomial adverb" in this manner. A similar construction can also be made with *hier*, as with the English "herewith" and "hereby".

Take a look at these nearly fascinating dialogues:

Sieglinde:	Ich arbeite **an meiner Diplomarbeit**.	I am working **on my senior project (thesis)**.
Bobfried:	**Woran** arbeitest du?	**What** are you working **on?**
Sieglinde:	**An meiner Diplomarbeit!**	**On my senior project (thesis)!**
Bobfried:	Ich arbeite auch **daran!**	I'm working **on that** too!

Ute:	Ich warte **auf den Bus**.	I am waiting **for the bus**.
Hilde:	**Worauf** wartest du?	**What** are you waiting **for?**
Ute:	**Auf den Bus** warte ich.	I am waiting **for the bus**.
Hilde:	**Darauf** warte ich auch!	I'm waiting **for it** too!

The bus will be here sooner than you think – that's the Graf von Anderson Advantage!

You have probably noticed that prepositions combine with verbs in ways that you could not always predict. For example, *arbeiten an* (dative) is similar to the English "working on", but *warten auf* (accusative) is rather unlike the English "waiting for", although it does resemble the regional expression "waiting on", as in, "I've been waiting on this bus for an hour!"

Going forward, when you learn a new verb, you will want to learn the prepositions that are used with it. If the preposition is a two-way preposition, you will need to learn the appropriate case as well.

Take a look at the following enticing examples:

Worin liegt der Unterschied zwischen Astronomie und Astrologie?	**In what** lies the difference between astronomy and astrology?
Worüber redet ihr?	**What** are you talking **about?**
Wovor hast du Angst?	**What** are you afraid **of?**
Beispiele **dafür** gibt es zuhauf.	There are many examples **of it**.
Ich würde **darauf** nicht wetten!	I wouldn't bet **on it!**
Hör auf **damit!**	Stop **with that** (cut it out)!

Learning the verb and preposition pairs takes time, but now that you know how it works, you probably have nothing other than time (and potential).

Certain prepositions do not form *da-* and *wo-*compounds. *Bis* and *seit*, for example are always used with *wann*, when forming a question:

Bis wann bleibst du in Berlin?	**Until when** are you staying in Berlin?
Seit wann wohnst du in Berlin?	**Since when** are you living in Berlin?

Likewise, even though *wozu* and *wonach* exist, they are seldom used to ask questions about destinations, since *wohin* covers that:

Wohin fliegst du diesen Sommer?	**To where** are you flying this summer?
Ich fliege **nach Amsterdam**.	I am flying **to Amsterdam**.

Wohin gehst du jetzt?	**To where** are you going now?
Ich gehe **zum Supermarkt**.	I am going **to the supermarket**.

Of course, you will see *wonach*, *wozu*, *danach*, and *dazu* in other situations:

Das Essen schmeckt **nach Knoblauch**.	The food tastes **of garlic** (tastes garlicky).
Wonach schmeckt es?	**Of what** (like what) does it taste?
Nach Knoblauch schmeckt es!	It tastes **of garlic**!

You could spend a profitable half hour looking at each of the entries in LEO under *wonach*, *wozu*, *danach*, and *dazu*. You will emerge with a wider understanding of these compounds, which abound in German. By learning them as you encounter them you will get to know them well. Rejoice!

Brief introduction to the genitive case

Before you can learn the genitive prepositions, you should become familiar with the GENITIVE CASE.

A quick review of dative preposition *von* will make the genitive case crystal clear for you.

"Faust" ist eine Tragödie **von dem deutschen Schriftsteller** Johann Wolfgang von Goethe.	"Faust" is a tragedy **by the German writer** Johann Wolfgang von Goethe.

The genitive case works as a replacement for *von*.

"Faust" ist eine Tragödie **des deutschen Schriftstellers** Johann Wolfgang von Goethe.	"Faust" is a tragedy **by the German writer** Johann Wolfgang von Goethe.

Essentially, *des Schriftstellers* is another way to say *von dem Schriftsteller*.
Look at these examples:

"Jenseits der Stille" ist ein Film **von der deutschen Regisseurin** Karoline Link.	"Beyond Silence" is a film **by the German director** Karoline Link.
"Jenseits der Stille" ist ein Film **der deutschen Regisseurin** Karoline Link.	"Beyond Silence" is a film **by the German director** Karoline Link.

"Ich liebe dich, Graf von Anderson!" ist ein Gedicht **von einem anonymen Verehrer**.	"I love you, Graf von Anderson!" is a poem **by an anonymous admirer**.
"Ich liebe dich, Graf von Anderson!" ist ein Gedicht **eines anonymen Verehrers**.	"I love you, Graf von Anderson!" is a poem **by an anonymous admirer**.

"Das Schreien macht Spaß" ist ein Lied **von den singenden Schmetterlingen**.	"Screaming is fun" is a song **by the singing butterflies**.
"Das Schreien macht Spaß" ist ein Lied **der singenden Schmetterlinge**.	"Screaming is fun" is a song **by the singing butterflies**.

Essentially, *der Regisseurin* is another way to say *von der Regisseurin, eines Verehrers* is another way to express *von einem Verehrer*, and *der Schmetterlinge* is another way to construct the concept *von den Schmetterlingen*.

Here is a chart of the nominative and genitive case:

	Nominative	*Genitive*
Masculine:	der Mann	des Mannes
	ein Mann	eines Mannes
Neuter:	das Kind	des Kindes
	ein Kind	eines Kindes
Feminine:	die Frau	der Frau
	eine Frau	einer Frau
Plural:	die Kinder	der Kinder
	meine Kinder	meiner Kinder

Notice that the masculine and neuter add an *-s* or *-es* to the noun. Also notice that the genitive plural, unlike the dative plural, does not require an *-n* at the end. Finally, notice that the masculine and neuter are formed identically, as are the feminine and plural.

We could at this point revise the triangles from Chapter 3 to form squares, but being good Pythagoreans, we will not do so. The triangles are easier to conceptualize, and your brain seems to prefer learning with the mystical number 3.

Take a look at all of the different ways you could describe the ownership of a Porsche, or even an Audi:

Der Professor hat einen Porsche.	The professor has a Porsche.
Das ist der Porsche von dem Professor.	That is the Porsche of the professor.
Das ist der Porsche des Professors.	That is the professor's Porsche.
Das ist sein Porsche.	That is his Porsche.
Der Porsche gehört ihm.	The Porsche belongs to him.

Das Kind hat auch einen Porsche.	The child also has a Porsche.
Das ist der Porsche von dem Kind.	That is the Porsche of the child.
Das ist der Porsche des Kindes.	That is the child's Porsche.
Das ist sein Porsche.	That is his Porsche.
Der Porsche gehört ihm.	The Porsche belongs to him.

Auch die Ärztin hat einen Porsche.	The doctor has a Porsche as well.
Das ist der Porsche von der Ärztin.	That is the Porsche of the doctor.
Das ist der Porsche der Ärztin.	That is the doctor's Porsche.
Das ist ihr Porsche.	That is her Porsche.
Der Porsche gehört ihr.	The Porsche belongs to her.

Die Einhörner haben einen Audi.	The unicorns have an Audi.
Das ist der Audi von den Einhörnern.	That is the Audi of the unicorns.
Das ist der Audi der Einhörner.	That is the unicorns' Audi.
Das ist ihr Audi.	That is their Audi.
Der Audi gehört ihnen.	The Audi belongs to them.

Memorizing how these examples work could help you with understanding and expressing ownership forevermore.

The genitive case allows you to indicate ownership by adding an *-s* or *-es* to a person's name.

Karls Porsche ist rot, aber Friederikes Porsche ist grün.	Karl's Porsche is red, but Friederike's Porsche is green.

Unlike in English, there is no need for an apostrophe, unless the name ends in *s* or *x*.

Der Porsche von Boris ist schwarz.	The Porsche of Boris black.
Boris' Porsche ist schwarz.	Boris's Porsche is black.

The genitive description can occur before a noun as well.

Das ist meines Vaters Haus.	That is my father's house.

This last formulation sounds somewhat stilted and is far less common than *das Haus meines Vaters*.

Genitive prepositions

Now that you know how the genitive case works, you can move into the sophisticated splendor of the genitive prepositions.

Using these prepositions correctly is a sign of a proper education and will earn you respect from those who are also well educated. If you are hanging out on the street, you can use the ones marked with an asterisk in the dative case and you will fit right in; try a can of beer down in the U-Bahn while you're at it.

Genitive prepositions

(an)statt	instead of
außerhalb	outside of
innerhalb	inside of
jenseits	beyond
während*	during
wegen*	on account of / due to
trotz*	despite / in spite of

Take a look at the following mesmerizing examples:

Ich wünsche mir **anstatt der Geschenke** Geld für eine Europareise.	I would like to have money for a trip to Europe **instead of gifts**.
Die alte Grafenburg steht **außerhalb der Stadtmauer**.	The old castle of the count stands **outside of the city walls**.
Er hat **innerhalb eines Jahrzehnts** Deutsch gelernt.	He learned German within a decade.

Als transzendent gilt, was **außerhalb oder jenseits eines Bereiches möglicher Erfahrung, insbesondere des Bereiches der normalen Sinneswahrnehmung** liegt und nicht von ihm abhängig ist.	That which is classified as transcendent is that which lies **outside of or beyond the domain of possible experience, especially the domain of normal sense-perception**, and is not dependent on this domain.
Essen Sie **während des Trinkens**, um den Alkohol zu absorbieren.	Eat **while drinking** in order to absorb the alcohol.
Das Spiel musste am Dienstag **wegen des Wetters** abgesagt werden.	The match had to be canceled on Tuesday **due to the weather**.
Trotz Ihrer hervorragenden Qualifikationen haben wir uns für einen anderen Kandidaten entschieden.	**Despite your outstanding qualifications**, we have decided in favor of another candidate.

Perhaps if you learn enough German to understand that last sentence, you will never be faced with the shattering reality of an encounter with it. That's the Graf von Anderson Advantage!

Time expressions to ponder

Um, am, and *im* are the most important prepositions for basic time expressions. If you don't recall that *am* is a contraction of *an dem* and *im* is a contraction of *in dem*, then maybe you should review this chapter or take a break.

Of course, sometimes there is no need for a preposition:

Es ist neun Uhr.	It is nine o'clock.
Es ist neun Uhr abends.	It is nine o'clock in the evening (p.m.)
Es ist neun Uhr morgens.	It is nine o'clock in the morning (a.m.)

To express the exact time of an event, we use ***um*** and the time:

Wir treffen uns **um zwei Uhr**.	We meet **at two o'clock**.
Wir treffen uns **um vierzehn Uhr**.	We meet **at two o'clock p.m**.

To express the date, we can use either *sein* or *haben*:

Heute ist der 2. Mai 2076.	Today is the 2nd of May, 2076.
Heute haben wir den 2. Mai 2076.	Today we have the 2nd of May, 2076.

The first sentence expresses the date as *der zweite*, while the second sentence expresses it as *den zweiten*. You will learn about the endings on *zweit* in Chapter 7.

To express the exact date or the day of an event, we use ***am*** and the date or day:

Unser Termin ist **am 13. Januar**.	Our appointment is **on January 13th**.
Unser Termin ist **am Freitag**.	Our appointment is **on Friday**.

Am 13. is written and spoken as *am dreizehnten*. You will learn about this type of adjective ending in Chapter 7.

To express the month in which an event takes place, we use ***im*** and the month:

Unser Termin ist **im Januar**.	Our appointment is **in January**.

To express the year in which an event takes place, we use the expression *im Jahr*:

Unser Termin ist **im Jahr 2022**.	Our appointment is **in the year 2022**.

Generally speaking, avoid using *in* and the year. Either use *im Jahr* as above, or the year itself without a preposition as in the example below.

Wir fliegen 2022 nach Finnland.	In 2022 we fly to Finland.

Time expressions that do not use a preposition are always either nouns in the accusative case or adverbs.

Unser Termin ist heute.	Our appointment is today.
Nächste Woche lernen wir mehr davon!	Next week we learn more of this.

You will find time expressions like *nächste Woche* easier to master once you have learned the adjective endings in Chapter 7. For now, spend a moment marveling that the words *heute, hoy, oggi,* and *aujourd'hui* each express the idea of "today". Could it be that the languages are all related?[3]

Übungen

A   Translate the following sentences into German.

> She is from Switzerland.
> She lives with her son around the corner from here.
> We are flying to Paris.
> The wine is a gift from her.
> I work at a bank.
> Are you driving through the city?
> I get up at 7:00 a.m.
> The flowers are for my mother.
> I am going to the supermarket.
> *Star Wars* is my favorite film since the year 1977.
> Are you against the death penalty?
> We have German until 3:00 p.m.

B   Now answer these questions and translate your answers:

> Gegen wen kämpfen die Guten?
> Mit wem verbringst du am liebsten deine Freizeit?
> Zu welchem Musikfestival gehen wir nächsten Sommer?
> Aus welcher Stadt kommst du?

Seit wann wohnst du in Luxemburg?

Für wen kaufst du jedes Jahr ein Geschenk?

Von wem bekommst du jedes Jahr ein Geschenk?

An welchen Tagen kommt die Post? (use *außer* in your answer)

Gegen wieviel Uhr gehst du normalerweise ins Bett?

Um wieviel Uhr öffnet die Universitätsbibliothek?

Wie kommt Sonnenlicht in das Klassenzimmer? (use *durch* in your answer)

Bis wann bleibst du mittwochs auf dem Campus?

Ohne was kann man nicht unsichtbar werden?

C   Translate! If you need help forming the commands, refer back to Chapter 2.

The ice cream ball rolls (from somewhere else) between the cookies and the cakes.

The ice cream ball melts between the cookies and the cakes.

A spaceship is flying above the skyscrapers.

The athlete jumps over the skyscrapers.

The turtle goes over the bridge.

The turtle stands on the bridge and waves.

Set the plates onto the table!

The dog goes under the table.

The dog sleeps under the table.

The cat goes to the window.

The cat sits at the window.

A tree stands in front of the house.

The cat sneaks up to the tree. (sich an einen Ort schleichen)

A bird sings in the tree.

Drive me in front of the house right away!

The count brings the musicians into the castle.

The count lives in the castle.

The driver drives up next to the Porsche on the highway.

The driver sits next to the passenger in the Porsche.

They drive the Porsche to the sea.

They don't drive the Porsche into the sea.

They go to the beach.

We live at the beach.

D   For each of the following sentences, write a question using either a *wo*-compound or a preposition and a question word for which the bolded phrase would be the answer. Translate the question and the answer into English.

In der Küche riecht es **nach Knoblauch und Tomaten**.

Er arbeitet **an seinem Roman**.

Wir haben Angst **vor dem Überwachungskapitalismus**.

Wir reden gern **über Politik**.

Wir hoffen **auf eine bessere Zukunft**.

Alles erinnert ihn **an seine Vergangenheit**.

Er beginnt **mit seiner Kindheit**.

Das war **für ihn** eine sehr gute Zeit.

Wasser besteht **aus Wasserstoff und Sauerstoff**.

E Rewrite the following questions using the genitive instead of the dative for the bolded phrase, then translate.

Ist das das Schloss **von dem Grafen**?
Ist das nicht die Nichte **von der Professorin**?
Siehst du das Schicksal **von meiner Freundin**?
Siehst du das Schicksal **von meinem Freund**?
Siehst du das Schicksal **von meinem Kind**?
Siehst du das Schicksal **von meinen Kindern**?
Welche Musik **von den 80er Jahren** findest du besonders cool?

F Figure out what the first sentence means, then use the words in brackets to form a logically related second sentence.

Ich kann diese Sache nicht verstehen.	[liegen / jenseits / mein Verständnis]
Sie arbeitet in Frankfurt, aber sie wohnt in Kronberg.	[ihre Wohnung / liegen / außerhalb / Stadt]
Der Lehrer will nicht nass werden!	[wir spielen / drinnen / wegen / Regen]
Der Graf will auf jeden Fall draußen sein!	[wir spielen / draußen / trotz / Wetter]
Die Reisenden wollen nicht nur übernachten, sondern auch kochen.	[sollen mieten / Ferienwohnung / statt / Hotelzimmer]
Sie fahren mit dem Zug von Florenz nach Turin.	[machen / Reise / innerhalb / Italien]
Wenn ich in Luzern bin, ist Bobfried der Chef.	[während / Abwesenheit]

Travel: Vienna and Budapest

The Alps form the southern frontier of Germanic Europe; Italy and the beautiful Mediterranean are south of the Alps. To reach Vienna from Bolzano, one could travel back through Salzburg, and then onward through the culturally rich city of Linz. Alternatively, one could visit the Italian city of Venice, although wise people have said that the journey to what is perhaps the world's most romantic and beautiful city should be reserved for taking with a true love so that you can experience it together. Nearby Trieste, on the other hand, is a sophisticated, cosmopolitan city with strong elements of Italian, Austrian, and Slovene cultures, which is worth a visit even if you are traveling alone or with a band of backpackers. The incredible *Schloss Miramar*, on the Gulf of Trieste, was constructed in 1860 for Austrian Archduke Ferdinand Maximilian and his wife, Charlotte of Belgium, who later became Emperor Maximilian I and Empress Carlota of Mexico. Make a note to explore the fabulous Adriatic beaches and cities of Croatia and Montenegro on your next visit, before boarding the train to Vienna. You could punctuate the journey to Vienna by visiting the Austrian cities of Klagenfurt, which was founded by dragon-slayers, according to legend, and Graz, with its well-preserved *Altstadt*, along the way.

The beautiful, monumental capital of Austria is called *Wien* in German. Architecturally, there is not another large city in German-speaking Europe that can compete with it. The city reminds one of Paris, but with strong Central European and subtle Southern and Eastern influences that contribute to its unique and enduring charm. Moreover, the quality of life in the former *Kaiserliche und Königliche Hauptstadt* consistently ranks at the top of the list of world cities, which certainly comes as no surprise to the many well-educated, stylish Viennese who actively participate in the centuries-old cultural traditions that thrive there. A visit to Vienna should last at least a week. Since the city is not inexpensive, you might consider booking a room well in advance. The Hotel Fürstenhof, across from the *Westbahnhof* at the top of the Mariahilfer Straße, is an atmospheric gem with attractive, if also basic, clean and affordable rooms. The adjacent *Café Westend* is a fine place to spend an afternoon, or a few months or years, reading, writing, and thinking in the authentic Viennese manner.

Stephansdom, the central cathedral, which dates back to the reign of Archduke Rudolf IV of Austria (1353–1365), the Habsburg ruler known as *der Stifter* (the founder), is an excellent first destination after unpacking. Walking from the Fürstenhof, one will enjoy the plentiful and diverse shopping opportunities on the pedestrian Mariahilfer Straße before crossing into the *Museumsquartier*, where a number of museums with collections covering architecture, fine art, fashion, and various other media await. Continuing in the direction of *Stephansdom*, one encounters a fine statue of the Habsburg Empress Maria Theresa (1717–1780) flanked by two grand, stately museums: the *Naturhistorisches Museum*, with an impressive collection of dinosaur fossils, precious stones, and pre-historic art, and the *Kunsthistorisches Museum*, with breathtaking works of art from Raphael, Dürer, Michelangelo, and Benvenuto Cellini, just to name a few. The nearby *Wiener Rathaus* and the *Parlamentsgebäude* are also worth visiting. During summer, *Rathausplatz* is transformed into a cultural festival with screenings of concerts, plays, and sporting events. The same area is home to Vienna's unparalleled *Christkindlmarkt*, which might make Vienna the best place on earth to experience the Christmas season.

Continuing in the direction of *Stephansdom*, the *Hofburg*, residence of the Holy Roman Emperors from 1438 until 1806, during which time Vienna was the imperial capital,[4] and of the Habsburg rulers of the Austrian and Austro-Hungarian Empires from 1806 until the 1918 Revolution, is surely a highlight of a trip to the city. The areas adjacent to the *Hofburg* contain several remarkable churches and palaces, as well as famous hotels, restaurants, and shops. The *Staatsoper* and the *Burgtheater*, each of which represents the *de facto* world standard for live performing arts, are located nearby. Among the many outstanding smaller theaters in Vienna, the Odeon Theater, home of the Serapions Ensemble, is worthy of special mention. Their mind-altering production of *Nunaki* in the bitter cold winter of 2002 was the single most impactful theater experience of Graf von Anderson's lifetime. May it soon return for an encore!

After finally arriving at *Stephansdom*, another long walk is in order, this time to *Schloss Belvedere*. The *Österreichische Galerie Belvedere*, an art museum housed inside of the Upper Belvedere Palace, includes masterpieces by Austrian artists Gustav Klimt, Oskar Kokoschka, and Egon Schiele and should not be missed under any circumstances. Walking back to the Fürstenhof, one can visit the *Naschmarkt*, a three-hundred-year-old market that features a robust mixture of fruit and vegetables, artisanal foods and baked goods, several cafes and restaurants, and an excellent flea market on Saturdays. The nearby *Secessionsgebäude*, which houses Klimt's astonishing *Beethovenfries*, is another highlight. Of the classic Viennese coffee shops, *Café Hawelka*, *Café Landtmann*, and *Café Central* capture the spirit of the classic Viennese institution very well. The restaurant *Zum Leupold* is unparalleled for traditional Viennese dining.

A ride or a very long walk to the Grinzing district in the hilly wine-growing region on the outskirts of the city will reward you, perhaps with a visit to a *Heuriger*, a Viennese wine tasting room where you can sample some of the local white wine, called *Grüner Veltliner*, and certainly with the lovely surroundings. A hike into the hills of the adjacent *Wienerwald* is worth it for the pretty vineyards and exceptional views of Vienna that one experiences there. Try to climb the Kahlenberg, just beyond Heiligenstadt, for starters. At some point,

Schloss Schönbrunn should make it onto your itinerary, as should a visit to the *Donauinsel*, weather permitting.

Budapest is absolutely necessary to visit in conjunction with Vienna. This vibrant city, the capital of neighboring Hungary, was part of the Austro-Hungarian Empire until 1918 and is easily reached by train from the new *Wiener Hauptbahnhof*. The views of the Danube flowing under the various lovely bridges connecting the twin cities of Buda and Pest are without parallel, especially the one from Gellért Hill. Visits to Heroes' Square, the Hungarian Parliament, and the city's many thermal baths (especially the Lukács Bath during the magical Saturday night EDM parties) are highlights. The people in Budapest are friendly and well educated, and many speak English, German, and other languages in addition to Hungarian. While in Budapest, be sure to sample as many of the excellent Hungarian wines as possible, perhaps in conjunction with a hearty portion of delicious *Pörkölt, Gulasch,* or *Paprikasch.*

German history in the *Goethezeit*

If there is only one statue in a town or city in German-speaking Europe and it does not depict a local hero or ancestral ruler, then it is most likely a statue of Johann Wolfgang von Goethe (1749–1832). Goethe's literary contributions to German, European, and world culture secure him a place in the public imagination of the same magnitude as William Shakespeare from the English-speaking world. Goethe's other accomplishments, as a gentleman scientist, traveler, lover, and statesman, lend him the aura of a national hero, rather like George Washington in the United States, with whom Goethe shares a general similarity of style and demeanor. Indeed, the era in which Goethe lived is called the *Goethezeit* in German. Goethe's encounters with leading figures of the time, including Napoleon and Beethoven, his famous journey to Italy in 1786, and his work with Duke Karl August to transform the small Duchy of Weimar into the cultural capital of the emerging German nation of *Dichter und Denker* constitute a series of episodes that represent the highest hopes of the emerging bourgeois consciousness that grew from the Enlightenment and continues to seek maturity in our time.

If there is another statue, either on the same pedestal or simply nearby, it very likely depicts Goethe's closest friend and intellectual collaborator, Friedrich Schiller (1759–1805). Whereas Goethe cultivated progressive dreams of the future from the perspective of a wealthy merchant's son adopted by the *Ancien Régime*, Schiller's political views were more modern, culminating in the seminal *Über die ästhetische Erziehung des Menschen in einer Reihe von Briefen* (1794), which describes a process of aesthetic education that would prepare citizens for enlightened self-government. Cultivation of the individual to create an optimized human being who could co-create an ideal society as envisioned by the ancient Greeks was the central preoccupation of Goethe, Schiller, and the other writers and thinkers who, together, created *Weimarer Klassik*. The contribution of Johann Joachim Winckelmann (1717–1768), the father of art history and archaeology, to the worldwide neo-classical movement of which Weimar Classicism is a part cannot be overstated. Winckelmann's *Geschichte der Kunst des Alterthums* (1764) remains in print today.

Hier, oder nirgend ist Amerika! exclaims one of the characters in Goethe's *Wilhelm Meisters Lehrjahre* (1796), the quintessential German *Bildungsroman* (novel of intellectual and spiritual adolescence), referencing the emigration of progressive-minded people from German-speaking lands to the New World that was taking place at the time. This emigration would accelerate in the 19th and 20th centuries. Indeed, the story of the German people, were it to be told fully, would extend across the plains of North and South America, and indeed to every continent on Earth, where the descendants of German-speaking immigrants now live.

Text and translation: Goethe

There was a time during which a college-educated person surely would have read Milton's *Paradise Lost* (1674), Cervantes's *Don Quixote* (1615), and Goethe's *Faust* (first part 1808, second part 1832). Students who memorize and recite the following passage from *Faust* are certain to make a favorable impression on their German-speaking friends and acquaintances. Students who read and ponder *Faust* in its entirety are certain to experience intellectual and spiritual growth.

Nacht.	Night.
In einem hochgewölbten, engen gotischen Zimmer Faust, unruhig auf seinem Sessel am Pulte.	*In a high-vaulted, narrow, Gothic room, Faust, restless in his chair at his desk.*
Habe nun, ach! Philosophie,	I have now, ugh! with blazing effort
Juristerei und Medizin,	Thoroughly studied philosophy, law, and medicine
Und leider auch Theologie	And unfortunately also theology.
Durchaus studiert, mit heißem Bemühn.	Yet I stand before you, a poor fool!
Da steh ich nun, ich armer Tor!	Just as wise and knowledgeable as I was before my studies;
Und bin so klug als wie zuvor;	My title is Master, Doctor even,
Heiße Magister, heiße Doktor gar	And up and down and across and in squiggled lines –
Und ziehe schon an die zehen Jahr	I have pulled my students around by their noses
Herauf, herab und quer und krumm	For a solid ten years, post-graduate school –
Meine Schüler an der Nase herum –	And what I see is this: we can know nothing!
Und sehe, daß wir nichts wissen können!	That fact wants to almost totally burn away my heart.
Das will mir schier das Herz verbrennen.	Of course, I understand more
Zwar bin ich gescheiter als all die Laffen,	Than all of these other ridiculous losers,
Doktoren, Magister, Schreiber und Pfaffen;	Doctors, masters, writers, and pastors.
Mich plagen keine Skrupel noch Zweifel,	No scruples are holding me back, no doubts are plaguing me,
Fürchte mich weder vor Hölle noch Teufel –	I fear neither hell nor the devil,
Dafür ist mir auch alle Freud entrissen,	But as a result of that, all joy has been ripped away from me.
Bilde mir nicht ein, was Rechts zu wissen,	I cannot imagine that I really know anything
Bilde mir nicht ein, ich könnte was lehren,	I cannot imagine that I could teach something
Die Menschen zu bessern und zu bekehren.	That would improve people or convert them (to what?).
Auch hab ich weder Gut noch Geld,	I have neither real estate nor money,
Noch Ehr und Herrlichkeit der Welt;	Neither glory nor worldly splendor;
Es möchte kein Hund so länger leben!	No dog would want to go on living this way!
Drum hab ich mich der Magie ergeben,	So, I have given myself over to the world of magic.
Ob mir durch Geistes Kraft und Mund	To see if through the power and words of spirit and mind
Nicht manch Geheimnis würde kund;	Some secret knowledge might not make itself known to me;
Daß ich nicht mehr mit saurem Schweiß	So that I no longer have to stand in sour sweat
Zu sagen brauche, was ich nicht weiß;	And talk about all the things I don't know, but rather
Daß ich erkenne, was die Welt	That I will become aware of, perceive, and realize –
Im Innersten zusammenhält,	That I will find out! – what holds the world together at its core.
Schau alle Wirkenskraft und Samen,	I will see each and every one of the forces and energies
Und tu nicht mehr in Worten kramen.	That can and do and could possibly cause effects in the world,
	And there will be no more reading for me!

German music: Beethoven

Ludwig van Beethoven (1770–1827) was born in Bonn, on the Rhine near Cologne, and spent his adult life in Vienna. Beethoven's music is the high point of Western culture. One could say that everything since Beethoven, not only in music, but in art and literature as well, has been either an attempt to reach a Beethoven-like high or to achieve success with works that are radically different from those of Beethoven. One way to evaluate this outrageous claim is to listen to large quantities of Beethoven and then decide for yourself. Beethoven's music will open your mind to the amazing potential of human life.

Graf von Anderson enthusiastically endorses the following recordings:

Wilhelm Furtwängler, Berliner Philharmoniker, *Beethoven: 9th Symphony* (1942)
Furtwängler, Schwarzkopf, Bayreuther Festspiele, *Beethoven: 9th Symphony* (1951)
Furtwängler, Berliner Philharmoniker, *Beethoven: 7th Symphony* (1943)
Furtwängler, Wiener Philharmoniker, *Beethoven Symphonies Nos. 5 & 7* (1950, 1954)
Erich Kleiber, Concertgebau Orchestra, *Beethoven: Symphonies 3 and 5* (1953)
Claudio Abbado, Wiener Philharmoniker, *Beethoven: Symphony No. 6, Choral Fantasy, etc.*
Claudio Abbado, Berliner Philharmoniker, *Beethoven: Die Sinfonien*
Osmo Vänskä, Minnesota Orchestra, *Beethoven: The Symphonies*
Cappella Amsterdam, Daniel Reuss, *Beethoven: Missa Solemnis*
Sir Simon Rattle, Berliner Philharmoniker, *Beethoven: Fidelio*
Orpheus Chamber Orchestra, *Beethoven: The Creatures of Prometheus*
Herbert von Karajan, Berliner Philharmoniker, *Beethoven: Triple Concerto, Overtures*
Itzhak Perlman, Berliner Philharmoniker, *Beethoven: Violin Concerto*
Wilhelm Kempff, Berliner Philharmoniker, *Beethoven: Piano Concertos*
Ashkenazy, Perlman, *Beethoven: Violin Sonatas Nos. 5 "Spring" and 9 "Kreuzer"*
Jacqueline du Pré, *Beethoven: The Five Cello Sonatas*
Wilhelm Kempff, *Beethoven: Piano Sonatas Op. 13, 27, 53, 57*
Alfred Brendel, *Beethoven: Bagatelles, Op. 33, 119, 136*
Adrian Brendel, Alfred Brendel, *Beethoven: Complete Works for Piano and Cello*
Nash Ensemble, *Beethoven: Clarinet Trio and Septet in E flat major*
Emerson String Quartet, *Beethoven: The String Quartets*
Eroica Quartet, *Beethoven: String Quartets, Op. 74, 95, 135*
Takács Quartet, *Beethoven: String Quartets (3 volumes)*
Peter Oundjian, Amsterdam Sinfonietta, *Beethoven: String Quartet No. 14, Grosse Fuge*

There are many different versions of Wilhelm Furtwängler's recordings, hence the inclusion of dates. The performance history, including the contemporary newsreel footage of Furtwängler conducting the 9th Symphony with the Berlin Philharmonic in 1942, is worth investigating in your free time.

Recommended films

Die freudlose Gasse (G.W. Pabst, 1925)
Faust (F.W. Murnau, 1926)
Letter from an Unknown Woman (Max Ophüls, 1948)
The Third Man (Carol Reed, 1949)
Sissi (Ernst Marischka, 1955)
Faust (Peter Gorski, Gustaf Gründgens, 1960)
Kontroll (Nimród Antal, 2003)

Notes

1 Cafe Kreuzberg is one of the many fine cultural institutions on California's legendary Central Coast.
2 Think of it this way: he goes from not being next to her, to being next to her. *Wohin? Neben sie.* And after he does this: *Wo ist er? Neben ihr.*
3 Search for "Indo-European Language Tree" and prepare to be amazed.
4 With the exception of the years from 1583 until 1612, during which Rudolf II moved the capital (back) to Prague.

5 Modal verbs, tenses, and passive voices

This chapter begins with a close look at the present tense and then gets wild.

The present tense

We have already learned how to form basic sentences with a subject, a verb, and some combination of predicates, direct and indirect objects, and prepositional phrases.

Ich bin der Koch.	I am the cook.	I am being the cook.	I do be the cook.[1]
Ich koche.	I cook.	I am cooking.	I do cook.
Ich koche Nudeln.	I cook noodles.	I am cooking noodles.	I do cook noodles.
Ich koche dir Nudeln.	I cook you noodles.	I am cooking you noodles.	I do cook you noodles.
Ich koche dir am Freitag Nudeln.	I cook you noodles on Friday.	I am cooking you noodles on Friday.	I do cook you noodles on Friday.

As you can see, the present tense in German has triple the power of any of the present tenses in English. This works in your favor. Imagine the poor German who needs to learn English, then express gratitude in whatever way seems appropriate to you.

Now let's add a level of complexity by introducing the modal verbs.

Modal verbs

Imagine that I, in fact, **am not the cook**, but that I **want to be** the cook. You would need two verbs: one to express "I want" and another for "to be".

Ich will der Koch sein.	I want to be the cook.	I am wanting to be the cook.	I do want to be the cook.
Ich will kochen.	I want to cook.	I am wanting to cook.	I do want to cook.
Ich will Nudeln kochen.	I want to cook noodles.	I am wanting to cook noodles.	I do want to cook noodles.
Ich will dir Nudeln kochen.	I want to cook you noodles.	I am wanting to cook you noodles.	I do want to cook you noodles.
Ich will dir am Freitag Nudeln kochen.	I want to cook you noodles on Friday.	I am wanting to cook you noodles on Friday.	I do want to cook you noodles on Friday.

Modal verbs are conjugated in the second place and are used in combination with an infinitive, which is placed at the end of the sentence.

The six modal verbs are:

wollen	to want, related to der Wille (will, volition)
sollen	should, etymologically related to das Soll (debit)
können	to be able to, as in: Ich kann fliegen!
müssen	to have to, as in: Ich muss Deutsch lernen!
dürfen	to be allowed to
mögen (möchten)	means "would like" when used in the *Konjunktiv II* form (more about that in Chapter 6)

The modal verbs allow us to make magical transformations in meaning:

Ich will der Koch sein.	I want to be the cook.
Ich will dir Nudeln kochen.	I want to cook you noodles.
Ich soll der Koch sein.	I should be the cook.
Ich soll dir Nudeln kochen.	I should cook you noodles.
Ich kann der Koch sein.	I am able be the cook.
Ich kann dir Nudeln kochen.	I am able to cook you noodles.
Ich muss der Koch sein.	I have to be the cook.
Ich muss dir Nudeln kochen.	I have to cook you noodles.
Ich darf der Koch sein.	I am allowed to be the cook.
Ich darf dir Nudeln kochen.	I am allowed to cook you noodles.
Ich möchte der Koch sein.	I would like to be the cook.
Ich möchte dir Nudeln kochen.	I would like to cook you noodles.

The whole universe would like to cook you noodles, so keep working up an appetite!

Future tense

If you loved the relative simplicity and elegance of the modal verbs, then you might be ready for the shocking ease of the future tense.

Imagine that you are not, in fact, the cook. This tragedy could be overcome by imagining a future in which you will be the cook. Behold the future tense ushering in an image of the coming revolution!

Ich **bin** nicht der Koch.	I **am** not the cook.
Ich **werde** der Koch **sein**!	I **will be** the cook!

The future tense is formed by using the verb *werden* and an infinitive, like *kochen*. *Werden* is conjugated in the second place, and the infinitive goes to the last place in the sentence.

You might recall that the verb *werden* means "to become". Watch these transformations of meaning to understand how the verb works its magic:

Ich **werde** der Koch.	I **am becoming** the cook.[2]
Ich **werde** der Koch **werden**.	I **will become** the cook.
Ich **will** der Koch **werden**!	I **want to become** the cook.

You should be able to see the structural similarity between the modal verbs and the future tense. The difference of course is that the modal verbs involve complex ideas – not only "to cook" or "to want", but "to want to cook" – whereas the future tense shifts the verb from the present to the future.

You can even place a modal verb pair in the future tense!

Ich **will** der Koch **werden**!	I **want to become** the cook.
Ich **werde** der Koch **werden wollen**.	I **will want to become** the cook.

The process of forming the future of a modal verb pair is exactly the same as a simple future construction: the verb *werden* is conjugated in second place, and the infinitive form of *wollen* is placed at the end of the sentence.

Take another look at the noodles to see if you understand how the modal verbs and the future tense work:

Ich **koche** dir Nudeln.	I **am cooking** you noodles.
Ich **werde** dir Nudeln **kochen**.	I **will cook** you noodles.
Ich **will** dir Nudeln **kochen**.	I **want to cook** you noodles.
Ich **werde** dir Nudeln **kochen wollen**.	I **will want to cook** you noodles.

Notice how, in each example, the conjugated verb from the previous example is placed at the end of the sentence in the infinitive form. This basic pattern of a conjugated verb in second place and the remaining verbs (in the infinitive form, as above, or as a past participle, as you will soon see) at the end of the sentence will occur again and again. Perhaps there is nothing more quintessentially German than this placement of the verbs.

Spoken past tense: *das Perfekt*

The structure of the past tense is very similar to the structure of the future tense and the modal verbs, but also has some important differences that you will notice.

Present tense	Ich **koche** dir Nudeln.	Verb conjugated in second place
Future tense	Ich **werde** dir Nudeln **kochen**.	Werden conjugated in second place, infinitive at end
Past tense	Ich **habe** dir Nudeln **gekocht**.	Haben conjugated in second place, past participle at end

The spoken past tense (as opposed to the written past tense, which is the subject of the next section) is formed by conjugating *haben* or *sein* in the second place and by placing the past participle at the end of the sentence. Most, but not all, past participles begin with "ge" and end with "t".

Let's begin by looking at the most important German verb, *sein*.

Present tense	Ich **bin** ein reicher Mann.	I **am** a rich man.
Future tense	Ich **werde** ein reicher Mann **sein**.	I **will be** a rich man.
Past tense	Ich **bin** ein reicher Mann **gewesen**.	I **was** a rich man.

Now, let's take a look at *haben*.

Present tense	Ich **habe** einen Audi.	I **have** an Audi.
Future tense	Ich **werde** einen Audi haben.	I **will have** an Audi.
Past tense	Ich **habe** einen Audi **gehabt**.	I **had** an Audi.

And now, let's take a look at *werden*.

Present tense	Ich **werde** müde.	I **am becoming** tired.
Future tense	Ich **werde** müde **werden**.	I **will become** tired.
Past tense	Ich **bin** müde **geworden**.	I **became** tired.

To begin with, notice that *sein* and *werden* both form the *Perfekt* with *sein* and that the *Perfekt* form of *haben* uses *haben*. The past participles *gewesen* and *geworden* are irregular – they simply need to be memorized, as will many others.

The past participle *gehabt* is regular and deserves our attention for a moment.

To form the past participle of a regular verb, the following procedure is followed:

1. locate the infinitive	haben	kicken	einstellen
2. remove the "en" to find the stem	hab	kick	einstell
3. add a "ge" to the beginning and "t" to the end of the stem	gehabt	gekickt	eingestellt

If the stem ends in "t", "d", "gn", or "fn", rather than a "t", add an "et" to the ending so that the word can be pronounced:

1. locate the infinitive	arbeiten	regnen	spenden
2. remove the "en" to find the stem	arbeit	regn	spend
3. add a "ge" to the beginning and "et" to the end of the stem	gearbeitet	geregnet	gespendet

Infinitives that begin with inseparable prefixes, like "be", "ver", or "er", or that end in "ieren" do not get a "ge".

1. locate the infinitive	bedeuten	verlieben	studieren
2. remove the "en" to find the stem	bedeut	verlieb	studier
3. add a "t" or an "et", as appropriate, to the end of the stem	bedeutet	verliebt	studiert

Some verbs follow an alternate pattern; they are irregular. Some people call them "strong verbs", which seems to imply that the ones we have already covered are "weak". How much strength does it take to be irregular? Ponder that in your free time.

The participles for these "strong verbs" begin with "ge" and end with "en". They essentially follow a two-step procedure with one possible extra step, to which we shall turn in a moment:

| 1. locate the infinitive | geben | essen | lesen |
| 2. add a "ge" to the infinitive | gegeben | gegessen | gelesen |

The extra step, of course, is that some of the strong verbs also change their stems, making the following additional two-step procedure advisable:

1. locate the infinitive	werfen	nehmen	sprechen
2. look up the past participle in the dictionary	geworfen	genommen	gesprochen

Some verbs are called "mixed verbs" – they have a changed stem but follow the pattern of regular (so-called weak) verbs:

1. locate the infinitive	denken	wissen	kennen
2. look up the past participle in the dictionary	gedacht	gewusst	gekannt

If all of these rules about forming participles seem like a lot to remember, then you will probably agree that simply memorizing the past participle as you learn each verb is the easiest and most reliable way to get them right every time. They are in the dictionary.

Start by looking up the past participles for each of the 110 verbs that you memorized in Chapter 2.

Figuring out whether or not the *Perfekt* is formed with *sein* or *haben* is not complicated. The simplest rule (assuming you have already internalized the instruction to use *sein* with *sein* and *werden*) is to default to *haben* – you will be right most of the time, since most verbs form the *Perfekt* with *haben*, but when you are wrong, it will sound terrible to German ears.

A better approach would be to read the next two sentences. If the subject, by performing the action of the verb, undergoes a change of location or of state, then *sein* is used. Otherwise, *haben* is used.

Der Mann **ist** nach Paris **geflogen**.	The man **flew** to Paris.	**Change of location**. The man, by flying, changes location (from not being in Paris to being in Paris).
Der Mann **hat** mich nach Paris **geflogen**.	The man **flew** me to Paris.	**No change of location for the subject.** The man sends me (a direct object) to Paris, but his location is not affected by this action.
Der Mann **ist** in Schweden **aufgewachsen**.	The man **grew up** in Sweden.	**Change of state**. The man, by growing up, changes state (from not being grown up to being grown up).
Der Mann **ist** um 8.00 Uhr **aufgewacht**.	The man **woke up** at 8:00.	**Change of state**. The man, by waking up, changes state (from not being awake to being awake).

In addition to the examples already given, the most common verbs that use *sein* are:

gehen	Die Frau **ist** ins Kino **gegangen**.	The woman **went** to the movies.
fahren	Wir **sind** nach Florida **gefahren**.	We **drove** to Florida.
laufen	Ich **bin** durch die Stadt **gelaufen**.	I **walked** through the city.
rennen	**Bist** du **gerannt**?	**Did** you **run**?
bleiben	Der Mann **ist** in Frankfurt **geblieben**.	The man **remained** in Frankfurt.

Sometimes students ask about *bleiben*. Think of it as a synonym for *sein*, or as the anti-*werden*, a case of "anti-change" (of state or of location). Or just accept that it forms the *Perfekt* with *sein*, and move on with your life.

The modal verbs are quite interesting in the *Perfekt*:

Present tense	Ich **kann** Deutsch **sprechen**.	I **can speak** German.
Future tense	Ich **werde** Deutsch **sprechen können**.	I **will be able to speak** German.
Past tense (modal and other verb)	Ich **habe** Deutsch **sprechen können**.	I **was able to speak** German.
Past tense (modal verb only)	Ich **habe** es **gekonnt**.	I **was able** to do it.

What's going on with the double infinitive in the third example? Take a look at the next table, just to make sure it was not a typo:

Present tense	Ich **will** Deutsch **lernen**.	I **want to learn** German.
Future tense	Ich **werde** Deutsch **lernen wollen**.	I **will want to learn** German.
Past tense (modal and other verb)	Ich **habe** Deutsch **lernen wollen**.	I **wanted to learn** German.
Past tense (modal verb only)	Ich **habe** es **gewollt**.	I **wanted** it.

As you can see, when both the modal verb and the other verb are present, the *Perfekt* is formed with two infinitives, resembling strongly the future tense. If only the modal verb is present, then the past participle is used, just like every other verb.

The future past, called *Futur II* in German, is also interesting, much like icing on an already rich cake:

Future tense	Ich **werde** Deutsch **lernen**.	I **will learn** German.
Past tense	Ich **habe** Deutsch **gelernt**.	I **have learned** German.
Future past tense	Ich **werde** Deutsch **gelernt haben**.	I **will have learned** German.

Die ganze Welt wird Deutsch gelernt haben – that's the Graf von Anderson Advantage!

Präteritum

The other form of the past tense is called *das Präteritum*. Unlike the *Perfekt*, the *Präteritum* does not require two verbs, but only one. For most verbs, the *Präteritum* exists as a written form that is used frequently in texts and less frequently in conversation. There are, however, several verbs that are frequently used in the *Präteritum* in spoken German: these are the ones you should learn first.

Three verbs that you should certainly know inside and out are *sein*, *haben*, and *werden*.

sein		*haben*		*werden*	
ich war	wir waren	ich hatte	wir hatten	ich wurde	wir wurden
du warst	ihr wart	du hattest	ihr hattet	du wurdest	ihr wurdet
er war	sie waren	er hatte	sie hatten	er wurde	sie wurden

Relative to the *Perfekt*, the simplicity of the *Präteritum* should be obvious:

Er **ist** mein Freund **gewesen**.	Er **war** mein Freund.	He **was** my friend.
Sie **hat** einen Porsche **gehabt**.	Sie **hatte** einen Porsche.	She **had** a Porsche.
Sie **sind** müde **geworden**.	Sie **wurden** müde.	They **became** tired.

Once again, unlike in other languages, there is not a difference in meaning (completed versus ongoing action, *par exemple*) between the *Perfekt* and the *Präteritum*.

The *Präteritum* forms of the modal verbs should also be memorized, with the exception of *mögen*, to which we will return in the following chapter.

dürfen		*können*		*müssen*	
ich durfte	wir durften	ich konnte	wir konnten	ich musste	wir mussten
du durftest	ihr durftet	du konntest	ihr konntet	du musstest	ihr musstet
er durfte	sie durften	er konnte	sie konnten	er musste	sie mussten
sollen		*wollen*			
ich sollte	wir sollten	ich wollte	wir wollten		
du solltest	ihr solltet	du wolltest	ihr wolltet		
er sollte	sie sollten	er wollte	sie wollten		

You can probably see why the *Präteritum* forms of the modal verbs are so useful, but just in case you cannot see, here are some examples:

Present tense	Wir **wollen** Pizza **essen**.	We **want to eat** pizza.
Präteritum	Wir **wollten** Pizza **essen**.	We **wanted to eat** pizza.
Perfekt	Wir **haben** Pizza **essen wollen**.	We **wanted to eat** pizza.
Perfekt	Wir **haben** es **gewollt**.	We **wanted** it.

Present tense	Er **kann** Deutsch **sprechen**.	He is able to **speak** German.
Präteritum	Er **konnte** Deutsch **sprechen**.	He was able **speak** German.
Perfekt	Er **hat** Deutsch **sprechen können**.	He was able **speak** German.
Perfekt	Er **hat** es **gekonnt**.	He **was able** to do it.

Of course, German speakers use both forms of the past tense, but the efficiency of the *Präteritum* forms of the modal verbs make it an efficient and compelling choice.

Regular verbs form the *Präteritum* in the following manner:

arbeiten		*kaufen*		*öffnen*	
ich arbeit**ete**	wir arbeit**eten**	ich kauf**te**	wir kauf**ten**	ich öffn**ete**	wir öffn**eten**
du arbeit**etest**	ihr arbeit**etet**	du kauf**test**	ihr kauf**tet**	du öffn**etest**	ihr öffn**etet**
er arbeit**ete**	sie arbeit**eten**	er kauf**te**	sie kauf**ten**	er öffn**ete**	sie öffn**eten**

You can probably see that the principle difference between the *Präteritum* and the present tense endings is the addition of a "t" or an "et".

Present:	ich arbeite	ich kaufe	ich öffne
Präteritum:	ich arbeit**ete**	ich kauf**te**	ich öffn**ete**

You probably also noticed that the *ich* and *er* forms are identical.

The irregular, allegedly strong, verbs are quite irregular. Take a look at these:

fliegen		*gehen*		*sprechen*	
ich flog	wir flog**en**	ich ging	wir ging**en**	ich sprach	wir sprach**en**
du flog**st**	ihr flog**t**	du ging**est**	ihr ging**et**	du sprach**st**	ihr sprach**t**
er flog	sie flog**en**	er ging	sie ging**en**	er sprach	sie sprach**en**

The lack of endings in the *ich* and *er* forms should be noted.

The so-called mixed verbs have changed stems just like in the *Perfekt*, and the *ich* and *er* forms each have an "e" ending.

denken		*kennen*		*wissen*	
ich dach**te**	wir dach**ten**	ich kann**te**	wir kann**ten**	ich wuss**te**	wir wuss**ten**
du dach**test**	ihr dach**tet**	du kann**test**	ihr kann**tet**	du wuss**test**	ihr wuss**tet**
er dach**te**	sie dach**ten**	er kann**te**	sie kann**ten**	er wuss**te**	sie wuss**ten**

As noted earlier, pondering the alleged strength, weakness, or "mixedness" of a verb is not always helpful – memorizing the actual verb forms works one hundred percent of the time.

You will most often encounter the *Präteritum* while reading, so the best way to practice it is to read. German newspapers and German literary texts (with a glossary or a handy English translation) are the best way to go. You will quickly discover which *Präteritum* forms are commonly used, and you can learn the others in graduate school or in your retirement.

Setting you up for lifelong learning – that's the Graf von Anderson Advantage!

Passive voice with *werden*

In English we are discouraged from using the passive voice. That last sentence is an example of the passive voice: the subject is "we", but we are not doing the discouraging – we are being discouraged. When the subject of a sentence is not doing the verb, then it is a passive sentence.

Active	English professors **discourage** us from using the passive voice.
Passive	We **are discouraged** from using the passive voice.

In the active voice example, English professors (the subject) are doing the discouraging. In the passive voice example, it is not clear who is doing the discouraging; the subject of the sentence is "we", and as stated above, "we" are not actively doing anything – that's what makes the sentence passive.

Auf Deutsch **wird** das Passiv sehr oft **benutzt**.	In German the passive voice **is used** quite frequently.

The combination of *werden* plus a past participle creates the passive voice. In the example above, *wird benuzt* translates into "is used". If you recall that the future tense is made with *werden* and an infinitive, then you might see how *werden* plus a past participle translates into the present tense.

Here are some common examples:

Werden Sie schon **bedient**?	**Are** you already **being served**?
Hier **wird** Deutsch **gesprochen**.	German **is spoken** here.
Hier **wird** Geschichte **geschrieben**.	History **is being made** here.
Für Garderobe **wird** nicht **gehaftet**.	For the cloakroom **liability is not taken**.

The final example might seem odd. *Haften* is a German verb that means "to be responsible" or "to be liable". Not surprisingly, it is paired with the preposition *für*.

Eltern **haften** für ihre Kinder.	Parents **are liable** for their children.

The sentence above is clearly active. Imagine this sentence on a sign in an expensive lamp shop, and then recall that in the past there were leashes for children.

Returning to the original *Garderobe* example, you might notice several things.

Für Garderobe **wird** nicht **gehaftet**.	For the cloakroom **liability is not taken**.

Für Garderobe translates more or less exactly as "for the cloakroom". Notice that there is not a subject in the sentence above! This is one of the only grammatical structures in German where a subject is not required. Simply stated, nobody is taking responsibility for the cloakroom, so maybe take your phone and car keys out of your pocket before hanging up your cloak!

Of course, the passive can also be used in the past tense, either in the *Perfekt* or in the *Präteritum*:

Perfekt	Für Garderobe **ist** nicht **gehaftet worden**.	For the cloakroom **liability was not taken**.
Präteritum	Für Garderobe **wurde** nicht **gehaftet**.	For the cloakroom **liability was not taken**.
Perfekt	Rom **ist** auch nicht an einem Tag **erbaut worden**.	Rome **wasn't built** in a day.
Präteritum	Rom **wurde** auch nicht an einem Tag **erbaut**.	Rome **wasn't built** in a day.

You will notice that the past participle *worden* is used to form the *Perfekt* of *werden* in the passive voice. Essentially, the use of *worden* signifies that *werden* is being used to create a passive voice sentence. Otherwise, *geworden* is used. As usual, *werden* forms the *Perfekt* with *sein*.

Here are some exciting examples of the passive voice from the life of Goethe:

Goethe **wurde** am 28. August 1749 **geboren**.	Goethe **was born** on August 28, 1749.
Goethe **ist** am 28. August 1749 **geboren worden**.	Goethe **was born** on August 28, 1749.
Goethe **wurde** 1782 in den Adelsstand **erhoben**.	Goethe **was elevated** to the nobility in 1782.
Goethe **ist** 1782 in den Adelsstand **erhoben worden**.	Goethe **was elevated** to the nobility in 1782.

Contrasting the last sentence with an active form might be useful:

Kaiser Joseph II. **erhob** Goethe am 10. April 1782 in den Adelsstand.	Kaiser Joseph II **elevated** Goethe to the nobility on April 10, 1782.
Kaiser Joseph II. **hat** Goethe am 10. April 1782 in den Adelsstand **erhoben**.	Kaiser Joseph II **elevated** Goethe to the nobility on April 10, 1782.

In order to use the passive voice and simultaneously show who the agent is, a prepositional phrase with *von* can be added.

Goethe **wurde** am 10. April 1782 **von Kaiser Joseph II.** in den Adelsstand **erhoben**.	Goethe **was elevated** to the nobility **by Kaiser Joseph II** on April 10, 1782.
Goethe ist am 10. April 1782 **von Kaiser Joseph II.** in den Adelsstand **erhoben worden**.	Goethe **was elevated** to the nobility **by Kaiser Joseph II** on April 10, 1782.
Wilhelm Meisters Lehrjahre **wurde** in den 1790er Jahren **von Goethe geschrieben**.	*William Meister's Apprenticeship* **was written** in 1790s **by Goethe**.
Wilhelm Meisters Lehrjahre **ist** in den 1790er Jahren **von Goethe geschrieben worden**.	*William Meister's Apprenticeship* **was written** in 1790s **by Goethe**.

As anyone who has ever written a book will tell you, the novel was written, but it certainly did not write itself.

Konjunktiv I

As a final treat, here is a brief explanation of *Konjunktiv I*, also known as "subjunctive one". These weird conjugations are used chiefly in news reports for the purpose of indirect quotation.

Take a look at the examples below.

Direct quote	Bobfried sagte, "Der König **ist** ein Dummkopf."	Bobfried said, "The king **is** an idiot."
Indirect quote	Bobfried sagte, der König **sei** ein Dummkopf.	Bobfried said the king **is** an idiot.

You can see in the first sentence that Bobfried is being quoted. His exact words are repeated in quotation marks. In the second sentence, Bobfried's exact words are not used, but rather, he is indirectly quoted.

Imagine that there are stiff penalties for *Majestätsbeleidigung* (insulting the monarchy): by using the *Konjunktiv I*, you will never be in danger of saying something nasty about His

Royal Highness – *Er sei ein Dummkopf* is clearly an indirect quotation, and you will be neither banished nor imprisoned for saying it, although you might be asked to give up the name of the person who said such a terrible thing. *Es lebe der König!*

An example from a recent report from the *Grafenkosmos Zeitung* should help to make the concept clear:

Die Einsatz vor der Insel Graflantis **habe** die ganze Nacht **angedauert**, berichtet das Staatsradio.	The state radio reports, the operation off the coast of the Isle of Graflantis **lasted** all night.

In this example, the *Grafenkosmos Zeitung* is not reporting that the operation lasted all night, but rather, it is indirectly quoting the *Staatsradio*. By using the *Konjunktiv I*, the content of the report is transmitted, but it is also shown that the newspaper itself is not making the report: the newspaper never said it lasted all night but rather indirectly quoted a source that did say that.

If you don't understand, here is the original report from the *Staatsradio*:

Die Einsatz vor der Insel Graflantis **hat** die ganze Nacht **angedauert**.	The operation off the coast of the Isle of Graflantis **lasted** all night.

Unless you start writing for a German news agency, you will never need to form the *Konjunktiv I*. If, however, you begin reading German news reports, you will be glad to know that all of the "incorrectly" conjugated verbs – *habe angedauert*, as opposed to *hat angedauert*, as in the example above – are actually intentional.

Deutsche Welle's *Langsam gesprochene Nachrichten* is an excellent resource for engaging with the news in German. You can begin your journey by pointing your browser in their direction and taking a step into a larger world filled with current events and the vocabulary needed to make sense of them.

Übungen

A Rewrite the following sentences in the future tense. Then rewrite each of the original sentences with each of the modal verbs.

Ich sehe dich!
Du sprichst mit deinem Vater.
Sie isst mit ihrer Tochter.
Wir lernen viel Deutsch!
Ihr fliegt nach Amsterdam.
Sie lieben einander.

Of course, you should translate each sentence into English to make sure you understand.

B Rewrite the following sentences in the future tense and in each past tense. Translate.

Friedrich lernt Deutsch.
Esst ihr noch Fleisch?

Ich spiele gern Gitarre.
Wann kommt der Zug in Wien an?
Die Kinder werden müde.
Um wieviel Uhr fliegst du nach Berlin?
Sie arbeitet bei der Deutschen Bank.
Wann wachen wir auf?
Wann müssen wir aufwachen?
Wir lesen *Das Glasperlenspiel* von Hermann Hesse.
Das Kind ist mein Sohn.
Die Frau hat einen Porsche.

C   Translate the following sentences and write them in the future, present, and each past tense, as in the model below.

Ich bin ein Graf.	**I am a count**.
Ich werde ein Graf sein.	I will be a count
Ich bin ein Graf gewesen.	I was a count.
Ich war ein Graf.	I was a count.

I am a human being.
I am getting smarter and stronger.
I have a future.
I am studying chemistry.
I drive with friends to Frankfurt.
I bring cookies to the party.
I show my friends the city.
I am able to fly!
I want to improve my German.

D   Rewrite the following sentences in the passive voice, using *von* to indicate agency. Bring each sentence into the future and each past tense.

Bobfried backt feines Vollkornbrot.
Im Park spielt ein Streichquartett schöne Musik.
Viele Personen lesen Zeitungen im Cafe.
In der Kneipe trinken die Leute Bier.
Im Büro erledigen die Angestellten alltägliche Aufgaben.
Die Mitarbeiter feiern am Freitagnachmittag.

Travel: Prague, Dresden, Leipzig, and Berlin

The train from Budapest to Prague passes through wealthy and cultured Bratislava, which formerly was known as *Preßberg* in German[3] and as *Pozsony* in Hungarian and which is the present capital of and largest city in Slovakia. Historically, Bratislava was a favored residence of the Austrian Empress Maria Theresa, as well as the capital of the Kingdom of Hungary from 1536 to 1783. The Church of St. Elizabeth, known as the Blue Church, is remarkable, as are the ruins of the Roman military camp, Gerulata, which formed part of the *Limes*. The train also passes through Brno, the second largest city in the Czech Republic. Brno has many interesting modernist buildings and was historically the capital of the Duchy of Moravia, which was part of the Holy Roman Empire and later part of the Austro-Hungarian Empire before becoming part of Czechoslovakia after it declared independence from Austria in 1918.

Prague is the capital of the Czech Republic, which was founded in 1993 following the 1989 Velvet Revolution. Prague was historically the capital of Bohemia, called *Böhmen* in German, one of the electoral principalities of the Holy Roman Empire. *Königreich Böhmen* was ruled by the Habsburgs from 1526 until 1918. Prague was the capital of the Holy Roman Empire at various times during the 14th and 17th centuries and remains one of the most beautiful cities in Europe, a festive and gregarious place like Munich, best explored in the company of the fortunate people who live there. The Prague Castle complex is noteworthy, especially the St. Vitus Cathedral, in which a replica of the Crown of Saint Wenceslas is displayed. The crown was created for Holy Roman Emperor Charles IV of the House of Luxembourg (1316–1378), who was the first King of Bohemia to become Holy Roman Emperor. The crown was used in the 1836 coronation of King Ferdinand V of Bohemia (1793–1875), who is also known as Kaiser Ferdinand I of Austria. After Ferdinand's abdication in favor of his nephew, Franz Joseph I (1830–1916), Ferdinand lived in the Prague Castle for the remainder of his days. Prague seems most beautiful in autumn, especially as the leaves change color across the Charles Bridge and the warm glow of the fading sun illuminates the Vltava River below. If time allows, an excursion to neighboring and charming Pilsen, with its well-preserved *Altstadt*, will bring you to the original source, *der Urquell*, of the pilsner style of beer.

The scenic train ride from Prague to Dresden takes just over two hours. Dresden is the capital of Saxony, *Sachsen* in German, which historically was an electoral principality of the Holy Roman Empire. Unlike Prague, Dresden was nearly totally destroyed during World War II, and much of it was rebuilt from prefabricated concrete panels, a style, called *Plattenbau* in German, which is fairly common in the former East German *Bundesländer* (federal states). Nevertheless, several areas have been restored magnificently, reminding visitors that Dresden was once referred to as Florence on the Elbe. A walk on the *Brühlsche Terrasse*, called "the Balcony of Europe", is essential, as are visits to the *Zwinger*, the *Semperoper*, the *Frauenkirche*, and the *Dresdner Residenzschloss*. The largest city in Saxony is Leipzig, which is only an hour away from Dresden by train. Home of Johann Sebastian Bach and of *Auerbachs Keller*, this city is sometimes mentioned by young, hip people as the "new Berlin". While in Leipzig, visit the *Nikolaikirche*, the *Völkerschlachtdenkmal*, and the new *Paulinum – Aula und Universitätskirche St. Pauli* at the University of Leipzig.

Of course, one could also travel directly from Budapest to Berlin, saving visits to the other cities for another time. The advantage of this approach would be the extended period of anticipation, during which one would be free to reflect for several hours on the astonishing history of the former capital of the Margraviate of Brandenburg, the Kingdom of Prussia, the *Kaiserreich*, the Weimar Republic, the Third Reich, and the *Deutsche Demokratische Republik* (East Germany), and the present capital of the *Bundesrepublik Deutschland* (Federal Republic of Germany). Contemporary Berlin rivals its historical and imaginary iterations with a palpable energy and pulsating magnetism that exist in few other places on the planet. Berlin surely numbers among the greatest cities of the world.

A first visit to Berlin should begin with a walk along Unter den Linden, the broad, tree-lined avenue that connects the newly reconstructed *Berliner Stadtschloss* to the *Brandenburger Tor*. This area is one of the centers of Berlin and is filled with embassies, theaters, and important monuments. Berlin has several other central areas: to the east of Unter den Linden is *Alexanderplatz*, a large square dominated by the iconic *Berliner Fernsehturm* and enclosed by East German high-rise housing blocks. South of Unter den Linden is the modernistic *Potsdamer Platz*, where the Sony Center and the German Film Museum await. Further afield, hipsters of various generations and subcultures will be attracted to the Kreuzberg, Prenzlau-erberg, and Friedrichshain districts, while the less hip might enjoy the newly renovated shops and cafes on *Kurfürstendamm*. Graf von Anderson endorses taking a ride on the *S-Bahn* through the *Grünewald* to the lovely *Wannsee* and then continuing the trip on the public ferry to Alt Kladow, where, at the top of the hill above the ferry terminal, the restaurant *Zum Dorfkrug* beckons with Jever, schnapps, and hearty fare.

A list of destinations in Berlin could fill several pages, if not volumes. Everyone should visit the *Neue Wache* and read the plaques there in respectful silence. Likewise, the memorial at *Bebelplazt* is easily overlooked at first, but then becomes unforgettable. Take the time to walk meditatively through the *Denkmal für die ermordeten Juden Europas*, allowing the massive dimensions of that memorial to resonate with your understanding of the scale and enduring legacy of the mass murders perpetrated in the name of the German people by the criminal National Socialist regime. The *Kaiser-Wilhelm-Gedächtniskirche* is a harsh reminder of the price of violence; it preserves and evokes the appearance of the ruined city in the years immediately following World War II.

On the *Museumsinsel* one can see the reconstructed Ishtar Gate, from ancient Babylon, and the Pergamon Altar, from ancient Greece, in the world-class *Pergamonmuseum*. Master-pieces of painting and sculpture, including the sublime *Mönch am Meer* by German Roman-tic painter Caspar David Friedrich, are on display in the various other outstanding museums on the island, which contribute to Berlin's reputation as the *Spree-Athen* (Athens on the River Spree). For those who are still awake after dark (and possibly also at sunrise), *Berghain* remains the *de facto* world standard for the electronic dance club experience, although surely the friends you make in Berlin will take you to places even more interesting than those men-tioned in your elementary German grammar and culture textbook.

German history in the early 19th century

The 1813 Battle of Leipzig, called the *Völkerschlacht* in German, was a key moment in the eventual liberation of the German people from Napoleon. Several monuments to this battle exist in Germany, including one in the shape of a cross on a hilltop in Berlin which gives the Kreuzberg district its name. The Congress of Vienna, held in the Austrian capital from November 1814 through June 1815 and dominated by Austrian stateman Klemens von Met-ternich (1773–1859), provided a forum for negotiating the political outcomes of the French Revolutionary and Napoleonic Wars and ultimately returned political power to the hereditary aristocracy while redrawing the map of Europe in a way that accelerated the rise of Prussia during the remainder of the 19th century.

The brothers Wilhelm von Humboldt (1767–1835) and Alexander von Humboldt (1769–1859) are icons of the progressive Prussian spirit that dominated public life during and fol-lowing the Napoleonic era. Majestic Humboldt County in Northern California is named for the explorer Alexander von Humboldt, whose landmark work, *Kosmos*, attempted to synthe-size the totality of the scientific knowledge of his day into a single, coherent account. Berlin's excellent Humboldt University is named for both Alexander and his brother Wilhelm, who was an important educational and linguistic theorist and who, along with the philosophers Johann Gottlieb Fichte (1762–1814) and Friedrich Schleiermacher (1768–1834), founded the university in 1809 under Prussian king Friedrich Wilhelm III (1770–1840). Other key figures in the development of the Prussian state included Prince Karl August von Hardenberg (1750–1822) and Baron Heinrich Friedrich Karl vom Stein (1757–1831), each of whom advocated for the abolishment of serfdom and the opening of the state bureaucracy to people of all social classes, as well as Gerhard von Scharnhorst (1755–1813) and Count August von Gneisenau (1760–1831), each of whom contributed to the reorganization of the Prussian army.

Although the aesthetic movement known as German Romanticism began before the occupation of German territory by the French, the presence of foreign troops on German soil intensified it. Writers and thinkers of the Romantic period include Friedrich Hölderlin (1770–1843), whose works remain among the highlights of world literature; Novalis (1772–1801), whose *Heinrich von Ofterdingen* supplements Goethe's *Wilhelm Meister* with a commitment to transcendental poetry; E.T.A. Hofmann (1776–1822), whose fantasies and horror stories inspired Schumann's *Kriesleriana* and Tchaikovsky's famous ballet, "The Nutcracker"; Joseph Freiherr von Eichendorff (1788–1857), whose *Aus dem Leben eines Taugenichts* seems to provide justification for some contemporary American university study abroad programs; and the brothers Jacob Grimm (1785–1863) and Wilhelm Grimm (1786–1859), whose collection of *Märchen*, as well as their pioneering German dictionary, earns them a place among the founders of the academic study of German literature and culture.

The Congress of Vienna reestablished the ruling power of the aristocracy but did not manage to silence the growing number of voices in favor of political change across the various German principalities. The rise of German nationalism was bound together with dreams of a constitutional, republican form of government and made a powerful early appearance at the *Wartburgfest* of 1817, during which hundreds of German university students who were members of *Burschenschaften* (fraternities) celebrated the fourth anniversary of the German victory over Napoleon as well as the four hundredth anniversary of Martin Luther's 95 Theses by marching to the fortress in which Luther had sought refuge from the political powers of his time centuries earlier. The 1832 *Hambacher Fest* saw thousands of people from various walks of life demonstrate in favor of national unity, freedom, and popular sovereignty. Writers and intellectuals associated with the *Junges Deutschland* (Young Germany) movement, an early flowering of progressive, social-democratic German consciousness, rejected absolutism in politics and Romanticism in the arts and prepared the way for the social-critical activism that would characterize the increasingly revolutionary period that began in the 1840s and that continues to address the unresolved issues of the present day.

Text and translation: Hölderlin

Friedrich Hölderlin was a key figure in German Romanticism. Like Goethe and Schiller, Hölderlin was fascinated by the ancient Greeks, and many of his works have themes and settings that originate in classical antiquity. Hölderlin's writing reaches us today from the sacred place, near the horizon from beyond which Being attempts to disclose itself to us, where the words of the ancient poets, dramatists, and philosophers first gave form to the immanence of the transcendental realm. With Hölderlin, we begin to recover the magic of existence that we first experienced as children, opening our eyes in genuine wonder at the dazzling world around us.

Buonaparte	**Bonaparte**
Heilige Gefäße sind die Dichter,	Holy vessels are the poets,
Worin des Lebens Wein, der Geist	In which the wine of life, the spirit
Der Helden, sich aufbewahrt,	Of heroes, preserves itself.
Aber der Geist dieses Jünglings,	But the spirit of this youth,
Der schnelle, müßt er es nicht zersprengen,	The swift one, would he not have to blow it up,
Wo es ihn fassen wollte, das Gefäß?	Where it would want to contain him, the vessel?

Der Dichter laß ihn unberührt wie den
Geist der Natur,
An solchem Stoffe wird zum Knaben der
Meister.
Er kann im Gedichte nicht leben und
bleiben,
Er lebt und bleibt in der Welt.

The poet leaves him untouched, like the spirit of
nature,
With such material, the master becomes an
apprentice.
He cannot live and remain in a poem,
He lives and remains in the world.

Der Zeitgeist

Zu lang schon waltest über dem Haupte mir,
Du in der dunkeln Wolke, du Gott der Zeit!
Zu wild, zu bang ists ringsum, und es
Trümmert und wankt ja, wohin ich blicke.
Ach! wie ein Knabe, seh ich zu Boden oft,
Such in der Höhle Rettung von dir, und
möcht,
Ich Blöder, eine Stelle finden,
Alleserschüttrer! wo du nicht wärest.
Laß endlich, Vater! offenen Augs mich dir
Begegnen! hast denn du nicht zuerst den Geist
Mit deinem Strahl aus mir geweckt? mich
Herrlich ans Leben gebracht, o Vater! –
Wohl keimt aus jungen Reben uns heilge
Kraft;
In milder Luft begegnet den Sterblichen,
Und wenn sie still im Haine wandeln,
Heiternd ein Gott; doch allmächtger
weckst du
Die reine Seele Jünglingen auf, und lehrst
Die Alten weise Künste; der Schlimme nur
Wird schlimmer, daß er bälder ende,
Wenn du, Erschütterer! ihn ergreifest.

The Spirit of the Times

Already too long presiding over my head,
You in the dark cloud, you god of time!
Too wild, too anxious it is all around, and it
Turns to ruins and totters, wherever I look.
Oh! Like a boy, I look to the ground often,
Seek in the cave rescue from you, and would
like,
I the foolish one, to find a place,
All-shattering-one! where you would not be.
Allow me finally, father! with open eyes to
Encounter you! Did you not first awaken the spirit
With your ray out of me? I,
Gloriously brought to life, oh father! –
Surely out of young vines holy power shoots to
us;
In mild air, encountering the mortals,
And when they transform quietly in the grove,
Serenely a god; but, all powerful one, you
awaken
The pure souls of youths, and teach
The old ones' wise arts; the evil one only
Becomes worse, such that he sooner ends,
When you, destroyer! seize him.

An die Deutschen

Spottet nimmer des Kinds, wenn noch das
alberne
Auf dem Rosse von Holz herrlich und viel
sich dünkt,
O ihr Guten! auch wir sind
Tatenarm und gedankenvoll!
Aber kommt, wie der Strahl aus dem
Gewölke kommt,
Aus Gedanken vielleicht, geistig und reif
die Tat?
Folgt die Frucht, wie des Haines
Dunklem Blatte, der stillen Schrift?

To the Germans

Do not make fun of the child, even if the silly one
On the horse of wood thinks much of its glorious
self,
O you good ones! also we are
Poor in action and full of thoughts!
But does it come, like a ray comes out of the
cloud,
From thoughts perhaps, intelligent and mature,
the deed?
Does the fruit follow, as with the grove's
Dark leaf, the silent writing?

German music: Schubert, Mendelssohn, Schumann, and Brahms

Italian composer Gioachino Rossini (1792–1868), Austrian composer Franz Schubert (1797–1828), and the German composers Felix Mendelssohn (1809–1847) and Robert Schumann (1810–1856) are recognized as leading figures of 19th century Romantic music. There are many who consider Johannes Brahms (1833–1897) to be a towering giant, representing an extension of Beethoven's genius into even higher realms of musical delight. Some of the 19th century composers are especially interesting on account of their *Lieder*, in which texts from

Goethe, Schiller, and other leading German writers are set to music. Listening to (and singing along with) *Lieder* is an excellent way to combine an interest in German music with the development of proficiency in the German language.

Graf von Anderson recommends the following recordings:

Claudio Abbado, London Symphony Orchestra, *Rossini: Il Barbiere di Siviglia*
Herbert von Karajan, Berlin Philharmoniker, *Schubert: Symphony No. 8 "Unfinished"*
Wilhelm Kempff, *Schubert: The Piano Sonatas*
Borodin Quartet, Sviatoslav Richter, *Schubert: String Quartet 14*; *Schumann: Piano Quintet*
Amadeus Quartet, Emil Gilels, *Schubert: Piano Quintet "The Trout"*
Matthias Goerner, *Schubert: Goethe Lieder*
Renée Fleming, *Schubert: Lieder*
Frank Braley, Ensemble Explorations, *Mendelssohn: Octet Op. 20, Romance sans Paroles*
Hilary Hahn, *Mendelssohn & Shostakovich: Violin Concertos*
Andre Previn, London Symphony Orchestra, *Mendelssohn: A Midsummer Night's Dream*
Mitsuko Uchida, *Schumann: Carnaval*; *Kreisleriana*
Mitsuko Uchida, *Schumann: G Minor Sonata*; *Waldszenen*; *Gesänge der Frühe*
Sviatoslav Richter, *Schumann: Fantasy in C*; *Faschingsschwank aus Wien, Papillons*
Emerson String Quartet, Leon Fleisher, *Brahms: String Quartets and Piano Quintet*
Otto Klemperer, Philharmonia Chorus and Orchestra, *Brahms: Ein deutsches Requiem*
Royal Concertgebouw Orchestra, Emanuel Ax, *Brahms: Violin Concerto, Piano Concerto No. 1*
Furtwängler, Berliner Philharmoniker, *Brahms: Symphony No.1*; *Schubert: Overture "Rosamunde"*; *Schumann: Overture "Manfred"*
Furtwängler, Berliner Philharmoniker, *Brahms: Symphony No. 4*; *Variations on a Theme by Haydn*

Schubert's unfinished symphony transports the attentive listener into the shadow world of German Romanticism. Perhaps, like Novalis's *Heinrich von Ofterdingen*, it could only be completed on the other side of this reality.

Recommended films

Berlin: Die Sinfonie der Großstadt (Walter Ruttmann, 1927)
Kuhle Wampe, oder: Wem gehört die Welt? (Slatan Dudow, Bertolt Brecht, 1932)
Hangmen Also Die! (Fritz Lang, 1943)
Die Legende von Paul und Paula (Heiner Carow,1973)
Der Himmel über Berlin (Wim Wenders, 1987)
Herr Lehmann (Leander Haußmann, 2003)
Das Leben der Anderen (Florian Henckel von Donnersmarck, 2006)
Victoria (Sebastian Schipper, 2015)

Notes

1 Rare. Also: not right.
2 Also: I become the cook, I do become the cook. Including all three English translations quickly becomes tedious.
3 The German populations of the Czech and Slovak lands were expelled by the occupying Soviet forces following World War II. The Nazi German invasion, occupation, and war crimes constitute a painful and tragic chapter in the history of these countries.

6 Clauses, conjunctions, relative pronouns, *Konjunktiv II*, and *Plusquamperfekt*

German grammar is about to get really interesting.

Simple clauses

Take a look at the following sentences, each of which consists of one clause.

Santa ist ein guter Mann.	Santa is a good man.
Santa trägt einen roten Anzug.	Santa wears a red suit.
Santa schenkt den Kindern viele Spielzeuge.	Santa gives the children many toys.

Enjoy the last moments of your single-clause existence.

Coordinating conjunctions

Clauses can be combined by using a coordinating conjunction, such as *und* (and).

Santa ist ein guter Mann **und** er trägt einen roten Anzug.
Santa ist ein guter Mann **und** er schenkt den Kindern viele Spielzeuge.

You should notice that the coordinating conjunction does not affect the placement of the verb within its clause:

Santa	ist	ein guter Mann	und	er	trägt	einen roten Anzug.
1.	2.	3.	0.	1.	2.	3.

As you can see, each verb remains in second place within its clause. The conjunction can be imagined to occupy space zero, resetting the numbers so that the next clause begins with the number one.

Other coordinating conjunctions include: *denn* (because), *aber* (but), *oder* (or), and *sondern* (but rather).

Santa ist ein guter Mann, **denn** er schenkt den Kindern viele Spielzeuge.	Santa is a good man **because** he gives the children many toys.
Santa trägt einen roten Anzug, **aber** er ist (trotzdem) ein guter Mann.	Santa wears a red suit, **but** he is (nevertheless) a good man.
Ist Santa ein guter Mann, **oder** ist er ein böser Mann?	Is Santa a good man, **or** is he a bad man?
Santa ist kein böser Mann, **sondern** er ist ein sehr guter Mann!	Santa is not a bad man, **but rather** he is a very good man!

Memorizing these five basic coordinating conjunctions will lead you onto a path of German glory.

Notice that a comma is not necessary with *und* and is absolutely necessary with *aber* and *sondern*. Commas are optional with the other coordinating conjunctions.

Subordinating conjunctions

Clauses also can be combined by using subordinating conjunctions, like *weil* (because).

Santa ist ein guter Mann, **weil** er den Kindern viele Spielzeuge schenkt.	Santa is a good man, **because** he gives the children many toys.

Subordinating conjunctions create a SUBORDINATE CLAUSE. The subordinate clause shows its subordination by placing its verb at the end, like the tail of a frightened and submissive canine, between its legs, which rattle and quake in fear at the very presence of the subordinating conjunction.

Perhaps you should read the rest of this section with the lights on!

Now, take another look at the sentence above:

Santa	ist	ein guter Mann	weil	er	den Kindern	viele Spielzeuge	schenkt.
1.	V2	3.	0.	1.	2.	3.	VE

The subordinate clause shows subordination by moving its verb to the end of the clause (VE). The main clause shows its dominance by maintaining its verb in second place in the sentence (V2).

The word order in the subordinate clause does not change, regardless of its position in the sentence:

Weil er den Kindern viele Spielzeuge schenkt,	ist	Santa	ein guter Mann
1.	V2	3.	4.

If a sentence begins with a subordinate clause, the entire clause counts as one grammatical space, which means it will be followed by the verb of the dominant clause. Take a moment to compare these two sentences:

Santa ist ein guter Mann, weil er den Kindern viele Spielzeuge schenkt.
Weil er den Kindern viele Spielzeuge schenkt, ist Santa ein guter Mann.

Do you see that *ist* is in second place in both sentences? Unlike the panic-frozen subordinate clause, the dominant clause is flexible. Like a Yogi, or water flowing in a stream around smooth rocks, it finds a way to maneuver its verb into second place in the sentence, thus signaling its irresistible dominance, like a lupine tail waving a menacing hello to the golden retrievers in a sunny, old-suburban park.

Look above once more to observe the stealthy dominance of the verb *sein* in each sentence.

Now, take a look at these fine exclamations:

Ich lerne Deutsch!	I am learning German!
Deutsch ist schön!	German is beautiful!

Hopefully, you see that each exclamation contains one clause. The verb is clearly in second place in each clause.

Now, observe how the verbs change when we transform *Deutsch ist schön* into *weil Deutsch schön ist*.

Ich **lerne** Deutsch, weil Deutsch schön ist!	I am learning German, because German is beautiful!
Weil Deutsch schön ist, **lerne** ich Deutsch!	Because German is beautiful, I am learning German!

Do you see that the verb of the dominant clause is in second place in each sentence? Do you see how the verb is at the end of the subordinate clause in each sentence? There is nothing else to see.

The best method for creating subordinate clauses is to write the simple clause and then transform it into a subordinate clause.

Simple clause	die Gräfin **wohnt** in Meran	the countess lives in Merano
Subordinate clause	weil die Gräfin in Meran **wohnt**	because the countess lives in Merano

Notice that a dominant clause needs to be added to the subordinate clause in order to create a sentence:

Er ist glücklich, weil die Gräfin in Meran wohnt.	He is happy, because the countess lives in Merano.
Weil die Gräfin in Meran wohnt, ist er glücklich.	Because the countess lives in Merano, he is happy.

Of course, to fully comprehend the sentence, one would need to know where "he" lives.

Other subordinating conjunctions include: *dass* (that), *ob* (whether), *wenn* (if and when), *als* (when), *damit* (in order that), *obwohl* (even though), *falls* (in the case that), *bevor* (before), and *seitdem* (since).

Ich weiß, **dass** die Gräfin in Meran wohnt.	I know **that** the countess lives in Merano.
Weißt du, **ob** die Gräfin in Meran wohnt?	Do you know **whether** the countess lives in Merano?
Die Gräfin geht jeden Tag spazieren, **wenn** sie in Meran ist.	The countess goes for a walk every day, **if and when** she is in Merano.

Als der Graf in Meran wohnte, hatte er die Gräfin noch nicht kennen gelernt.	**When** the count lived in Merano, he had not yet met the countess.
Damit sich die Gräfin nicht langweilt, muss sie jeden Tag etwas Neues erleben.	**In order that** the countess is not bored, she has to experience something new every day.
Die Gräfin wohnt gern in Meran, **obwohl** sie lieber in Davos wohnt.	The countess likes living in Merano, **although** she prefers living in Davos.
Falls Sie mit der Gräfin sprechen, begrüßen Sie sie bitte von mir.	**In the case that** you speak with the countess, please say hello to her from me.
Bevor die schöne Gräfin aufwacht, backt der gräfliche Bäcker ihr Lieblingsbrot.	**Before** the beautiful countess wakes up, the comital baker bakes her favorite bread.
Seitdem sie in Meran wohnt, ist die Gräfin immer glücklich.	**Since** she has been living in Merano, the countess is always happy.[1]

You should note that *als* is used only with the past tense and that *wenn* is the conditional "if" as well as the present and future "when".

Als ich Kind war, habe ich gern Schokolade gegessen.	**When** I was a child, I liked eating chocolate.
Wenn ich alt bin, werde ich immer noch gern Schokolade essen.	**When** I am old, I will still like eating chocolate.
Wenn es noch ein Stück Schokolade gibt, möchte ich dieses Stück essen.	**If** there is still a piece of chocolate, I would like to eat this piece.

Finally, to avoid the frequent confusion that students have with *wann* and *wenn*, you should note that *wann* is a question word:

Wann habe ich Schololade nicht gern gegessen?	**When** have I not liked eating chocolate?
Wann werde ich Schokolade nicht gern essen?	**When** will I not like eating chocolate?
Wann würde ich Schokolade nicht gern essen?	**When** would I not like eating chocolate?

That last question is rhetorical, so don't let it slow you down. We will look at it more closely when we arrive at the *Konjunktiv II* in just a few pages.

Question words

Subordinate clauses can be created with question words. To form these clauses, one simply uses the question word as if it were a subordinating conjunction.

Question (one clause):	Warum trägt Santa einen roten Anzug?	Why does Santa wear a red suit?
Answer (two clauses):	Ich weiß nicht, warum Santa einen roten Anzug trägt.	I don't know why Santa wears a red suit.

The answer could also be written with the subordinate clause first:

Answer (two clauses):	Warum Santa einen roten Anzug trägt, weiß ich nicht.	Why Santa wears a red suit, I don't know.

Notice that the verb of the dominant clause, *weiß*, is in second place. Notice also the verb in the subordinate clause is always located at the end of the subordinate clause.

Ich	weiß	nicht,	warum Santa einen roten Anzug trägt.
1.	V2	3.	4.
Warum Santa einen roten Anzug trägt,	weiß	ich	nicht.
1.	V2	3.	4.

Here are a few more tantalizing examples:

Question (one clause):	Wann fliegt Santa nach Tahiti?	When does Santa fly to Tahiti?
Answer (two clauses):	Ich habe vergessen, wann er nach Tahiti fliegt.	I have forgotten when he flies to Tahiti.
	Wann er nach Tahiti fliegt, habe ich vergessen.	When he flies to Tahiti I have forgotten.

Question (one clause):	Mit wem fliegt er nach Tahiti?	With whom is he flying to Tahiti?
Answer (two clauses):	Er hat mir nicht mitgeteilt, mit wem er nach Tahiti fliegt.	He did not tell me, with whom he is flying to Tahiti.
	Mit wem er nach Tahiti fliegt, hat er mir nicht mitgeteilt.	With whom he is flying to Tahiti he did not tell me.

Question (one clause):	Was will er auf Tahiti machen?	What does he want to do in Tahiti?
Answer (two clauses):	Ich darf euch nicht sagen, was er auf Tahiti machen will.	I am not allowed to tell you, what he wants to do in Tahiti.
	Was er auf Tahiti machen will, darf ich euch nicht sagen.	What he wants to do in Tahiti, I am not allowed to tell you.

Keeping quiet about Santa's secret plans in Tahiti – that's the Graf von Anderson Advantage!

Relative pronouns

The last type of subordinate clause is formed by using relative pronouns. These clauses are called "relative clauses", but don't let that fact confuse you.

Take a look at these simple clauses:

Mein Vater ist ein guter Mann.	My father is a good man.
Ich spreche mit meinem Vater.	I speak with my father.

As with all simple clauses, the verb is in second place. Now watch with slowly growing astonishment as a relative clause is formed:

Ich spreche mit meinem Vater, **der** ein guter Mann ist.	I speak with my father, **who** is a good man.

The relative pronoun refers to the noun directly preceding it. *Der* is used since *Vater* is masculine and is nominative in the relative clause.

If this concept is confusing to you, write out the relative clause as a simple sentence:

Der Vater ist ein guter Mann.	The father is a good man.

Then rewrite the sentence as a relative clause, essentially eliminating the noun and moving the verb to the end:

der ein guter Mann ist	**who** is a good man

The verb goes to the end of a relative clause, just like it does with subordinate clauses. Observe how the case of the relative pronoun shifts as the relative clauses change:

Nominative	Ich spreche mit meinem Vater, **der** ein guter Mann ist.	I speak with my father, **who** is a good man.
Accusative	Ich spreche mit meinem Vater, **den** ich gestern im Park gesehen habe.	I speak with my father, **whom** I saw yesterday in the park.
Dative	Mein Vater ist der gute Mann, mit **dem** ich spreche.	My father is the good man with **whom** I speak.
Genitive	Ich spreche mit meinem Vater, **dessen** Biographie ich schreibe.	I am speaking with my father, **whose** biography I am writing.

If the cases confuse you, write out the relative clause as a sentence, and then transform it into a relative clause.

Nominative	**Der** Vater ist ein guter Mann.
Accusative	Ich habe **den** Vater gestern im Park gesehen.
Dative	Ich spreche mit **dem** Mann.
Genitive	Die Biographie **des** Vaters schreibe ich.

Obviously, the genitive relative pronoun, *dessen*, breaks the pattern. We will return to *dessen* in a moment.

Let's look at a feminine noun:

Ich sehe eine schöne Frau.	I see a beautiful woman.
Die Frau ist meine Mutter.	The woman is my mother.

Watch the transformations of the relative pronouns below. Also, observe the two ways you can structure the relative clause. The relative pronoun comes directly after the noun to which it refers.

Nominative	Ich sehe eine schöne Frau, **die** meine Mutter ist.	I see a beautiful woman, **who** is my mother.
	Eine schöne Frau, **die** meine Mutter ist, sehe ich.	A beautiful woman, who is my mother, I see.

Accusative	Meine Mutter ist die schöne Frau, **die** ich sehe.	My mother is the beautiful woman **whom** I see.
	Die schöne Frau, **die** ich sehe, ist meine Mutter.	The beautiful woman **whom** I see is my mother.
Dative	Die Frau, mit **der** ich gern ins Kino gehe, ist meine Mutter.	The woman with **whom** I like going to the movies is my mother.
	Meine Mutter ist die Frau, mit **der** ich gern ins Kino gehe.	My mother is the woman with **whom** I like going to the movies.
Genitive	Die Frau, **deren** Schwester meine Tante ist, ist meine Mutter.	The woman, **whose** sister is my aunt, is my mother.
	Meine Mutter ist die Frau, **deren** Schwester meine Tante ist.	My mother is the woman **whose** sister is my aunt.

Note once again that in each of the examples above, the relative pronoun comes directly after *Frau*, which is the noun to which each relative pronoun refers.

The table below follows masculine, feminine, neuter, and plural relative pronouns through the nominative, accusative, dative, and genitive cases.

Masculine

der	Er ist der Mann, **der** mir ein Auto verkauft hat.	He is the man **who** sold me a car.
den	Er ist der Mann, **den** ich in der Kneipe gesehen habe.	He is the man **whom** I saw in the bar.
dem	Er ist der Mann, **dem** ich fünf Dollar gegeben habe.	He is the man **to whom** I gave five dollars.
dessen	Er ist der Mann, **dessen** Autos ich wasche.	He is the man **whose** cars I wash.

Feminine

die	Sie ist die Frau, **die** mir ein Auto verkauft hat.	She is the woman **who** sold me a car.
die	Sie ist die Frau, **die** ich in der Kneipe gesehen habe.	She is the woman **whom** I saw in the bar.
der	Sie ist die Frau, **der** ich fünf Dollar gegeben habe.	She is the woman **to whom** I gave five dollars.
deren	Sie ist die Frau, **deren** Autos ich wasche.	She is the woman **whose** cars I wash.

Neuter

das	Ich sehe das Kind, **das** mir ein Auto verkauft hat.	I see the child **who** sold me a car.
das	Ich sehe das Kind, **das** ich in der Kneipe gesehen habe.	I see the child **whom** I saw in the bar.
dem	Ich sehe das Kind, **dem** ich fünf Dollar gegeben habe.	I see the child **to whom** I gave five dollars.
dessen	Ich sehe das Kind, **dessen** Autos ich wasche.	I see the child **whose** cars I wash.

Plural

die	Ich sehe die Männer, **die** mir ein Auto verkauft haben.	I see the men **who** sold me a car.

die	Ich sehe die Männer, **die** ich in der Kneipe gesehen habe.	I see the men **whom** I saw in the bar.
denen	Ich sehe die Männer, **denen** ich fünf Dollar gegeben habe.	I see the men **to whom** I gave five dollars.
deren	Ich sehe die Männer, **deren** Autos ich wasche.	I see the men **whose** cars I wash.

Make sure that you notice the dative plural, *denen*. It might help you to recall that the dative plural uses *den* and adds an "n" or an "en" to the noun, hence, *denen*. *Dessen* and *deren* you will simply have to memorize.

Konjunktiv II – the imaginary subjunctive

The imaginary subjunctive, called *Konjunktiv II* in German (to distinguish it from *Konjunktiv I*, which you will undoubtedly recall is used for indirect quotation when reporting the news), is used to create a **subjunctive mood**, in which imaginary, speculative situations can be easily discussed without being mistaken for psychoses.

For example, imagine the following hypothetical primitive-tribal discussion:

Person 1	Wenn es regnet, bekommen wir Wasser vom Himmel.	When it rains, we get water from the sky.
Person 2	Es regnet nicht.	It is not raining.
Person 1	Es wird regnen! Und wenn es regnet, werden wir Wasser vom Himmel bekommen!	It will rain! And when it rains, we will get water from the sky!
Person 2	Es regnet aber nicht!	But it is not raining!
Person 1	In der Vergangenheit hat es geregnet, und als es geregnet hat, haben wir Wasser vom Himmel bekommen!	In the past it has rained, and when it has rained, we have gotten water from the sky!
Person 2	Es regnet nicht!!	It is not raining!!

Eventually these dialogues terminated in the type of violence that contributed to the nasty, brutish brevity of life before the subjunctive mood prevailed:

| Person 1 | Es regnet nicht, aber wenn es **regnen würde**, **würden** wir Wasser vom Himmel **bekommen**. | It is not raining, but if it **would rain**, we **would get** water from the sky. |
| Person 2 | Ja, klar. Wir **bekämen** Wasser vom Himmel, wenn es **regnete**. | Yes, clearly. We **would get** water from the sky if it **would rain**. |

As you can see, the *Konjunktiv II* brings about a subjunctive mood – no one is saying that it is raining, OK? Now, could you put down that club and please imagine a possible scenario in which it WOULD RAIN? Well done.

Take a look at this inauthentic fragment from the history of logic and zoology:

Faktum Nr. 1	Schweine sind keine Vögel.	Pigs are not birds.
Faktum Nr. 2	Schweine haben keine Flügel.	Pigs do not have wings.
Faktum Nr. 3	Schweine **wären** Vögel, wenn sie Flügel **hätten**.	Pigs **would be** birds, if they **had** wings.

Students who have studied basic science might recognize that *Faktum Nr. 3* might not be true.

Now, rejoice as you imagine the following states of affairs, taken straight from the daily life of Graf von Anderson:

Present	Ich will Pasta Norma essen, aber ich bin nicht in Catania.	I want to eat Pasta Norma, but I am not in Catania.
Future	Ich werde Pasta Norma essen, wenn ich in Catania bin.	I will eat Pasta Norma, when I am in Catania.
Konjunktiv II	Ich **würde** Pasta Norma **essen**, wenn ich in Catania **wäre**.	I **would eat** Pasta Norma, if I **were** in Catania.

As you have seen in the several of the sentences above, there are two ways to form the *Konjunktiv II*. The first way resembles the future tense.

Future	Ich **werde** Pasta in Palermo **essen**.
Konjunktiv II	Ich **würde** Pasta in Palermo **essen**.

In the example above, the verb *werden* is conjugated in its *Konjunktiv II* form and combined with the infinitive, producing a structure that resembles the English construction "would eat".

Here is *werden* in its *Konjunktiv II* forms:

ich würde	wir würden
du würdest	ihr würdet
er würde	sie würden

You can see that these forms are extremely similar to the *Präteritum* forms of *werden*. If you cannot see that, why not look them up right now? Do you see?

The other way to form the *Konjunktiv II* is to use the *Kojunktiv II* form of the verb by itself.

Konjunktiv II (with würden):	Ich **würde** in Catania **sein**.	I **would be** in Catania.
Konjunktiv II (without würden)	Ich **wäre** in Catania.	I **would be** in Catania.

Take a look at the *Konjunktiv II* forms of *sein* and *haben*:

sein		*haben*	
ich wäre	wir wären	ich hätte	wir hätten
du wärest	ihr wäret	du hättest	ihr hättet
er wäre	sie wären	er hätte	sie hätten

Hopefully, you can see that these forms are extremely similar to the *Präteritum* forms of each verb. If you cannot see that, you really should look them up. The one-word forms of the *Konjunktiv II* are based on (and sometimes identical with) the *Präteritum* forms.

You might now understand the use of *möchten* as a modal verb:

Ich **würde** ein Glas Wein **mögen**.	I **would like** a glass of wine.
Ich **möchte** ein Glas Wein.	I **would like** a glass of wine.
Ich **möchte** ein Glas Wein **haben**.	I **would like to have** a glass of wine.
Ich **möchte** ein Glas Wein **trinken**.	I **would like to drink** a glass of winne.

Can you see that the first two sentences are pure subjunctive uses of *mögen* (to like)? Do you wonder about the imaginary conditions under which this person "would like" a glass of wine? Maybe if it were friendly or voted consistently for enlightened environmental regulations?

Can you also see that in the last two sentences *möchte* is used as a modal verb? If not, review the modal verbs from the last chapter. How would the meaning of the sentences change if you substituted *möchte* with each of the other modal verbs? How would those meanings change if you were to place these modal verbs into the subjunctive?

Ich **möchte** ein Glas Wein **haben**.	I **would like to have** a glass of wine.
Ich **kann** ein Glas Wein **haben**.	I **am able to have** a glass of wine.
Ich **könnte** ein Glas Wein **haben**.	I **would be able to have** a glass of wine.

Although for the vast majority of verbs it is more common to form the *Konjunktiv II* with *würden* and an infinitive, there are few verbs for which the one-verb *Konjunktiv II* form is at least as common, or even preferable. *Sein, haben,* and the modal verbs fall into this last category.

Schweine könnten fliegen.	Pigs would be able to fly.
Schmetterlinge müssten lachen.	Butterflies would have to laugh.
Er dürfte singen.	He would be allowed to sing.
Die ganze Welt wollte tanzen.	The whole world would want to dance.
Du solltest mich anrufen.	You should call me.

You have probably noticed that *sollen* and *wollen* are conjugated exactly the same way in the *Konjunktiv II* and in the *Präteritum*. Context prevents this from causing difficulties.

You might also have noticed that the difference between the *Konjunktiv II* and *Präteritum* for *können, müssen,* and *dürfen,* as well as for *haben,* is an umlauted vowel: *konnten/könnten; mussten/müssten; durften/dürften; hatte/hätte.*

Other verbs add endings to the *Präteritum* forms, like *gehen,* for example: *ging/ginge*. Still other verbs, like *sein, fliegen,* and *kommen,* add an umlauted verb and an ending: *war/wäre; flog/flöge; kam/käme.*

As you have probably already realized, looking up these verbs in the dictionary is something you should do until you have somehow internalized them. Reading German texts will be extremely helpful with this process.

The real action in the *Konjunktiv II* takes place with the subordinating conjunction *wenn*:

Was würde passieren, wenn deine Freunde vorbeikommen würden?	What would happen if your friends were to come over?
Wenn meine Freunde vorbeikämen, würden wir viel Musik machen.	If my friends came over, we would make lots of music.

Was für Musik machtet ihr?	What kind of music would you make?
Wir würden Reggae spielen.	We would play reggae.
Würde es gut sein?	Would it be good?
Es wäre sehr gut, mein Freund. Sehr gut.	It would be very good, my friend. Very good.

Making grammar sound like music to our ears – that's the Graf von Anderson Advantage!

Before we leave the *Konjunktiv II*, we should turn to the past tense. The past-subjunctive might be the most useless form of human thought, but then again, it might be the most important. In German, the past-subjunctive is formed by using the *Konjunktiv II* forms of *sein* or *haben* with a past participle.

Perfekt	Ich habe Bier getrunken.	I drank beer.
Konjunktiv II	Ich hätte Bier getrunken.	I would have drunk beer.
Perfekt	Ich habe sie nicht hören können.	I was not able to hear her.
Konjunktiv II	Ich hätte sie nicht hören können.	I would not have been able to hear her.
Perfekt	Ich bin Professor gewesen.	I was a professor.
Konjunktiv II	Ich wäre Professor gewesen.	I would have been a professor.
Perfekt	Ich bin ins Kino gegangen.	I went to the movies.
Konjunktiv II	Ich wäre ins Kino gegangen.	I would have gone to the movies.

Notice that there is only one way to form the past-subjunctive – with the *Konjunktiv II* form of *sein* or *haben* and a past participle. This makes your life quite easy: all you need to do is write a sentence in the *Perfekt*, and then substitute the *Konjunktiv II* form for the present-tense form of *sein* or *haben* – everything else remains exactly the same.

Plusquamperfekt

Sometimes past events happen more or less simultaneously:

Als ich in Frankfurt wohnte, hatte ich viele Freunde.	When I lived in Frankfurt, I had many friends.
Als ich durch Frankreich fuhr, habe ich viele Schlösser gesehen.	When I drove through France, I saw many chateaus.
Als ich mit Doktor Frankenstein sprach, sind die Kinder ins Bett gegangen.	When I was speaking with Dr. Frankenstein, the kids went to bed.

We can use either (or both) of the past tenses to narrate these simultaneous events, as you can see above. But what do we do when two events in the past occur sequentially, one before the other?

Als ich ins Haus kam, **waren** die Kinder schon ins Bett **gegangen**.	When I came into the house, the children already **had gone** to bed.

As you can see, whichever action occurs farther back in the past is described with the *Plusquamperfekt*, which means, essentially, *more than Perfekt*. What is more past tense than past tense? *Plusquam*-past tense, dude.

The *Plusquamperfekt* is formed by conjugating *sein* or *haben* in the *Präteritum* form and combining it with a past participle. It resembles the *Perfekt* strongly, as the following examples demonstrate:

Perfekt	Ich **habe** schon **gegessen**.	I already **ate**.
Plusquamperfekt	Ich **hatte** schon **gegessen**.	I **had** already **eaten**.

Imagine if someone invited you to dinner, but you had already eaten:

Möchtest du mit mir zum Abendessen gehen?	Would you like to go to dinner with me?
Nein, danke. Ich habe schon gegessen.	No, thank you. I have already eaten.

Now imagine that weeks later the same friend is confronting you with examples of your antisocial behaviors, and you are defending yourself:

Du wolltest nicht mit mir zum Abendessen gehen!	You did not want to go to dinner with me!
Ich **hatte** schon **gegessen**, als du mich zum Abendessen **einludst**!	I **had** already **eaten** when you **invited** me to dinner!

You can see that the *Plusquamperfekt* partners very well with the *Präteritum*, which is the preferred tense for whichever action happened more recently. Of course, in spoken German, you might also hear:

Ich **hatte** schon **gegessen**, als du mich zum Abendessen **eingeladen hast**.	I **had** already **eaten** when you **invited** me to dinner.

Using the *Präteritum* with the *Plusquamperfekt* is a sign of a solid education and a strong mind, but using the *Perfekt* with the *Plusquamperfekt* is gradually becoming more acceptable.

The subordinating conjunction *nachdem* is often used with the *Plusquamperfekt*.

Take a look at these one-clause events from the past:

Perfekt	*Präteritum*	*Plusquamperfekt*
Ich **bin** nach Kopenhagen **geflogen**.	Ich flog nach Kopenhagen.	Ich **war** nach Kopenhagen **geflogen**.
Ich **habe** meine dänischen Freunde **besucht**.	Ich **besuchte** meine dänischen Freunde.	Ich **hatte** meine dänischen Freunde **besucht**.
Ich **bin** mit dem Zug nach Köln **gefahren**.	Ich **fuhr** mit dem Zug nach Köln.	Ich **war** mit dem Zug nach Köln **gefahren**.

Now, see how they tell a story when combined with *nachdem* into multi-clause sentences:

Nachdem ich nach Kopenhagen **geflogen war**, **besuchte** ich meine dänischen Freunde.	After I **had flown** to Copenhagen, I **visited** my Danish friends.

Ich **bin** mit dem Zug nach Köln **gefahren**, nachdem ich meine dänischen Freunde **besucht hatte**.	I **traveled** with the train to Cologne after I **had visited** my Danish friends.
Was **machte** ich, nachdem ich nach Köln **gefahren war**?	What **did I do** after I **had traveled** to Cologne?
Ich **darf** euch nicht **mitteilen**, was ich **machte**, nachdem ich nach Köln **gefahren war**.	I am not **allowed to tell** you what I **did** after I **had traveled** to Cologne.

At this point, a brief overview of all of the possible verb forms, from the simple present tense with which we started back in Chapter 2, all the way to the *Plusquamperfekt*, might be exciting:

Bobfried **spricht** Deutsch.	Bobfried **speaks** German.
Bobfried **kann** Deutsch **sprechen**.	Bobfried **is able to speak** German.
Bobfried **wird** Deutsch **sprechen**.	Bobfried **will speak** German.
Bobfried **wird** Deutsch **sprechen können**.	Bobfried **will be able to speak** German.
Bobfried **hat** Deutsch **gesprochen**.	Bobfried **spoke** German.
Bobfried **sprach** Deutsch.	Bobfried **spoke** German.
Bobfried **hat** Deutsch **sprechen können**.	Bobfried **was able to speak** German.
Bobfried **konnte** Deutsch **sprechen**.	Bobfried **was able to speak** German.
Bobfried **hatte** (schon) Deutsch **gesprochen**.	Bobfried (already) **had spoken** German.
Bobfried **hatte** Deutsch **sprechen können**.	Bobfried **had been able to speak** German.
Bobfried **würde** Deutsch **sprechen**.	Bobfried **would speak** German.
Bobfried **spräche** Deutsch.	Bobfried **would speak** German.
Bobfried **würde** Deutsch **sprechen können**.	Bobfried **would be able to speak** German.
Bobfried **hätte** Deutsch **gesprochen**.	Bobfried **would have spoken** German.
Bobfried **hätte** Deutsch **sprechen können**.	Bobfried **would have been able to speak** German.

How many German verbs do you know well enough to be able to write your own simple sentences (like those above) going through all of the tenses and moods? The number itself does not matter, so long as it increases over time.

To complete the mental journey that is Chapter 6, take a look at all of the above forms rendered as subordinate clauses with *weil*. You could recite these sentences every morning in front of the bathroom mirror, along with your other daily affirmations:

Jeder liebt mich, weil ich schönes Deutsch spreche.	Everyone loves me because I speak beautiful German.
Jeder liebt mich, weil ich schönes Deutsch sprechen kann.	Everyone loves me because I am able to speak beautiful German.
Jeder wird mich lieben, weil ich schönes Deutsch sprechen werde.	Everyone will love me because I will speak beautiful German.
Jeder wird mich lieben, weil ich schönes Deutsch sprechen können werde.	Everyone will love me because I will be able to speak beautiful German.
Jeder hat mich geliebt, weil ich schönes Deutsch gesprochen habe.	Everyone loved me because I spoke beautiful German.
Jeder hat mich geliebt, weil ich schönes Deutsch sprach.	Everyone loved me because I spoke beautiful German.
Jeder hat mich geliebt, weil ich schönes Deutsch habe sprechen können.	Everyone loved me because I was able to speak beautiful German.
Jeder hat mich geliebt, weil ich schönes Deutsch sprechen konnte.	Everyone loved me because I was able to speak beautiful German.

Jeder hat mich geliebt, weil ich schon schönes Deutsch gesprochen hatte.	Everyone loved me because I already had spoken beautiful German.
Jeder hat mich geliebt, weil ich schon schönes Deutsch hatte sprechen können.	Everyone loved me because I already had been able to speak beautiful German.
Jeder würde mich lieben, weil ich schönes Deutsch sprechen würde.	Everyone would love me because I would speak beautiful German.
Jeder würde mich lieben, weil ich schönes Deutsch sprechen können würde.	Everyone would love me because I would be able to speak beautiful German.
Jeder würde mich lieben, weil ich schönes Deutsch sprechen könnte.	Everyone would love me because I would be able to speak beautiful German.
Jeder hätte mich geliebt, weil ich schönes Deutsch gesprochen hätte.	Everyone would have loved me because I would have spoken beautiful German.
Jeder hätte mich geliebt, weil ich schönes Deutsch hätte sprechen können.	Everyone would have loved me because I would have been able to speak beautiful German.

At this point in your German career, you can read almost any text you might encounter, whether in a novel or a newspaper. All you need is a dictionary and some patience. Start by finding the subject and the verb in each clause, then stop and give yourself some applause!

That's the Graf von Anderson Advantage!

Übungen

A   Combine the following short sentences into a longer sentence using the conjunction in parentheses. Translate to make sure you understand.

Es regnet. Wir bleiben im Klassenzimmer. (und)

Es regnet. Wir bleiben im Klassenzimmer. (denn)

Es regnet. Wir bleiben im Klassenzimmer. (weil)

Du darfst nicht mit den anderen Kindern Fußball spielen. Du machst deine Hausaufgaben. (bevor)

Ich weiß. Ich darf nicht mit den anderen Kindern spielen. Ich habe meine Hausaufgaben gemacht. (dass, bevor).

Du darfst mit den anderen Kindern Fußball spielen. Du hast deine Hausaufgaben gemacht. (nachdem)

Gegen 20.00 Uhr darfst du mit deiner Freundin in Goa sprechen. Nach zwanzig Minuten musst du den Hörer auflegen. (aber)

Ferngespräche sind teuer. Nach zwanzig Minuten musst du den Hörer auflegen. (weil)

Gegen 3.00 Uhr darfst du mit deiner Freundin in Goa sprechen. Ferngespräche sind teuer. (obwohl)

B   Combine the following elements into a sentence with a subordinate clause. Translate to make sure you understand.

Ich weiß es nicht. Wo wohnt Bobfried?

Kannst du es für mich herausfinden? Welche Farbe ist seine Lieblingsfarbe?

Er hat es mir nicht sagen wollen. Mit wem ist er nach München gefahren?

Wir müssen den Schaffner fragen! Wann kommt der Zug in München an?

Er hat die Verkäuferin gefragt. Wieviel kostet der Pullover?

Seine Begleiterin konnte es nicht verstehen. Wieso kostet der Pullover so viel?

Die Verkäuferin hat es ihnen nicht erklären können. Warum ist der Preis so hoch?

Dem Taxifahrer sagte er es. Zu welchem Hotel wollte er fahren?

Er gab es auf dem Zimmerservice-Formular an. Was wollten sie zum Frühstück essen?

C   Combine the following elements into a sentence with a relative clause. Translate to make sure you understand.

Ich habe einen Bruder. Er wohnt in Budapest.

Ich habe in Budapest einen Bruder. Ich besuche ihn.

Ich habe zwei Tanten. Sie wohnen in Antwerpen.

Ich habe in Antwerpen zwei Tanten. Ich besuche sie.

Ich sehe ein Gespenst. Sein Gesicht leuchtet im Mondlicht.

Mein bester Freund wohnt in Berlin. Ich spiele gern Gitarre mit ihm.

Ich habe auch neue Freunde. Ich forme mit ihnen eine Band.

Wir spielen psychedelische elektronische Tanzmusik. Das ist unsre Lieblingsmusik.

Wir sollten einen Hund adoptieren. Sein Charakter passt zu uns.

D   Use the following situations to write a sentence in the *Konjunktiv II* beginning with *wenn*. Translate to make sure you understand.

Wir haben Hunger. Wir essen.

Die Sonne scheint. Wir tragen eine Sonnenbrille.

Wir sind allwissend. Wir wissen alles.

Sie hat ein Auto. Sie fährt zu dir.

Er hat Geld. Er nimmt ein Taxi.

Wir sind klüger. Es gibt mehr Umweltschutz.

Wir sind intelligenter gewesen. Es hat in den letzten vierzig Jahren mehr Umweltschutz gegeben.

Wir wollen vernünftiger sein. Wir verlangen mehr Umweltschutz.

Es gibt einen anderen bewohnbaren Planeten in der Nähe. Die bevorstehende Umweltkatastrophe ist immer noch echt tragisch.

Travel: Karlsruhe, Baden-Baden, Strasbourg, and Freiburg

Many people arrive in Berlin for a visit and find it impossible to imagine living anywhere else. Even Graf von Anderson, to paraphrase Marlene Dietrich, *hat noch einen Koffer in Berlin*, although he can't remember where he left it. If, however, you decide to continue your journey beyond Berlin, Hamburg is the next logical place to follow your *Wanderlust*. The Beatles liked it for a reason; imagine something like a hybrid of Amsterdam and midtown Manhattan spread out along the Elbe, and you will begin to understand the subtle cosmopolitanism of this Hanseatic city. Heading north toward the *Ostsee* (Baltic Sea), one could sail to Copenhagen, in Denmark, and then to Stockholm, in Sweden; Helsinki, in Finland; and St. Petersburg, in Russia, before stopping in Tallinn, formerly *Reval*, in Estonia; Klaipėda, formerly *Memel*, in Lithuania (and from there, making time to visit the stunning Lithuanian capital, Vilnius); Riga, in Latvia; Kaliningrad, formerly *Königsberg*, in a noncontiguous part of Russia; and Gdansk, formerly *Danzig*, in Poland, before visiting Rostock and Lübeck after returning to German waters. The high quality of life in the Baltic region is worth exploring, as is the area's rich history. Another option would be to explore the *Nordsee* (North Sea), sailing to Gothenburg, in Sweden; Oslo and Bergen, in Norway; perhaps reaching Edinburgh, in Scotland, if you are an experienced sailor; returning to Germany through Bremerhaven, making time to visit Bremen and Oldenburg; and enjoying an excursion to Groningen, in the Netherlands, as well.

After these adventures on and around the sea, an overnight train to Karlsruhe will make you happy to be back on land. Karlsruhe is home to several important universities, including the *Staatliche Hochschule für Gestaltung*, where the incomparable Peter Sloterdijk is a professor of philosophy and media theory. The *Karlsruher Schloss*, residence of the dukes and grand dukes of Baden from 1717 until 1918, is impressive and well situated. Nearby Baden-Baden, summer resort of the European aristocracy during the Victorian and Edwardian eras, deserves an extended stay. Graf von Anderson endorses squandering money at roulette in the casino, as well as spending several hours each day in the regally appointed thermal baths from which Baden-Baden derives its good name. Attending an opera at the *Festspielhaus* is also advised. The *Hotel am Markt* is centrally and discretely located on a hill above the *Friedrichsbad*. Baden-Baden makes an excellent base for exploring the numerous outdoor activities offered in the northern *Schwarzwald*.

Crossing to the French side of the Rhine, lovely Alsace, which is *Elsaß* in German, is filled with fertile vineyards and lovely towns. The historic city of Strasbourg, with roots going back to Roman times, is absolutely essential to visit. The *Straßburger Münster* is a fine example of high Gothic architecture – be sure to observe the sinister spectacle of its astronomical clock when it goes into motion. The fantastic food and wine available in Strasbourg and in nearby Colmar, where the early 16th century *Isenheimer Altar* simply must be seen, more than justify spending time in this beautiful part of the world. *Flammkuchen*, which is *Flammekueche* in the Alsatian dialect, and which also is, oddly, one of the few words which Germans will routinely correct if you do not say it in *Hochdeutsch*, is known in French and in English as *tarte flambée* and is delicious regardless of pronunciation; try some with a nice Pinot Gris. Visits to the Council of Europe and the European Parliament, both of which are located in Strasbourg, also will be of interest.

The lively university town of Freiburg is the sunniest and most environmentally friendly city in Germany. The city has excellent universities, a remarkable medieval cathedral, and a high quality of life. According to an ancient rumor, if you step into any of the *Bächle* (little waterways) that run through the town, you will marry someone from Freiburg. So be careful – or not – depending on your hopes and circumstances. Freiburg is located near the *Kaiserstuhl* wine-growing region, where the Gewürztraminer variety finds its finest expression – try an older bottle, perhaps with some *Käsespätzle* – and is a convenient gateway to the southern *Schwarzwald*, where winter sports are among the many highlights of this majestic outdoor paradise.

German history in the late 19th century

In the 19th century, political activism moved beyond the retrospectively obvious demands for popular sovereignty and participatory government that were formulated in the Enlightenment and fought for in the American, French, and Haitian Revolutions of the late 18th century toward the issues of abusive state power and material inequality that created and maintained systemic imbalances in political participation and limited the universal flourishing of human potential. The world was not turning into Goethe and Schiller's Weimar for most people, and the German principalities that emerged from the Congress of Vienna, including enlightened Prussia, increasingly displayed the reactionary tendencies of police states as the 19th century progressed. The Carlsbad Decrees of 1819 which imposed censorship, banned certain free associations, and removed liberal university professors from their posts, marked the beginning of this process, which lead many writers and intellectuals who engaged in the public critique of power to seek refuge in more liberal countries.

Heinrich Heine (1797–1856), a sharp-witted critic and perhaps the greatest German poet after Goethe, spent most of his adult life in exile in Paris. Heine's lyric poetry formed the basis of popular *Lieder* composed by Schumann and Mendelssohn, and his satirical yet also delightfully descriptive travel writing, especially the *Harzreise*, slowly contributed to his fame. His critical verse epic, *Deutschland ein Wintermärchen*, is a classic work of political satire, and his poem, *Die schlesischen Weber*, which brought attention to the plight of the exploited weavers in Silesia, remains a powerful example of the power of art to help raise awareness of social injustice. In Paris, Heine met another exiled German critic, the philosopher Karl Marx (1818–1883), whose seminal work *Das Kapital* provided a scientific materialist account of the capitalist production system and the alienation of labor inherent in that system. The concrete details of a more efficient system were left to future generations to work out, which has proven to be a difficult and enduring task.

The *Manifest der Kommunistischen Partei* was published in 1848, a year in which a series of revolutions gripped the European capitals, including Berlin, Vienna, and Budapest. These revolutions were, however, not based on the embryonic Marxist philosophy, but rather were belated attempts to regain the lost political progress that had seemed inevitable after 1789 and Napoleon. One interesting result of the 1848 revolutions was the abdication of Ferdinand I in favor of Franz Joseph I, who would remain kaiser of Austria until his death during World War I, earning the nickname *der ewige Kaiser*. In May of 1848, the first freely elected German parliament was convened in the *Paulskirche* in Frankfurt. Delegates succeeded in writing a liberal constitution that went on to influence both the constitution of the Weimar Republic (1919) and the current German *Grundgesetz* (1949), although it was not adopted at the time. The 1848 revolutions brought about minor successes, including a limited constitution in Prussia, and paved the way for German unification, as well as for later revolutions, in the following decades. The *Sozialdemokratische Partei Deutschlands*, known as the *SPD*, was founded on Marxist principles in 1863 and remains Germany's oldest political party.

Two novels from the decade following the 1848 revolutions present pictures of the aspirational, educated middle-class known as *Bildungsbürgertum*, the values of which remain a powerful force among good families in contemporary times. Austrian Adalbert Stifter's (1805–1868) *Der Nachsommer* provides a portrait of conscientious cultivation of the private sphere as well as the peaceful, cooperative participation in the public good based on a neoclassical aesthetic theory expanded to appreciate local, organic, and especially Gothic phenomena and supplemented by empirical science. Swiss author Gottfried Keller's (1819–1890) *Der grüne Heinrich* shows the dark side of these values, especially when followed selfishly and without the guidance of a strong community. The novels were written as industrialization swept across the face of Western Europe. Many of the features of modern times made their first appearance in the mid- and late 19th century, including trains, telegraphs, and photography. By the end of the century, the telephone and the automobile would be poised to make their impacts in the century to come. The spectacular progress of science associated with names like Justus von Liebig (1803–1873) in chemistry; Hermann von Helmholtz (1821–1894), Ernst Mach (1838–1916), Wilhelm Röntgen (1845–1923), and Heinrich Hertz (1857–1894) in physics; and Ernst Haeckel (1834–1919) and Robert Koch (1843–1910) in biology accelerated in the second half of the 19th century and continued to accelerate as the 20th century began. Firms like Krupp (1811), Villeroy & Boch (1836), Siemens (1847), Bayer (1863), Deutsche Bank[2] (1870), and Bosch (1886) were each founded during this period of unprecedented scientific and economic growth.

The rise of Prussia intensified after the failure of the Frankfurt Congress to create a united German state. During this period Otto von Bismarck (1815–1898) began his epoch-defining political career. Bismarck was the greatest European statesman since Metternich and had an impact of the magnitude of Napoleon. Not since Friedrich the Great had a German leader captured the popular imagination to such an extent. The rise of Prussia culminated in a series of wars against Denmark (1864), Austria (1866), and finally France (1870), each of which was orchestrated by Bismarck and which culminated in the creation of the *Deutsches Reich* in 1871. King Wilhelm I of Prussia was crowned *Deutscher Kaiser* in the Hall of Mirrors in Versailles in occupied France. The famous painting of the event by Anton von Werner is worth an extended viewing. The years following the foundation of the *Kaiserreich* are referred to as the *Gründerzeit*, the period in which modern Germany emerged onto the world stage, nominally under the rule of Kaiser Wilhelm I, but actually under the political genius of his chancellor, Bismarck. Bismarck pursued *Realpolitik*, flexibly attempting to maintain the power of the owners of capital and land and to forestall what appeared to be the inevitable rise of the working class; it was through *Realpolitik* that the first social welfare programs in Europe were established during Bismarck's chancellorship. Bismarck famously declared, "*Nicht durch Reden oder Majoritätsbeschlüsse werden die großen Fragen der Zeit entschieden – das ist der große Fehler von 1848 und 1849 gewesen – sondern durch Eisen und Blut*". Insofar as violence was exported for the sake of achieving domestic political and economic stability, the contours of political reality took on forms that remain all too recognizable in the present era. This militaristic trend would accelerate tragically after Kaiser Wilhelm II dismissed Bismarck in 1890.

Text and translation: Heinrich Heine and Karl Marx

Heinrich Heine

Jede Zeit ist eine Sphinx, die sich in den Abgrund stürzt, sobald man ihr Rätsel gelöst hat.	Every era is a sphinx that falls into oblivion as soon as one solves its riddle.
In dunkeln Zeiten wurden die Völker am besten durch die Religion geleitet, wie in stockfinstrer Nacht ein Blinder unser bester Wegweiser ist; er kennt dann Wege und Stege besser als ein Sehender. Es ist aber töricht, sobald es Tag ist, noch immer die alten Blinden als Wegweiser zu gebrauchen.	In dark times people are best led by religion, just like in pitch black night a blind person is our best guide; because he knows the paths and ways better than one who can see. It is insane, however, once it is daytime, to continue to use the blind person as our guide.
Von allen Welten, die der Mensch erschaffen hat, ist die der Bücher die Gewaltigste.	Of all the worlds that human beings have created, the world of books is the most powerful.

Karl Marx

Das Reich der Freiheit beginnt da, wo Arbeit aufhört.	The realm of freedom begins where work ends.
Das Geld ist der allgemeine, für sich selbst konstruierte Wert aller Dinge. Es hat daher die ganze Welt, die Menschheit wie die Natur, ihres eigentümlichen Wertes beraubt. Das Geld ist das den Menschen entfremdete Wesen seiner Arbeit und seines Daseins, und dieses fremde Wesen beherrscht ihn, und er betet es an.	Money is the general, constructed for itself, value of all things. It has therefore robbed the whole world, humanity as well as nature, of its own inherent value. Money is the alienated essence of the work and the existence of human beings, and this alien essence rules them, and they worship it.

Die Philosophen haben die Welt nur verschieden interpretiert; es kommt aber darauf an, sie zu verändern.	Philosophers have only interpreted the world in various ways; the point is to change it.

German music: Wagner, Bruckner, Wolf, and Mahler

The Polish composer Frédéric Chopin (1810–1849) and the Hungarian Franz Liszt (1811–1886), considered by many to be the two greatest pianists who ever lived, form another current of Romantic music in the 19th century. German composer, dramatist, and theorist Richard Wagner (1813–1883) is undeniably the next giant in the history of Western music after Beethoven. The George Solti box set of Wagner's *Der Ring des Nibelungen* was, in the CD era, the prized possession of many a budding Germanist. The cult of Wagner was and is based around the *Festspielhaus* in Bayreuth, which was constructed for the sole purpose of performing Wagner's elaborate *Gesamtkunstwerke*. As one matures, one spends relatively more time with Chopin, perhaps having become aware of the dangers of seduction, narcosis, and pathos – in music and in life.

Following Wagner, Austrian composer Anton Bruckner (1824–1896) expanded the symphonic form in ways that are unmistakably modern, foreshadowing the sound of the 20th century without succumbing to its worst excesses. The Austrian composer of Slovene origin Hugo Wolf (1860–1903) made important contributions to the repertoire of German *Lieder*. Austrian composer and conductor Gustav Mahler (1860–1911) remains a controversial figure in the history of music; there are some who rank his works as highly as those of Beethoven, and there are others who cannot imagine doing so.

Graf von Anderson recommends the following recordings:

Alfred Cortot, *Chopin: Preludes, Impromptus, Barcarolle & Berceuse*
Martha Argerich, *Chopin: The Legendary 1965 Recording*
Claudio Arrau, *Chopin: The Complete Nocturnes and Impromptus*
Martha Argerich, Beaux Arts Trio, *Chopin Complete Edition VIII: Waltzes; Chamber Music*
Claudio Arrau, *Liszt: 12 Etudes d'exécution transcendante*
Georges Cziffra, *Liszt: 7 Hungarian Rhapsodies*
Lazar Berman, *Liszt: Années de pèlerinage*
Diana Damrau, *Liszt Lieder*
Sviatoslav Richter, London Symphony Orchestra, *Liszt: The Two Piano Concertos; The Piano Sonata*
Karl Böhm, Bayreuther Festspiele, *Wagner: Tristan und Isolde*
Georg Solti, Wiener Philharmoniker *Wagner: Der Ring des Nibelungen*
Solti, Wiener Philharmoniker, *Wagner: Orchestral Favorites*
Edo de Waart, Netherlands Radio Philharmonic Orchestra, *Wagner: Orchestral Adventures*
Bruno Walter, Columbia Symphony Orchestra, *Bruckner: Symphony No. 4 "Romantic"*
Furwängler, *Bruckner: Symphony No. 7* and *Mahler: Lieder eines fahrenden Gesellen* (1949 and 1951)
Elisabeth Schwarzkopf, Gerald Moore, *Wolf: Lieder*
Sophie Karthäuser, Eugene Asti, *Wolf: Kennst du das Land?*
Sir Simon Rattle, Berliner Philharmoniker, *Mahler: Symphony No. 6*
Claudio Abbado, Berliner Philharmoniker, *Mahler: Symphony No. 9*
Pierre Boulez, Wiener Philharmoniker, *Mahler: Das Lied von der Erde*

Diana Damrau's version of Liszt's *Liebestraum No. 3* is especially moving. Wolf's *Lieder* are among Graf von Anderson's personal favorites, and the Sophie Karthäuser recording is excellent.

Recommended films

Bismarck (Wolfgang Liebeneiner, 1940)
Der Untertan (Wolfgang Staudte, 1951)
Mahler (Ken Russell, 1974)
Nordsee ist Mordsee (Hark Bohm, 1976)
Proteus: A Nineteenth Century Vision (David Lebrun, 2004)
Soul Kitchen (Fatih Akın, 2009)
Baden Baden (Rachel Lang, 2016)

Notes

1 Observant students will notice that *in Meran wohnt* translates into "is living in Merano" and not "has been living in Merano". Why the "error"? Think of it this way: this is why Germans sometimes say in English, "Since I am living in Merano, I am having more fun". We often know they mean to say, "Since I have been living in Merano I have been having more fun" – that's how we express the idea in English. In German, they express the idea with the present tense. Since you have accepted this fact, you have been happier. After you are accepting this fact, you are being even happier.
2 At the turn of the 21st century, Graf von Anderson was a proud member of the Equity Capital Markets Group in Frankfurt, where he developed a profound appreciation for the culture of this elite institution.

7 Adverbs, adjectives, and extended adjectives

This chapter begins with some of the easiest concepts in the German language and then expands into the most difficult ones. If you can make it to the end, you have really accomplished something.

Adverbs

An adverb modifies either a verb or an adjective. Take a look:

Der Schmetterling schreit **laut**.	The butterfly screams **loudly**.

As a quick review: the subject is *Schmetterling*, the verb is *schreit*, and *laut* modifies the verb.

Wie schreit der Schmetterling?	**How** does the butterfly scream?
Laut! Laut schreit der Schmetterling.	**Loudly!** The butterfly screams **loudly**.

The beauty of adverbs is that they DO NOT REQUIRE ENDINGS.

Predicate adjectives

The beauty of predicate adjectives is that they, like adverbs, DO NOT REQUIRE ENDINGS.

Der Schmetterling ist **schön**.	The butterfly is **beautiful**.

The subject is *Schmetterling*, the verb is *ist*, and the adjective is *schön*.

Wie ist der Schmetterling?	**How** is the butterfly?
Schön! Schön ist er.	**Beautiful!** It is **beautiful**.

Why is it called a "predicate adjective"? You might recall predicate nouns from Chapter 3. If not, you should review. You will need to understand predicate nouns in order to understand this chapter.

Predicate nouns and adjectives can be imagined as having some sort of equivalence to the subject of a clause:

Der Schmetterling	ist	schön.	The butterfly	is	beautiful.
subject	=	predicate adjective	subject	=	predicate adjective
Der Schmetterling	ist	ein Freund.	The butterfly	is	a friend.
subject	=	predicate noun	subject	=	predicate noun

Predicate nouns are in the nominative case, just like the subject. Predicate adjectives do not require endings, just like adverbs.

Here is an example of an adverb modifying a predicate adjective.

Der Schmetterling ist **sehr** schön.	The butterfly is **very** beautiful.

As you can see, *sehr* modifies *schön*.

Wie schön ist der Schmetterling?	How beautiful is the butterfly?
Sehr! Sehr schön ist er.	Very! It is very beautiful.

Adverbs and predicate adjectives are so simple, one wants to smile.

Attributive adjectives (adjectives attached to nouns)

If only the world were as simple as adverbs and predicate adjectives. Alas, sometimes we want to create a compound idea, as with "the beautiful butterfly".

See if you can follow this argument, freely adapted from a lost work of Plato:

Der Schmetterling ist schön.	The butterfly is beautiful.
Er schreit sehr laut.	It screams very loudly.
∴ **Der schöne Schmetterling** schreit sehr laut.	∴ **The beautiful butterfly** screams very loudly.

In this example, the adjective comes before the noun. It is an ATTRIBUTE rather than a PREDICATE. We have created a more complex subject – not only is it *der Schmetterling*, but rather *der schöne Schmetterling*.

Notice that the adverb *sehr* modifies the adverb *laut*, which in turn modifies the verb *schreit*.

Take a look at how easy it would be to add more adverbs to this sentence:

Der **sehr** schöne Schmetterling schreit **wirklich sehr** laut.	The **very** beautiful Butterfly screams **really very** loudly.

Adverbs do not require endings, no matter where you place them. Attributive adjectives, on the other hand, require endings. The endings depend on the article (the *der-* or *ein*-word) that proceeds the noun, and sometimes there is not an article; this also effects the adjective ending.

Take a look below at a chart of all of the adjective endings for a masculine noun.

	Der-words	*Ein-words*	*No article*
Nominative	der schön**e** Schmetterling	ein schön**er** Schmetterling	schön**er** Schmetterling
Accusative	den schön**en** Schmetterling	einen schön**en** Schmetterling	schön**en** Schmetterling
Dative	dem schön**en** Schmetterling	einem schön**en** Schmetterling	schön**em** Schmetterling
Genitive	des schön**en** Schmetterlings	eines schön**en** Schmetterlings	schön**en** Schmetterlings

You might find the last column a little odd, but imagine that you wanted to speak to a beautiful butterfly, whose name you did not know:

Schöner Schmettterling! Hörst du mich?   **Beautiful butterfly!** Do you hear me?

Maybe you are secretly in love with someone whose name you do not know. You could refer to this person as "beautiful butterfly" in your shyness anonymous group meetings, where you might say:

Heute habe ich **schönen Schmetterling** gesehen!   I saw **beautiful butterfly** today!

Of course, you could always send good vibrations through the Universal Grooviness Amplifier (UGA) to the unaware object of your obsession:

Ich schicke **schönem Schmetterling** gute Vibrationen!   I send **beautiful butterfly** good vibrations!

We all send beautiful butterfly good vibrations – that's the Graf von Anderson Advantage!

The important thing to have noticed in the example of *der schöne Schmetterling* is that the ending on the adjective changes depending on the ending (or lack of an ending) of the *der-* or *ein*-word.

Rejoice, for the adjective endings follow a pattern! The pattern involves PRIMARY and SECONDARY endings, which you will not be surprised to discover are called "strong" and "weak" in less "woke" German textbooks. Ignore their outdated classifications and see how the world really works by looking at the examples below.

Observe the pattern for the adjective endings for a masculine noun:

Nominative	der kleine Frosch
primary ending = er (like der)	ein kleiner Frosch
secondary ending = e	kleiner Frosch
Accusative	den kleinen Frosch
primary ending = en (like den)	einen kleinen Frosch
secondary ending = en	kleinen Frosch
Dative	dem kleinen Frosch
primary ending = em (like dem)	einem kleinen Frosch
secondary ending = en	kleinen Frosch
Genitive	des kleinen Frosches
primary ending = en (not like des)	eines kleinen Frosches
secondary ending = en	kleinen Frosches

The articles (*der*- and *ein*-words) will not change. You learned them in Chapter 3 with the help of the triangles. We will never add any endings to the articles – review Chapter 3 until this is clear to you. The question this chapter answers is, "What ending do we add to the attributive adjective?"

If we look at the *Frosch* above, we can easily determine which adjective ending to add by asking ourselves one simple question: does the article have the primary ending? If it does, then the adjective needs the secondary ending. If it does not, then the adjective needs the primary ending.

Notice that the masculine genitive endings are unlike those of the other three cases, but they still follow the same rule. Does *des* have the primary ending? No, it does not.

Finally, notice that in the accusative and genitive cases, the primary and secondary adjective endings are identical, which makes things easier.

Let's look now at the adjective endings for a feminine noun:

Nominative	die schöne Elfin
primary ending = e (like die)	eine schöne Elfin
secondary ending = e	schöne Elfin
Accusative	die schöne Elfin
primary ending = e (like die)	eine schöne Elfin
secondary ending = e	schöne Elfin
Dative	der schönen Elfin
primary ending = er (like der)	einer schönen Elfin
secondary ending = en	schöner Elfin
Genitive	der schönen Elfin
primary ending = er (like der)	einer schönen Elfin
secondary ending = en	schöner Elfin

As you can see, the nominative and accusative endings are all "e", and the dative and genitive patterns are identical.

Let's look now at the adjective endings for a neuter noun:

Nominative	das schöne Pferd
primary ending = es (like das)[1]	ein schönes Pferd
secondary ending = e	schönes Pferd
Accusative	das schöne Pferd
primary ending = es (like das)	ein schönes Pferd
secondary ending = e	schönes Pferd
Dative	dem schönen Pferd
primary ending = em (like dem)	einem schönen Pferd
secondary ending = en	schönem Pferd
Genitive	des schönen Pferdes
primary ending = en (not like des)	eines schönen Pferdes
secondary ending = en	schönen Pferdes

And now take a look at a plural noun:

Nominative	die guten Hexen
primary ending = e (like die)	meine guten Hexen
secondary ending = en	gute Hexen

Accusative	die gut**en** Hexen
primary ending = e (like die)	meine gut**en** Hexen
secondary ending = en	gut**e** Hexen
Dative	den gut**en** Hexen
primary ending = en (like den)	meine**n** gut**en** Hexen
secondary ending = en	gut**en** Hexen
Genitive	der gut**en** Hexen
primary ending = er (like der)	mein**er** gut**en** Hexen
secondary ending = en	gut**er** Hexen

To really test your understanding, attempt to create a sentence in which a beautiful golden butterfly sings a mesmerizingly powerful song:

ein Schmetterling	a butterfly
ein schöner goldener Schmetterling	a beautiful golden butterfly
ein Lied	a song
ein hypnotisierend starkes Lied	a mesmerizingly powerful song
Ein schöner goldener Schmetterling singt ein hypnotisierend starkes Lied.	A beautiful golden butterfly sings a mesmerizingly powerful song.

You should notice that when there are multiple adjectives, as in *schöner goldener*, they take the same ending. You can, but need not separate the adjectives with commas.

You should also take another look at the adverb *hypnotisierend*. It does not take an ending, since it modifies the adjective *stark*.

But imagine if the song were not "mesmerizingly powerful" but rather "mesmerizing" and "powerful":

Ein schöner goldener Schmetterling singt ein hypnotisierendes starkes Lied.

Now *hypnotisierend* is used as an adjective that modifies *Lied*, and therefore it requires an ending: *hypnotisierendes*.

To test your abilities, could you assert that you see the beautiful golden butterfly and that you are happy with its mesmerizing, powerful song?

Ich sehe einen schönen goldenen Schmetterling und ich bin mit seinem hypnotisierenden starken Lied zufrieden.

To recapitulate the major theme of this section: if the *der-* or *ein-*word uses the primary ending, then the adjective(s) will use the secondary ending. If not, then the adjective(s) will use the primary ending.

The following chart simplifies the matter by presenting the primary and secondary endings for each type of word in each case:

	Masculine	*Feminine*	*Neuter*	*Plural*
Nominative	er/e	e/e	es/e	e/en
Accusative	en/en	e/e	es/e	e/en
Dative	em/en	er/en	em/en	en/en
Genitive	en/en	er/en	en/en	er/en

You can find another copy of this chart in the Executive Summary at the end of the book.

Hopefully you can see that if you have to make a guess, "en" is a good guess and "es" is a rather poor guess.

Adjectival nouns

We can turn an adjective into a noun by capitalizing it and following the rules for the adjective endings. Let's begin with a simple subject and predicate adjective:

Der Mann ist deutsch.	The man is German.

Recall the simple days of predicate adjectives with fondness, and then observe the following transformation:

Der Mann ist Deutscher.	The man is a German.

The adjective *deutsch* becomes the noun *Deutscher*.
What if the woman is German?

Die Frau ist deutsch.	The woman is German.
Die Frau ist Deutsche.	The woman is a German.

And what if there are many Germans?

Diese Leute sind deutsch.	The people are German.
Diese Leute sind Deutsche.	The people are Germans.

Before you congratulate yourself for understanding, take a look at what happens when we use an *ein*-word and compare these results to those for a *der*-word:

Der Mann ist ein Deutscher.	The man is a German.
Er ist der Deutsche.	He is the German.
Die Frau ist eine Deutsche.	The woman is a German.
Sie ist die Deutsche.	She is the German.
Die Leute sind Deutsche.	The people are Germans.
Sie sind die Deutschen.	They are the Germans.

In each example, you can see that the noun *Deutsch-* requires an ending! The ending it requires is determined by the same rules (primary/secondary) that are used for adjective endings.

Nominative	Er ist Deutscher.	Primary ending on Deutscher
Accusative	Ich sehe einen Deutschen.	Primary ending on einen, secondary on Deutschen
Dative	Wir werfen dem Deutschen den Ball zu.	Primary ending on dem, secondary on Deutschen
Genitive	Das ist das Haus des Deutschen.	Primary ending on Deutschen

For added practice, rewrite the sentences above using the feminine and plural forms.

To understand *Deutsch*, you really need to understand *die Deutschen*, so hopefully your elementary language and culture course includes several large doses of German literature, philosophy, history, music, and art along with all of this *der-die-das*.

	Masculine	*Feminine*	*Plural*
Nominative	der Deutsche	die Deutsche	die Deutschen
	ein Deutscher	eine Deutsche	keine Deutschen
	Deutscher	Deutsche	Deutsche
Accusative	den Deutschen	die Deutsche	die Deutschen
	einen Deutschen	eine Deutsche	keine Deutschen
	Deutschen	Deutsche	Deutsche
Dative	dem Deutschen	der Deutschen	den Deutschen
	einem Deutschen	einer Deutschen	keinen Deutschen
	Deutschem	Deutscher	Deutschen
Genitive	des Deutschen	der Deutschen	der Deutschen
	eines Deutschen	einer Deutschen	keiner Deutschen
	Deutschen	Deutscher	Deutscher

Comparatives and superlatives

The basic pattern for comparatives and superlatives is observed in the following plain-vanilla adjective.

nett, netter, nettest-	*nice, nicer, nicest*
Meine Freunde sind nett.	My friends are nice.
Meine Freunde sind netter (als deine Freunde).	My friends are nicer (than your friends).
Meine Freunde sind am nettesten.	My friends are the nicest.
Meine Freunde sind die nettesten Freunde.	My friends are the nicest friends.

Notice that the predicate adjective form of the superlative differs from its attributive adjectival form. What does that mean? You cannot say that anything is *nettest* – you must use the construction *am nettesten*, which roughly corresponds to saying that something is at the highest location in the matrix of niceness.

Some German texts (and teachers) overemphasize the *am nettesten* construction. While it is true that *am nettesten* is necessary for use as a predicate adjective, the basic form of the superlative is, exactly as in English, *nettest*. If your teacher starts to cry as you explain this to them, just go along with whatever they say.

Here's another example:

klein, kleiner, kleinst-	*small, smaller, smallest*
Mein Hund ist klein.	My dog is small.
Mein Hund ist kleiner.	My dog is smaller.
Mein Hund ist am kleinsten.	My dog is the smallest.
Mein Hund ist der kleinste Hund.	My dog is the smallest dog.

Once again, you can see with *am kleinsten* that the predicate adjective is formed by following the simple rule of adjective endings from earlier in the chapter.

am kleinsten = an d**em** kleinst**en** Rang	primary ending d**em**, secondary ending **en**

Sometimes there will be an alteration of the vowel, as in the following examples:

groß, größer, größt-	*large, larger, largest*
Mein Mercedes ist groß.	My Mercedes is large.
Mein Mercedes ist größer.	My Mercedes is larger.
Mein Mercedes ist am größten.	My Mercedes is the largest.
Mein Mercedes ist das größte Auto.	My Mercedes is the largest car.

lang, länger, längst-	*long, longer, longest*
Dieser Weg ist lang.	This way is long.
Dieser Weg ist länger.	This way is longer.
Dieser Weg ist am längsten.	This way is the longest.
Dieser Weg ist der längste Weg.	This way is the longest way.

Finally, there are some cases where the comparative and/or superlative does not seem to resemble the original adjective:

gut, besser, best-	*good, better, best*
Der VW ist ein guter deutscher Wagen.	VW is a good German car.
Der Audi ist ein besserer deutscher Wagen.	Audi is a better German car.
Der Porsche ist der beste deutsche Wagen.	Porsche is the best German car.
Der Porsche ist am besten.	Porsche is the best.

Finally, here is an example with both predicate and attributive adjective forms:

hoch, höher, höchst-	*high, higher, highest*
Der Kangchendzönga ist sehr hoch.	Kangchenjunga is very high.
Er ist ein sehr hoher Berg.	It is a very high mountain.
Der K2 ist höher als Kangchendzönga.	K2 is higher than Kangchenjunga.
Er ist ein höherer Berg.	It is a higher mountain.
Der Mount Everest ist am höchsten.	Mount Everest is the highest.
Er ist der höchste Berg der Erde.	It is the highest mountain in the world.

When in doubt about a comparative or superlative, checking in the dictionary will always work.

Turning verbs into adjectives

We can all agree that sometimes the man is running.

Der Mann rennt.	The man is running.

What if we want to say something about the running man? We can turn the verb *rennen* into an adjective!

Der rennende Mann ist mein Onkel.	The running man is my uncle.

This magical transformation was completed by adding a "d" to the infinitive form of the verb, using the following formula:

$$rennen + d = rennend$$

All that remains is to add the appropriate adjective ending:

Ein rennender Mann geht in eine Kneipe.	A running man walks into a bar.
Ich sehe einen rennenden Mann.	I see a running man.
Ich gebe dem rennenden Mann ein Glas Wasser.	I give the running man a glass of water.
Der Schatten eines rennenden Mannes vergeht schnell.	The shadow of a running man passes quickly.

Some students regress at this point in their education and produce horrible sentences with *rennend* as a predicate in order to express the idea "the man is running". Don't be one of those people:

Der Mann rennt.	The man is running.

Past participles can also be used to form adjectives. Take the example of bread that one has already consumed:

Gegessenes Brot ist schwer zu verdienen.	Eaten bread is difficult to earn.

Think about credit, debt, and motivation some other time. For now, notice that all one must do is add an adjective ending to the past participle, and the story is over.

And quite honestly, that's all the grammar you need to get started. *Geh fort und sprich Deutsch* – that's the Graf von Anderson Advantage!

Übungen

A   In each of the following sentences, insert the adjective *gut* in front of *Lehrer*, *intelligent* in front of *Frau*, and *nett* in front of any other nouns. Be sure to translate each sentence.

Der Lehrer ist ein Mann.
Seine Frau liebt unsren Lehrer.

Unser Lehrer kocht mit seiner Frau ein Abendessen.
Seine Frau kocht mit unsrem Lehrer das Abendessen.
Ein Lehrer soll einen Volvo Kombiwagen haben.
Die Frau eines Lehrers sollte immer die Farbe des
Volvos wählen.

B   For each of the following sentences, write four new sentences as in the model below.

Der Ball ist rund.
Das ist ein runder Ball.
Das ist sogar der rundeste Ball der Welt.
Ich sehe einen runden Ball.
Ich sehe den rundesten Ball der Welt.

Das Haus ist groß.
Die Professorin ist intelligent.
Der Hund ist freundlich.
Die Kinder sind nett.
Die Katze ist alt.
Die Studenten sind arm.
Das Fenster ist schön.
Der Audi ist technisch fortschrittlich.
Der Prinz ist weit gereist.

Could it be unnecessary to repeat the instruction to translate each exercise? Perhaps.

C   For each of the following sentences, write two new sentences as in the model below.

Die Stadt ist alt und historisch.
Es gibt eine alte historische Stadt.
Ich wohne in einer alten historischen Stadt.

Der Dorf ist klein und freundlich.
Das Land ist interessant und tolerant.
Die Burg ist schneebedeckt.
Der Turm ist hoch.
Das Schloss ist elegant.
Die Wohnung ist klein, aber hell.
Der Keller ist dunkel und nass.
Das Hotel ist fein und teuer.
Das Gasthaus ist gemütlich.

D   For each of the following sentences, write four new sentences as in the model below,
paying close attention to the adjective endings.

Der Mann ist intelligent.
Hallo! Intelligenter Mann! Achtung!

Ich sehe den intelligenten Mann.
Ich spreche mit dem intelligenten Mann.
Ich schreibe die E-Mail-Adresse des intelligenten Mannes auf.

Der Student ist jung.
Die Studentin sieht athletisch aus.
Die StudentInnen sind fleißig.
Die Professorin ist weltberühmt.
Der Professor singt.
Die ProfessorInnen lesen.
Der Graf ist edel.
Die Gräfin ist gnädig.
Die Grafen und Gräfinnen werden von allen geliebt.

Travel: Basel, Zurich, Bern, and Lucerne

Traveling south from Freiburg leads one to culturally rich Basel, Switzerland.[2] Basel is famous for its high quality of life, its outstanding museums and excellent university, as well as for the annual Art Basel art fair, the resounding success of which has led to the creation of a second Art Basel event each year in Miami Beach. The entire *Basler Altstadt* is listed on the *Schweizerisches Inventar der Kulturgüter von nationaler und regionaler Bedeutung*; wander around and visit everything that strikes your interest, and then take one of the excellent guided tours to see what you might have missed. Basel's carnival rivals those of Cologne, Düsseldorf, and Mainz, and since it begins one week after the other celebrations end, you could arrange to make a personal comparison. Basel is home to several important companies, including Novartis and Swiss Air Lines. The Swiss chemist and author Albert Hofmann (1906–2008) worked at Sandoz Laboratories in Basel when he discovered LSD in 1943.

From Basel, one can make several journeys within Switzerland, most of which involve changing trains in Zürich. Zürich is Switzerland's largest city and is consistently ranked among the top cities in the world for quality of life. Its setting, surrounded by the Alps on the northern end of majestic Lake Zürich, is breathtaking, and the options for dining and entertainment rival those of any of the other great European cities. The *Schauspielhaus Zürich*, which is also known as the *Pfauenbühne*, is one of the most important theaters in the German-speaking world – attending performances there will contribute to your general education, as will reading each of the plays that premiered there over the last century. Smart travelers will also visit the *Kunsthaus Zürich*, take a short trip to Schaffhausen to see the dramatic *Rheinfall*, and climb the *Üetliberg*, before taking the train to Bern.

Bern is famous for its Renaissance *Altstadt*. Amazingly, you can jump into the Aare River and let the current carry you from one side of the *Altstadt* to the other; maybe ask a local before you take the plunge. Four bears live in the *Bärengraben* and the adjacent *BärenPark*, located near the *Nydeggbrücke*. Even if you never visit Bern, find a photograph of the *Kindlifresserbrunnen* and use it to keep your younger siblings in line. Perhaps the most visually impressive city in Switzerland is Lucerne, *Luzern* in German, which is picturesquely located on the *Vierwaldstättersee* as it flows into the Reuss River. The medieval *Kapellbrücke* and the adjacent *Wasserturm* are among Switzerland's most popular tourist attractions.

Depending on the size of your budget, you might have already run out of money upon reaching Lucerne. If not, the resort towns of Davos, St. Moritz, Montreux (which hosts an excellent jazz festival in July), and Locarno (which offers an excellent film festival in August) should be on your itinerary. Further afield, St. Gallen is home to one of Europe's finest business schools as well as one of its most beautiful Baroque cathedrals. Southern Switzerland was periodically home to Friedrich Nietzsche (1844–1900), who spent many summers in Sils Maria, near St. Moritz, before moving to Turin. Herman Hesse (1877–1962) lived in Montagnola, near the Italian-speaking Swiss city of Lugano, for the last four decades of his life. This part of the country remains famous for its pleasant climate and colorful scenery, as the hills roll down to Italy and the Mediterranean, where new adventures have beckoned since before the dawn of civilization.

German history from 1900 to the present

Friedrich Nietzsche, who died in 1900 after a decade of madness, wrote works that crossed the boundaries between literature, intellectual history, and philosophy, profoundly influencing many of the leading artists, writers, and thinkers of the 20th century. Nietzsche's radical visions of the coming crises and opportunities of a transcendental future are intellectual achievements that have not yet been absorbed fully into human consciousness; Nietzsche's writings remain essential reading. The two decades prior to the outbreak of World War I in 1914 were a period of rich cultural production, especially in Vienna, where Sigmund Freud (1856–1939), Arthur Schnitzler (1862–1931), Karl Kraus (1874–1936), Gustav Klimt (1862–1918), Egon Schiele (1890–1918), Oscar Kokoschka (1886–1980), Otto Wagner (1841–1918), Adolf Loos (1870–1933), and Ludwig Wittgenstein (1889–1951), among dozens of others, co-created many of the recognizable landmarks of the modern world. This fertile period was not limited to Vienna, as demonstrated by the sublime poetic masterpieces of Rainer Maria Rilke (1875–1926), the disturbing narratives of Franz Kafka (1882–1924), and the epic, realist novels of Heinrich Mann (1871–1950) and his brother Thomas Mann (1875–1955).

Wilhelm II (1859–1941) ascended the throne of the German Empire after the death of his father, Kaiser Friedrich III (1831–1888), which followed that of Wilhelm's grandfather, Kaiser Wilhelm I (1797–1888). Since there were three different Kaisers during 1888, the year is called the *Dreikaiserjahr* in German. The militarism that had been a feature of European life since before the *Hermannsschlacht* and which Bismarck, to his lasting credit, had managed and controlled, creating a system of international alliances that maintained a period of peace and stability in Western Europe from 1871 until 1914, was unleashed into the mechanized hell of World War I by the bombastic and narcissistic Kaiser. Had he lived, Wilhelm's liberal, anglophone father, Friedrich III, might have pursued a more peaceful path. As the senseless war approached – and, courageously, even after it broke out – the political philosophers and activists Rosa Luxemburg (1871–1919) and Karl Liebknecht (1871–1919) spoke loudly in favor of peace and against the mass slaughter of the working classes taking place under the command of an international ruling class that was primarily focused on their own interests and not on the welfare of their subjects. Luxemburg and Liebknecht were honored posthumously later in the century, when prominent streets were named for them in East Berlin.

As German and Austrian defeat in the First World War became certain, due in large part to the intervention of the United States, the revolutions of 1918 broke out, finally deposing the German and Austrian aristocracies. The Habsburgs were forced to flee Austria, and the Hohenzollerns were forced to flee Germany. Wilhelm II lived out the remainder of his days on a small estate in Doorn, in the Netherlands, while the young Crown Prince Otto von Habsburg (1912–2011) spent his early life in Spain. The Weimar Republic (1919–1933) and the First Austrian Republic (1919–1934) were formed from the chaos of the defeat in World War I. Despite the high hopes of many, the murders of Luxemburg and Liebknecht in January 1919 by right wing reactionary forces did not bode well for the future. The Weimar Republic never enjoyed the support of a solid majority of the population, which was fragmented into various interest groups that had multiplied and ossified since the time of Bismarck. The malevolent personality of Adolf Hitler and the group of opportunistic and violently national-ist, colonialist, and racist criminals who surrounded him and formed the leadership of the Nazi Party preyed on the fears and ignorance of the public, establishing a dictatorship in 1933 in Germany. The Austrians created a fascist government of their own in 1934, prior to the *Anschluss* with Germany in 1938.

Even before the Nazis had taken power, resistance to them had been met with violence. The combination of Stormtroopers, SS, *Konzentrationslager*, and the Gestapo remain frightening long after they have faded from existence; state terrorism, along with an end-less barrage of state propaganda, kept the German people behind the leaders they had nominally chosen long after their doom had become inevitable. By the time Josef Goebbels asked the German people *Wollt ihr den totalen Krieg?* in February 1943, the answer was a foregone conclusion. After the war and the Holocaust left millions of people dead – six million murdered Jews and a long list of others, including but not limited to political oppo-nents, homosexuals, people with mental and physical disabilities, Soviet citizens, and prisoners of war – and reduced many of the cities of Europe to rubble, the narratives of German, European, and world history had been disfigured forever. As the composer Rich-ard Strauss, who remained in Germany during the Third Reich, noted in his diary at the end of the war, "The most terrible period of human history came to an end, the twelve-year reign of bestiality, ignorance and anti-culture under the greatest criminals, during which Germany's 2000 years of cultural evolution met its doom".[3]

Many Germans who had the necessary means emigrated when the Nazis came to power. Bertolt Brecht (1898–1956) moved to several different European cities, eventu-ally settling in Denmark, then Sweden, and finally Finland, before spending the remain-der of the war years in the United States. Brecht's play *Mutter Courage und ihre Kinder* premiered in Zurich in 1941 and ranks among the greatest anti-war artworks ever created. For those who remained in Nazi Germany, questions of complicity in the Nazi crimes would follow them after the war. The outright denial of high-ranking Nazi official and Hitler confidant Albert Speer (1905–1981) of knowledge of the Holocaust provided a penumbra of plausible deniability to many other Germans who had spent the war at greater distances from the centers of power. The silence of Nazi party member Martin Heidegger (1889–1976) towers over the achievements of his work in philosophy, while Hermann Hesse's (1877–1962) emigration to Switzerland in 1913 allowed him to remain an advocate of a peaceful, spiritual, and progressive German culture that was suppressed and perverted by the militant racists who left Germany in ruins in 1945. The German resistance, especially the *Weiße Rose* group based in Munich and the group surrounding Claus von Stauffenberg (1907–1944) that attempted to assassinate Hitler in 1944, are noteworthy for their courage. *Vergangenheitsbewältigung*, the coming to terms with the crimes and horrors of the Nazi past, began in the rubble of what has been called *Stunde Null* and continues to this day.

Postwar West German chancellors, including Konrad Adenauer (1876–1967), Willy Brandt (1913–1992), and Helmut Schmidt (1918–2015), led through the difficulty of the division of Germany into two countries – the *Deutsche Demokratische Republik (DDR)*, which we know as East Germany in the English-speaking world, and the *Bundesrepublik*

Deutschland (BRD), or West Germany. The sad story of the high ideals and grim realities of the *DDR* is of interest to many Germanists and non-Germanists alike; the Berlin Wall, built to prevent East Germans from fleeing to the West, served and continues to serve as a powerful symbol of the repressive East German regime. West Germany grew into a strong democracy with a robust economy that produced many high-end export products, providing opportunities for a high standard of living and educational attainment as well as a strong social safety net for those who lived there. After the decades-long Cold War and nuclear arms race were forced to a head by the aggressive policies of US president Ronald Reagan (1911–2004), Soviet leader Mikhail Gorbachev (b. 1931) introduced reforms in the Soviet Union and in Soviet-dominated Eastern Europe that led to the fall of the Berlin Wall in November 1989. The street protests of the East Germans, especially in Leipzig, surely hastened the end of the East German police state. German reunification took place a year later, and the dissolution of the Soviet Union followed in 1991.

Throughout the postwar period, the idea of a European integration was pursued and cultivated, beginning with the creation of the Council of Europe in 1949, expanding into the European Coal and Steel Community in 1952, and culminating in the formation of the European Union in 1993. Otto von Habsburg, who spurned the Nazis' repeated attempts to gain his endorsement, dedicated his life to the European project; watching his 2011 funeral in the *Stephansdom* and hearing the old Austrian anthem played on the pipe organ was a moment of high emotion, a belated, final ending of the 20th century, and certainly of an older era as well. The years since German reunification and the creation of the EU have witnessed increased German presence on the world stage, including limited military engagements as a member of NATO, the EU, and the UN. In recent years, a series of immigration crises fueled by wars in the Middle East have fed into a resurgence of the far right in Germany, and in other European nations, that was unimaginable during the euphoric years following the fall of the Berlin Wall. In 2005, Angela Merkel (b. 1954), a former East German quantum chemist and member of the center-right *Christlich Demokratische Union Deutschlands, (CDU)*, became chancellor of Germany. As *Bundeskanzlerin*, Merkel has navigated the complexities of domestic and international politics with a blend of conservative principle and cosmopolitan responsibility that has led many, in Europe and beyond, to see her as the current leader of the free world, especially in the wake of the surprising Brexit, the nasty 2016 US election, and the depressing aftermaths of these events.

As always, there are bright spots on the horizon. The European Green Party and the national parties that constitute it have made progress in many countries across Europe, achieving partnership with the *SPD* in a coalition government in Germany from 1998 to 2005 and holding at present both the presidency and a plurality of seats in the *Landtag* in the wealthy, technology-rich *Bundesland* of Baden-Württemberg. *Die Grünen* are the number-two party in Bavaria, Hamburg, and Hessen. In Austria, the Greens entered the national government for the first time in 2020, forming an unlikely partnership with the nationalist *Österreichische Volkspartei*. The Swiss have two Green parties, one of which is centrist, the *Grünliberale Partei*, and one of which is leftist and slightly more popular, the *Grüne Partei der Schweiz*. The European Pirate Party promises to do for privacy and copyright reform, as well as for government and corporate transparency, what the Greens are doing for environmental issues, but at present their political success has been limited. As longtime Merkel cabinet minister Ursula von der Leyen (b. 1958) assumed office as president of the European Commission in 2019, the future of the European Union appeared to be in competent hands.

Text and translation: Nietzsche

Friedrich Nietzsche considered *Also sprach Zarathustra* to be his greatest gift to humankind.

Als Zarathustra dreissig Jahr alt war, verliess er seine Heimat und den See seiner Heimat und ging in das Gebirge. Hier genoss er seines Geistes und seiner Einsamkeit und wurde dessen zehn Jahr nicht müde. Endlich aber verwandelte sich sein Herz, – und eines Morgens stand er mit der Morgenröthe auf, trat vor die Sonne hin und sprach zu ihr also:

"Du grosses Gestirn! Was wäre dein Glück, wenn du nicht Die hättest, welchen du leuchtest!

Zehn Jahre kamst du hier herauf zu meiner Höhle: du würdest deines Lichtes und dieses Weges satt geworden sein, ohne mich, meinen Adler und meine Schlange.

Aber wir warteten deiner an jedem Morgen, nahmen dir deinen Überfluss ab und segneten dich dafür.

Siehe! Ich bin meiner Weisheit überdrüssig, wie die Biene, die des Honigs zu viel gesammelt hat, ich bedarf der Hände, die sich ausstrecken.

Ich möchte verschenken und austheilen, bis die Weisen unter den Menschen wieder einmal ihrer Thorheit und die Armen einmal ihres Reichthums froh geworden sind.

Dazu muss ich in die Tiefe steigen: wie du des Abends thust, wenn du hinter das Meer gehst und noch der Unterwelt Licht bringst, du überreiches Gestirn!

Ich muss, gleich dir, *untergehen*, wie die Menschen es nennen, zu denen ich hinab will.

So segne mich denn, du ruhiges Auge, das ohne Neid auch ein allzugrosses Glück sehen kann!

Segne den Becher, welcher überfliessen will, dass das Wasser golden aus ihm fliesse und überallhin den Abglanz deiner Wonne trage!

Siehe! Dieser Becher will wieder leer werden, und Zarathustra will wieder Mensch werden."

– Also begann Zarathustra's Untergang.

When Zarathustra was thirty years old, he left his home and the lake of his home and went into the mountains. Here he enjoyed his spirit and his loneliness and never became tired in these in ten years. Finally, however, his heart changed, and one morning he rose with the dawn, stepped before the sun, and spoke to it thus:

"You great star! What would be your joy if you did not have those whom you illuminate!

For ten years you came up here to my cave: you would have become tired of your light and of this path, without me, my eagle and my serpent.

But we waited for you on every morning, took from you your abundance, and blessed you for it.

Behold! I am weary of my wisdom, like the bee, which has collected too much honey, I am in need of hands that stretch themselves out.

I would like to give away and distribute, until the wise ones among the humans once again become glad of their folly and the poor ones once again become glad of their wealth.

For this I have to climb into the depths: as you do in the evening, when you go behind the sea and bring light even to the underworld, you overabundant star!

I must, like you, go under, as the people call it, to those to whom I want to descend.

So bless me then, you calm eye, which without envy can also see an all too great happiness!

Bless the cup which wants to overflow, such that the water will flow golden from it and carry in all directions the reflection of your blissfulness!

Behold! This cup wants to become empty again, and Zarathustra wants to become human again."

– Thus began Zarathustra's descent.

German music: Modernist and contemporary

Music after Wagner develops in some exciting new directions. The Hungarian Béla Bartók's (1881–1945) string quartets, which stand out even among his other well-regarded works, are excellent pieces of music that capture the frenetic, disjointed spirit of the early 20th century while remaining spiritually uplifting. The German composers Richard Strauss

(1864–1949) and Carl Orff (1895–1982) wrote fantastic music in the early 20th century that is accessible and is performed frequently throughout the world. Don't worry if the text of Orff's *Carmina Burana* is difficult for you to understand, since the singing is in Latin, not German. The music of the Austrian composers Arnold Schoenberg (1874–1951) and Alban Berg (1885–1935), as well as that of the other composers associated with the Second Viennese School, is, as with the music of Mahler, held in high esteem by many well-educated people.

Karlheinz Stockhausen (1928–2007) was one of the more interesting German composers of the postwar period. His pioneering work with electronic and aleatoric music left a lasting impression on a generation of Avant Garde musicians, ranging from Igor Stravinsky and Pierre Boulez to Miles Davis and various members of the Grateful Dead. Hungarian György Ligeti (1923–2006), who spent his productive years in Vienna during the communist occupation of his native country, was an astonishing composer whose atmospheric and transcendental soundscapes are unparalleled. Sicilian composer Salvatore Sciarrino (b. 1947) numbers among the living giants on the contemporary musical horizon.

Graf von Anderson recommends the following recordings:

Herbert von Karajan, Berliner Philharmoniker, *Richard Strauss: Also sprach Zarathustra, Til Eulenspiegel, etc.*

Karajan, Wiener Philharmoniker, *R. Strauss: Der Rosenkavalier*

Karajan, Bell, Berliner Philharmoniker, *R. Strauss: An Alpine Symphony*

Karajan, Janowitz, Berliner Philharmoniker, *R. Strauss: Tod und Verklärung, Metamorphosen, Vier letzte Lieder*

Kolisch Quartet, *Schoenberg: String Quartets Nos. 1–4*

Orpheus Chamber Orchestra, *Schoenberg: Verklärte Nacht, Chamber Symphonies Nos. 1 & 2*

Belcea Quartet, *Berg, Webern, and Schönberg: Chamber Music*

Takács Quartet, *Bartok: Complete String Quartets*

Yehudi Menuhin, *Bartok: Violin Concertos 1 & 2, Viola Concerto, Rhapsodies 1 & 2*

Patricia Kopatchinskaja, Peter Eötvös, *Bartok, Eötvös, Ligeti*

Isabelle Faust, *Bartok: Violin Sonatas*

Zoltan Kocsis, *Bartok: Complete Solo Piano Works*

Eugen Jochum, Orchester der Deutschen Oper Berlin, *Orff: Carmina Burana*

Wolfgang Sawallisch, Philharmonia Orchestra, *Orff: Der Mond, Die Kluge*

Daniel Reuss, Cappella Amsterdam, *Ligeti: Lux aeterna*

Hagen Quartet, *Ligeti: String Quartets 1&2, Ramifications*

Reinbert de Leeuw, Asko|Schönberg Ensemble, *Ligeti Project (5 volumes)*

Karl Heinz Stockhausen, *Gesang der Jünglinge*

Bojé and Eötvös, *Stockhausen: Spiral I & II, Pole, Wach, Japan, Zyklus, Tierkreis, In Freundschaft*

Ensemble Recherche, *Stockhausen: kontra-punkte + refrain*

Paul Mefano, Ensemble CLSI, *Stockhausen: Kurzwellen*

Garlitsky, Fromanger, *Sciarrino: Musique de Chambre*

Otto Katzameier, Klangforum Wien, *Sciarrino: Quaderno di strada*

Neue Vocalsoloisten Freiburg, *Sciarrino, 12 Madrigali (Live)*

The Takács Quartet performance of Bartok's string quartets ranks among Graf von Anderson's all-time favorite classical music recordings.[4]

Recommended films

Von morgens bis mitternachts (Karlheinz Martin, 1920)
Metropolis (Fritz Lang, 1927)
Triumph of the Will (Leni Riefenstahl, 1935)
Die Mörder sind unter uns (Wolfgang Staudte, 1946)
Germania anno zero (Roberto Rossellini, 1948)
Dr. Strangelove (Stanley Kubrick, 1964)
Ich war neunzehn (Konrad Wolf, 1968)
Die Verlorene Ehre der Katharina Blum (Volker Schlöndorff, Margarethe von Trotta, 1975)
Die Ehe der Maria Braun (Rainer Werner Fassbinder, 1979)
Stalingrad (Joseph Vilsmaier, 1993)
Jenseits der Stille (Caroline Link, 1996)
Die Stille nach dem Schuss (Volker Schlöndorff, 2000)
Gegen die Wand (Fatih Akin, 2004)
Sophie Scholl – Die letzten Tage (Marc Rothemund, 2005)
The Turin Horse (Béla Tarr, Ágnes Hranitzky, 2011)

Notes

1 *Das* is enough like "es" to count. If you have a problem with it, contact the German Consulate or switch to another language.
2 A general note on Switzerland: if you are fortunate enough to have an opportunity to work or study anywhere in this country, you should take it without a second thought. The future looks increasingly Swiss.
3 Michael Kennedy, Richard Strauss: Man, Musician, Enigma. Cambridge University Press (1999), p. 361.
4 As the photographs that accompany each section of this book were being taken in the autumn of 2007, Graf von Anderson was listening to this recording nearly every day while researching and writing a dissertation chapter on Novalis and attempting to avoid freezing to death through a combination of strong East Frisian tea and the antique coal-burning furnace in his small apartment on the Isländische Straße in Prenzlauerberg.

Further reading

Overviews

A Little History of the World: Illustrated Edition by E.H. Gombrich (Translated by Caroline Mustill, 2011)
A Concise History of Germany by Mary Fulbrook (Third Edition, 2019)
The Habsburg Monarchy, 1618–1815 by Charles W. Ingrao (Third Edition, 2020)
Iron Kingdom: The Rise and Downfall of Prussia, 1600–1947 by Christopher Clark (2007)
The German Genius: Europe's Third Renaissance, the Second Scientific Revolution, and the Twentieth Century by Peter Watson (2010)
Germany: Memories of a Nation by Neil MacGregor (2014)
Deutsche Geschichte by Manfred Mai (1999)
Swiss Watching: Inside the Land of Milk and Honey by Diccon Brewes (Third Edition, 2018)

Ancient and medieval

The Agricola and the Germania by Tacitus
The History of Medieval Europe by Lynn Thorndike (1917)
The Nibelungenlied
Tristan by Gottfried von Strassburg
Parzival by Wolfram von Eschenbach
The Emperor and the Saint: Frederick II of Hohenstaufen, Francis of Assisi, and Journeys to Medieval Places by Richard Cassady (2011)
The Mystical Thought of Meister Eckhart: The Man from Whom God Hid Nothing by Bernard McGinn (2001)

Renaissance and Baroque

The Civilization of the Renaissance in Italy by Jacob Burckhardt (1860)
The Life and Art of Albrecht Dürer by Erwin Panofsky (1955)
Martin Luther: Visionary Reformer by Scott H. Hendrix (2015)
Götz von Berlichingen by Johann Wolfgang von Goethe (1773)
Galileo by Bertolt Brecht (1938)
The Adventures of Simplicius Simplicissimus by Hans Jakob Christoffel von Grimmelshausen

Late Baroque and Enlightenment

Bach: Music in the Castle of Heaven by John Eliot Gardiner (2013)
A Book Forged in Hell: Spinoza's Scandalous Treatise and the Birth of the Secular Age by Steven Nadler (2011)

Frederick the Great: King of Prussia by Tim Blanning (2015)
Candide by Voltaire
Nathan the Wise by Gotthold Ephraim Lessing
Critique of Pure Reason by Immanuel Kant
Napoleon: A Life by Andrew Roberts (2014)
Hegel, Haiti, and Universal History by Susan Buck-Morss (2009)

Goethezeit through 1848

Goethe: The Poet and the Age by Nicholas Boyle (1991, 2000)
Faust by Johann Wolfgang von Goethe (Translated by Stuart Atkins)
Wilhelm Meister's Apprenticeship by Johann Wolfgang von Goethe (Translated by Eric A. Blackall)
Henry von Ofterdingen by Novalis (Translated by Palmer Hilty)
On the Aesthetic Education of Man by Friedrich Schiller (Translated by Reginald Snell)
Hyperion by Friedrich Hölderlin (Translated by Ross Benjamin)
The Golden Pot and other Tales by E.T.A. Hoffmann (Translated by Ritchie Robertson)
A World Restored: Metternich, Castlereagh, and the Problems of Peace, 1812–22 by Henry Kissinger (1954)
The Invention of Nature: Alexander von Humboldt's New World by Andrea Wulf (2015)
Alexander und Wilhelm – Die Humboldts by Magdalena and Gunnar Schupelius (2010)

Middle to late 19th century

Germany. A Winter Tale by Heinrich Heine (Mondial Bilingual Edition, 2007)
The Communist Manifesto by Karl Marx and Friedrich Engels
Indian Summer by Adalbert Stifter (Translated by Wendell Frye)
Green Henry by Gottfried Keller (Translated by A.M. Holt)
Marx's Capital Illustrated by David Smith, Illustrated by Phil Evans (2013)
Bismarck: A Life by Jonathan Steinberg (2011)
The Gay Science by Friedrich Nietzsche (Translated by Walter Kaufmann)
Nietzsche: A Philosophical Biography by Rüdiger Safranski (Translated by Shelley Frisch, 2000/2010)

20th century and beyond

The Selected Poetry of Rainer Maria Rilke: Bilingual Edition (Edited and translated by Stephen Mitchell)
Kaiser Wilhelm II: A Concise Life by John C. G. Röhl (2014)
Storm of Steel by Ernst Jünger
Red Rosa: A Graphic Biography of Rosa Luxemburg by Kate Evans (2015)
Freud: A Life for Our Time by Peter Gay (1988)
Tractatus Logico-Philosophicus by Ludwig Wittgenstein
The Man without Qualities by Robert Musil
Weimar: A Cultural History by Walter Laqueur (1974)
Berlin Alexanderplatz by Alfred Döblin
The Battle for the Streets of Berlin by Molly Loberg (2019)
Mother Courage and Her Children by Bertolt Brecht (Translated by Eric Bentley)
Inside the Third Reich by Albert Speer (1969)
Ordinary Men: Reserve Police Battalion 101 and the Final Solution in Poland by Christopher Browning (1992)
The Years of Extermination: Nazi Germany and the Jews, 1939–1945 by Saul Friedländer (2007)
Adolf Hitler by Ian Kernshaw (Abridged edition, 2008)

The Glass Bead Game (Magister Ludi) by Hermann Hesse
Postwar: A History of Europe Since 1945 by Tony Judt (2005)
Operation Paperclip: The Secret Intelligence Program that Brought Nazi Scientists to America by Annie Jacobsen (2014)
Basic Writings by Martin Heidegger (Edited by David Farrell Krell)
Eumeswil by Ernst Jünger
Critique of Cynical Reason by Peter Sloterdijk
Extinction by Thomas Bernhard (Translated by David McLintock)
How Will Capitalism End?: Essays on a Failing System by Wolfgang Streeck (2017)

Executive summary

Conjugations of *sein, haben,* and *werden* in the PRESENT TENSE:

	Singular	Plural
1st person	Ich **bin** sehr schön. Ich **habe** viele Freunde. Ich **werde** stärker und netter.	Wir **sind** sehr schön. Wir **haben** viele Freunde. Wir **werden** stärker und netter.
2nd person (familiar)	Du **bist** sehr schön. Du **hast** viele Freunde. Du **wirst** stärker und netter.	Ihr **seid** sehr schön. Ihr **habt** viele Freunde. Ihr **werdet** stärker und netter.
3rd person	Er/sie/es **ist** sehr schön. Er/sie/es **hat** viele Freunde. Er/sie/es **wird** stärker und netter.	Sie **sind** sehr schön. Sie **haben** viele Freunde. Sie **werden** stärker und netter.

Conjugations of selected verbs in the PRESENT TENSE:

	Singular	Plural
1st person	Ich **arbeite** in Köln. Ich **spreche** Deutsch. Ich **ziehe** mich **an.** Ich **putze** mir die Zähne.	Wir **arbeiten** in Köln. Wir **sprechen** Deutsch. Wir **ziehen** uns **an.** Wir **putzen** uns die Zähne.
2nd person (familiar)	Du **arbeitest** in Köln. Du **sprichst** Deutsch. Du **ziehst** dich **an.** Du **putzt** dir die Zähne.	Ihr **arbeitet** in Köln. Ihr **sprecht** Deutsch. Ihr **zieht** euch **an.** Ihr **putzt** euch die Zähne.
3rd person	Er/sie/es **arbeitet** in Köln. Er/sie/es **spricht** Deutsch. Er/sie/es **zieht** sich **an.** Er/sie/es **putzt** sich die Zähne.	Sie **arbeiten** in Köln. Sie **sprechen** Deutsch. Sie **ziehen** sich **an.** Sie **putzen** sich die Zähne.

NOMINATIVE, ACCUSATIVE, and DATIVE CASES, with the POSSESSIVE ARTICLES:

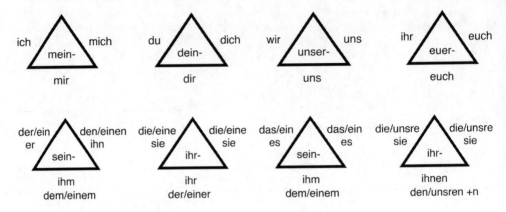

The VERB *sprechen*, conjugated across TIMES and MOODS:

PRESENT

Bobfried **spricht** Deutsch. — Bobfried speaks / does speak / is speaking German.

Bobfried **kann** Deutsch **sprechen**. — Bobfried is able to speak German.

FUTURE

Bobfried **wird** Deutsch **sprechen**. — Bobfried will speak German.
Bobfried **wird** Deutsch **sprechen können**. — Bobfried will be able to speak German.

PAST

Bobfried **hat** Deutsch **gesprochen**. — Bobfried spoke / did speak / was speaking German.

Bobfried **sprach** Deutsch. — Bobfried spoke / did speak / was speaking German.

Bobfried **hat** Deutsch **sprechen können**. — Bobfried was able to speak German.
Bobfried **konnte** Deutsch **sprechen**. — Bobfried was able to speak German.

PLUSQUAMPERFEKT

Bobfried **hatte** (schon) Deutsch **gesprochen**. — Bobfried (already) had spoken German.
Bobfried **hatte** (schon) Deutsch **sprechen können**. — Bobfried (already) had been able to speak German.

KONJUNKTIV II

Bobfried **würde** Deutsch **sprechen**. — Bobfried would speak German.
Bobfried **spräche** Deutsch. — Bobfried would speak German.
Bobfried **würde** Deutsch **sprechen können**. — Bobfried would be able to speak German.
Bobfried **könnte** Deutsch **sprechen**. — Bobfried would be able to speak German.
Bobfried **hätte** Deutsch **gesprochen**. — Bobfried would have spoken German.
Bobfried **hätte** Deutsch **sprechen können**. — Bobfried would have been able to speak German.

Sentences transformed into SUBORDINATE CLAUSES:

PRESENT

..., weil Bobfried Deutsch spricht.

... because Bobfried speaks / does speak / is speaking German.

..., weil Bobfried Deutsch sprechen kann.

... because Bobfried is able to speak German.

FUTURE

..., weil Bobfried Deutsch sprechen wird.

... because Bobfried will speak German.

..., weil Bobfried Deutsch sprechen können wird.

... because Bobfried will be able to speak German.

PAST

..., weil Bobfried Deutsch gesprochen hat.

... because Bobfried spoke / did speak / was speaking German.

..., weil Bobfried Deutsch sprach.

... because Bobfried spoke / did speak / was speaking German.

..., weil Bobfried Deutsch hat sprechen können.

... because Bobfried was able to speak German.

..., weil Bobfried Deutsch sprechen konnte.

... because Bobfried was able to speak German.

PLUSQUAMPERFEKT

..., weil Bobfried (schon) Deutsch gesprochen hatte.

... because Bobfried (already) had spoken German.

..., weil Bobfried (schon) Deutsch hatte sprechen können.

... because Bobfried (already) had been able to speak German.

KONJUNKTIV II

..., weil Bobfried Deutsch sprechen würde.

... because Bobfried would speak German.

..., weil Bobfried Deutsch spräche.

... because Bobfried would speak German.

..., weil Bobfried Deutsch sprechen können würde.

... because Bobfried would be able to speak German.

..., weil Bobfried Deutsch sprechen könnte.

... because Bobfried would be able to speak German.

..., weil Bobfried Deutsch gesprochen hätte.

... because Bobfried would have spoken German.

..., weil Bobfried Deutsch hätte sprechen können.

... because Bobfried would have been able to speak German.

ADJECTIVE ENDINGS (primary/secondary):

	Masculine	*Feminine*	*Neuter*	*Plural*
Nominative	er/e	e/e	es/e	e/en
Accusative	en/en	e/e	es/e	e/en
Dative	em/en	er/en	em/en	en/en
Genitive	en/en	er/en	en/en	er/en

Answer key

Chapter 1

A   Are you really looking for the answer to this one here?

B   Rather than looking here, you should look in a dictionary. Graf von Anderson recommends www.leo.org.

C   The noun in each sentence below has been replaced with the appropriate pronoun.

Er ist groß.	Sie ist unsterblich.	Er ist stark.
Sie ist intelligent.	Sie sind unsterblich.	Sie sind stark.
Es ist klein.	Es ist grau.	Sie ist schwarz.
Sie sind nett.	Sie sind grau.	Es ist durchsichtig.
Sie sind stark.	Er ist braun.	Sie sind weiß.
Sie sind schön.	Sie sind braun.	Sie sind schmutzig.

D   Here is a list of the nouns with articles and plurals. Did you find them in the dictionary?

das Lehen, die Lehen	die Welt, die Welten	der Hornung, die Hornunge	die Zehe, die Zehen
der Herr, die Herren	der König, die Könige	der Sommer, die Sommer	die Luft, die Lüfte
der Winter, die Winter	die Hitze	der Nachbar, die Nachbarn	der Buhmann, die Buhmänner
das Verschulden	die Schelte, die Schelten	der Atem	der Sang, die Sänge

Chapter 2

A   The answers are in the dictionary.

B   The following sentences have been rewritten, changing *ich* to *du*.

Du studierst Philosophie und Betriebswirtschaftslehre (BWL).	You study philosophy and business administration.
Du hilfst dem alten Mann.	You help the old man.
Du brauchst einen Kaffee.	You need a coffee.
Du bekommst eine E-Mail.	You receive an email.
Du trägst jeden Tag Jeans und ein T-Shirt.	You wear jeans and a t-shirt every day.

Du denkst immer positiv.	You always think positively.
Du erzählst gern alte Geschichten.	You like to tell old stories.
Du hörst gern klassische Musik.	You like to listen to classical music.
Du weißt, wie schön die Welt ist.	You know how beautiful the world is.
Du kennst Angela, und du kennst Berlin.	You know Angela, and you know Berlin.
Du erscheinst jeden Tag auf dem Campus.	You appear on campus every day.
Du bestehst alle Prüfungen.	You pass all tests.
Du vergisst nie.	You never forget.
Du magst Käse.	You like cheese.
Du willst nach Amsterdam fliegen.	You want to fly to Amsterdam.
Du kommst aus Hamburg.	You are from Hamburg.
Du tanzt unter den Sternen.	You dance under the stars.
Du rennst durch den Wald.	You run through the forest.
Du sitzt in der Kneipe.	You sit in the pub.
Du sprichst Deutsch und Englisch.	You speak German and English.
Du wohnst in Bonn.	You live in Bonn.
Du machst immer das Fenster auf.	You always open the window.
Du wirfst meinem Sohn den Ball zu.	You throw the ball to my son.
Du singst gern.	You like to sing.

The following sentences have been rewritten, changing *du* to *ihr*.

Ihr studiert Philosophie und Betriebswirtschaftslehre (BWL).	You study philosophy and business administration.
Ihr helft dem alten Mann.	You help the old man.
Ihr braucht einen Kaffee.	You need a coffee.
Ihr bekommt eine E-Mail.	You receive an email.
Ihr tragt jeden Tag Jeans und ein T-Shirt.	You wear jeans and a t-shirt every day.
Ihr denkt immer positiv.	You always think positively.
Ihr erzählt gern alte Geschichten.	You like to tell old stories.
Ihr hört gern klassische Musik.	You like to listen to classical music.
Ihr wisst, wie schön die Welt ist.	You know how beautiful the world is.
Ihr kennt Angela, und ihr kennt Berlin.	You know Angela, and you know Berlin.
Ihr erscheint jeden Tag auf dem Campus.	You appear on campus every day.
Ihr besteht alle Prüfungen.	You pass all tests.
Ihr vergesst nie.	You never forget.
Ihr mögt Käse.	You like cheese.
Ihr wollt nach Amsterdam fliegen.	You want to fly to Amsterdam.
Ihr kommt aus Hamburg.	You are from Hamburg.
Ihr tanzt unter den Sternen.	You dance under the stars.
Ihr rennt durch den Wald.	You run through the forest.
Ihr sitzt in der Kneipe.	You sit in the pub.
Ihr sprecht Deutsch und Englisch.	You speak German and English.
Ihr wohnt in Bonn.	You live in Bonn.
Ihr macht immer das Fenster auf.	You always open the window.
Ihr werft meinem Sohn den Ball zu.	You throw the ball to my son.
Ihr singt gern.	You like to sing.

The following sentences have been rewritten, changing *ihr* to *er*.

Er studiert Philosophie und Betriebswirtschaftslehre (BWL).	He studies philosophy and business administration.
Er hilft dem alten Mann.	He helps the old man.
Er braucht einen Kaffee.	He needs a coffee.
Er bekommt eine E-Mail.	He receives an email.
Er trägt jeden Tag Jeans und ein T-Shirt.	He wears jeans and a t-shirt every day.
Er denkt immer positiv.	He always thinks positively.
Er erzählt gern alte Geschichten.	He likes to tell old stories.
Er hört gern klassische Musik.	He likes to listen to classical music.
Er weiß, wie schön die Welt ist.	He knows how beautiful the world is.
Er kennt Angela, und er kennt Berlin.	He knows Angela, and he knows Berlin.
Er erscheint jeden Tag auf dem Campus.	He appears on campus every day.
Er besteht alle Prüfungen.	He passes all tests.
Er vergisst nie.	He never forgets.
Er mag Käse.	He likes cheese.
Er will nach Amsterdam fliegen.	He wants to fly to Amsterdam.
Er kommt aus Hamburg.	He is from Hamburg.
Er tanzt unter den Sternen.	He dances under the stars.
Er rennt durch den Wald.	He runs through the forest.
Er sitzt in der Kneipe.	He sits in the pub.
Er spricht Deutsch und Englisch.	He speaks German and English.
Er wohnt in Bonn.	He lives in Bonn.
Er macht immer das Fenster auf.	He always opens the window.
Er wirft meinem Sohn den Ball zu.	He throws the ball to my son.
Er singt gern.	He likes to sing.

The following sentences have been rewritten, changing *er* to the plural *sie*.

Sie studieren Philosophie und Betriebswirtschaftslehre (BWL).	They study philosophy and business administration.
Sie helfen dem alten Mann.	They help the old man.
Sie brauchen einen Kaffee.	They need a coffee.
Sie bekommen eine E-Mail.	They receive an email.
Sie tragen jeden Tag Jeans und ein T-Shirt.	They wear jeans and a t-shirt every day.
Sie denken immer positiv.	They always think positively.
Sie erzählen gern alte Geschichten.	They like to tell old stories.
Sie hören gern klassische Musik.	They like to listen to classical music.
Sie wissen, wie schön die Welt ist.	They know how beautiful the world is.
Sie kennen Angela, und sie kennen Berlin.	They know Angela, and they know Berlin.
Sie erscheinen jeden Tag auf dem Campus.	They appear on campus every day.
Sie bestehen alle Prüfungen.	They pass all tests.
Sie vergessen nie.	They never forget.
Sie mögen Käse.	They like cheese.
Sie wollen nach Amsterdam fliegen.	They want to fly to Amsterdam.
Sie kommen aus Hamburg.	They are from Hamburg.
Sie tanzen unter den Sternen.	They dance under the stars.
Sie rennen durch den Wald.	They run through the forest.
Sie sitzen in der Kneipe.	They sit in the pub.

Sie sprechen Deutsch und Englisch.	They speak German and English.
Sie wohnen in Bonn.	They live in Bonn.
Sie machen immer das Fenster auf.	They always open the window.
Sie werfen meinem Sohn den Ball zu.	They throw the ball to my son.
Sie singen gern.	They like to sing.

C   The *du* version of each sentence above has been transformed into a yes/no question.

Studierst du Philosophie und Betriebswirtschaftslehre (BWL)?	Are you studying philosophy and business administration?
Hilfst du dem alten Mann?	Are you helping the old man?
Brauchst du einen Kaffee?	Do you need a coffee?
Bekommst du eine E-Mail?	Are you receiving an email?
Trägst du jeden Tag Jeans und ein T-Shirt?	Do you wear jeans and a t-shirt every day?
Denkst du immer positiv?	Do you always think positively?
Erzählst du gern alte Geschichten?	Do you like to tell old stories?
Hörst du gern klassische Musik?	Do you like to listen to classical music?
Weißt du, wie schön die Welt ist?	Do you know how beautiful the world is?
Kennst du Angela? Kennst du Berlin?	Do you know Angela? Do you know Berlin?
Erscheinst du jeden Tag auf dem Campus?	Do you appear on campus every day?
Bestehst du alle Prüfungen?	Do you pass all tests?
Vergisst du nie?	Do you never forget?
Magst du Käse?	Do you like cheese?
Willst du nach Amsterdam fliegen?	Do you want to fly to Amsterdam?
Kommst du aus Hamburg?	Are you from Hamburg?
Tanzt du unter den Sternen?	Are you dancing under the stars?
Rennst du durch den Wald?	Do you run through the forest?
Sitzt du in der Kneipe?	Are you sitting in the pub?
Sprichst du Deutsch und Englisch?	Do you speak German and English?
Wohnst du in Bonn?	Are you living in Bonn?
Machst du immer das Fenster auf?	Do you always open the window?
Wirfst du meinem Sohn den Ball zu?	Are you throwing the ball to my son?
Singst du gern?	Do you like to sing?

D   The question word *wer* has been used to make an open-ended question out of the *er* versions of sentences above, and other questions with *was*, *wie*, *wo*, and *wann* have also been formed. To learn how to say "whom" and "to whom", turn to Chapter 3.

Wer studiert Philosophie und Betriebswirtschaftslehre (BWL)?	Who studies philosophy and business administration?
Was studiert er?	What does he study?
Wer hilft dem alten Mann?	Who helps the old man?
Wer braucht einen Kaffee?	Who needs a coffee?
Was braucht er?	What does he need?
Wer bekommt eine E-Mail?	Who receives an email?
Was bekommt er?	What does he receive?
Wer trägt jeden Tag Jeans und ein T-Shirt?	Who wears jeans and a t-shirt every day?
Was trägt er jeden Tag?	What does he wear every day?
Wer denkt immer positiv?	Who always thinks positively?

Wie denkt er immer?	How does he always think?
Wann denkt er positiv?	When does he think positively?
Wer erzählt gern alte Geschichten?	Who likes to tell old stories?
Was erzählt er gern?	What does he like to tell?
Wie erzählt er alte Geschichten? (Gern!)	How does he tell old stories? (He enjoys doing it!)
Wer hört gern klassische Musik?	Who likes to listen to classical music?
Was hört er gern?	What does he like to listen to?
Wer weiß, wie schön die Welt ist?	Who knows how beautiful the world is?
Was weiß er?	What does he know?
Wer kennt Angela? Wer kennt Berlin?	Who knows Angela? Who knows Berlin?
Was kennt er? (Berlin!)	What does he know? (Berlin!)
Wer erscheint jeden Tag auf dem Campus?	Who appears on campus every day?
Wo erscheint er jeden Tag?	Where does he appear every day?
Wann erscheint er auf dem Campus?	When does he appear on campus?
Wer besteht alle Prüfungen?	Who passes all tests?
Was besteht er?	What does he pass?
Wer vergisst nie?	Who never forgets?
Wann vergisst er?	When does he forget?
Wer mag Käse? (Dumme Frage. Jeder mag Käse!)	Who likes cheese? (Stupid question. Everyone!)
Was mag er?	What does he like?
Wer will nach Amsterdam fliegen?	Who wants to fly to Amsterdam?
Wer kommt aus Hamburg?	Who is from Hamburg?
Wer tanzt unter den Sternen?	Who dances under the stars?
Wo tanzt er?	Where does he dance?
Wer rennt durch den Wald?	Who runs through the forest?
Wo rennt er?	Where does he run?
Wer sitzt in der Kneipe?	Who sits in the pub?
Wo sitzt er?	Where is he sitting?
Wer spricht Deutsch und Englisch?	Who speaks German and English?
Wer wohnt in Bonn?	Who lives in Bonn?
Wo wohnt er?	Where does he live?
Wer macht immer das Fenster auf?	Who always opens the window?
Was macht er immer auf?	What does he always open?
Wann (wie oft) macht er das Fenster auf?	When (how often) does he open the window?
Wer wirft meinem Sohn den Ball zu?	Who throws the ball to my son?
Was wirft er meinem Sohn zu?	What is he throwing to my son?
Wer singt gern?	Who likes to sing?
Was macht er gern?	What does he like to do?

E   The translations appear next to each exercise, and the original sentences are translated below:

Ich studiere Philosophie und Betriebswirtschaftslehre (BWL).	I study philosophy and business administration.
Ich helfe dem alten Mann.	I help the old man.
Ich brauche einen Kaffee.	I need a coffee.
Ich bekomme eine E-Mail.	I receive an email.
Ich trage jeden Tag Jeans und ein T-Shirt.	I wear jeans and a t-shirt every day.
Ich denke immer positiv.	I always think positively.

Ich erzähle gern alte Geschichten.	I like to tell old stories.
Ich höre gern klassische Musik.	I like to listen to classical music.
Ich weiß, wie schön die Welt ist.	I know how beautiful the world is.
Ich kenne Angela, und ich kenne Berlin.	I know Angela, and I know Berlin.
Ich erscheine jeden Tag auf dem Campus.	I appear on campus every day.
Ich bestehe alle Prüfungen.	I pass all tests.
Ich vergesse nie.	I never forget.
Ich mag Käse.	I like cheese.
Ich will nach Amsterdam fliegen.	I want to fly to Amsterdam.
Ich komme aus Hamburg.	I am from Hamburg.
Ich tanze unter den Sternen.	I dance under the stars.
Ich renne durch den Wald.	I run through the forest.
Ich sitze in der Kneipe.	I sit in the pub.
Ich spreche Deutsch und Englisch.	I speak German and English.
Ich wohne in Bonn.	I live in Bonn.
Ich mache immer das Fenster auf.	I always open the window.
Ich werfe meinem Sohn den Ball zu.	I throw the ball to my son.
Ich singe gern.	I like to sing.

Chapter 3

A   The following questions have been written using the correct form of *welch* and have been answered using the correct form of *dies*.

Welches Einhorn ist weiß? (Which unicorn is white?)	Welche Frau ist reich? (Which woman is rich?)	Welcher Hund ist groß? (Which dog is big?)
Welcher Drache ist grün? (Which dragon is green?)	Welcher Mann ist intelligent? (Which man is intelligent?)	Welche Katze ist klein? (Which cat is small?)
Welche Zauberin ist attraktiv? (Which sorceress is attractive?)	Welches Kind ist nett? (Which child is nice?)	Welches Raumschiff ist schön? (Which spaceship is beautiful?)

Dieses Einhorn ist weiß. (This unicorn is white.)	Diese Frau ist reich. (This woman is rich.)	Dieser Hund ist groß. (This dog is big.)
Dieser Drache ist grün. (This dragon is green.)	Dieser Mann ist intelligent. (This man is intelligent.)	Diese Katze ist klein. (This cat is small.)
Diese Zauberin ist attraktiv. (This sorceress is attractive.)	Dieses Kind ist nett. (This child is nice.)	Dieses Raumschiff ist schön. (This spaceship is beautiful.)

B   Having taken care not to forget to re-conjugate the verb, the nouns in each sentence above have been transformed into plurals and combined with the correct form of *all*.

Alle Einhörner sind weiß. (All unicorns are white.)	Alle Frauen sind reich. (All women are rich.)	Alle Hunde sind groß. (All dogs are big.)
Alle Drachen sind grün. (All dragons are green.)	Alle Männer sind intelligent. (All men are intelligent.)	Alle Katzen sind klein. (All cats are small.)
Alle Zauberinnen sind attraktiv. (All sorceresses are attractive.)	Alle Kinder sind nett. (All children are nice.)	Alle Raumschiffe sind schön. (All spaceships are beautiful.)

C   Each of the sentences in A and B has been rewritten using each of the possessive articles. Why does doing something so tedious make sense? For the surprises and the mistakes, but also for the deep immersion in the grammatical pattern. Stick with it. Envision the white unicorns!

Mein Einhorn ist weiß. (My unicorn is white.)	Unser Einhorn ist weiß. (Our unicorn is white.)
Dein Einhorn ist weiß. (Your unicorn is white.)	Euer Einhorn ist weiß. (Your unicorn is white.)
Sein Einhorn ist weiß. (His unicorn is white.) Ihr Einhorn ist weiß. (Her unicorn is white.) Sein Einhorn ist weiß. (Its unicorn is white.)	Ihr Einhorn ist weiß. (Their unicorn is white.)
Meine Einhörner sind weiß. (My unicorns are white.)	Unsre Einhörner sind weiß. (Our unicorns are white.)
Deine Einhörner sind weiß. (Your unicorns are white.)	Eure Einhörner sind weiß. (Your unicorns are white.)
Seine Einhörner sind weiß. (His unicorns are white.) Ihre Einhörner sind weiß. (Her unicorns are white.) Seine Einhörner sind weiß. (Its unicorns are white.)	Ihre Einhörner sind weiß. (Their unicorns are white.)

One could also write *unsere* and *euere*, as explained in Chapter 2. We use the shorter forms for the sake of consistency and savings on ink.

Meine Frau ist reich. (My wife is rich.)	Unsre Frau ist reich. (Our wife is rich.)
Deine Frau ist reich. (Your wife is rich.)	Eure Frau ist reich. (Your wife is rich.)
Seine Frau ist reich. (His wife is rich.) Ihre Frau ist reich. (Her wife is rich.) Seine Frau ist reich. (Its wife is rich.)	Ihre Frau ist reich. (Their wife is rich.)
Meine Frauen sind reich. (My wives are rich.)	Unsre Frauen sind reich. (Our wives are rich.)
Deine Frauen sind reich. (Your wives are rich.)	Eure Frauen sind reich. (Your wives are rich.)
Seine Frauen sind reich. (His wives are rich.) Ihre Frauen sind reich. (Her wives are rich.) Seine Frauen sind reich. (Its wives are rich.)	Ihre Frauen sind reich. (Their wives are rich.)

Note that, when used with a possessive article, *Mann* and *Frau* generally refer to married partners, as in *Ehemann und Ehefrau, Gatte und Gattin*.

Mein Hund ist groß. (My dog is big.)	Unser Hund ist groß. (Our dog is big.)
Dein Hund ist groß. (Your dog is big.)	Euer Hund ist groß. (Your dog is big.)
Sein Hund ist groß. (His dog is big.) Ihr Hund ist groß. (Her dog is big.) Sein Hund ist groß. (Its dog is big.)	Ihr Hund ist groß. (Their dog is big.)

Meine Hunde sind groß. (My dogs are big.)	Unsre Hunde sind groß. (Our dogs are big.)
Deine Hunde sind groß. (Your dogs are big.)	Eure Hunde sind groß. (Your dogs are big.)
Seine Hunde sind groß. (His dogs are big.) Ihre Hunde sind groß. (Her dogs are big.) Seine Hunde sind groß. (Its dogs are big.)	Ihre Hunde sind groß. (Their dogs are big.)

Mein Drache ist grün. (My dragon is green.)
Dein Drache ist grün. (Your dragon is green.)
Sein Drache ist grün. (His dragon is green.)
Ihr Drache ist grün. (Her dragon is green.)
Sein Drache ist grün. (Its dragon is green.)

Unser Drache ist grün. (Our dragon is green.)
Euer Drache ist grün. (Your dragon is green.)
Ihr Drache ist grün. (Their dragon is green.)

Meine Drachen sind grün. (My dragons are green.)

Deine Drachen sind grün. (Your dragons are green.)
Seine Drachen sind grün. (His dragons are green.)
Ihre Drachen sind grün. (Her dragons are green.)
Seine Drachen sind grün. (Its dragons are green.)

Unsre Drachen sind grün. (Our dragons are green.)
Eure Drachen sind grün. (Your dragons are green.)
Ihre Drachen sind grün. (Their dragons are green.)

Mein Mann ist intelligent. (My husband is intelligent.)

Dein Mann ist intelligent. (Your husband is intelligent.)

Sein Mann ist intelligent. (His husband is intelligent.)
Ihr Mann ist intelligent. (Her husband is intelligent.)
Sein Mann ist intelligent. (Its husband is intelligent.)

Unser Mann ist intelligent. (Our husband is intelligent.)
Euer Mann ist intelligent. (Your husband is intelligent.)
Ihr Mann ist intelligent. (Their husband is intelligent.)

Meine Männer sind intelligent. (My husbands are intelligent.)

Deine Männer sind intelligent. (Your husbands are intelligent.)

Seine Männer sind intelligent. (His husbands are intelligent.)
Ihre Männer sind intelligent. (Her husbands are intelligent.)
Seine Männer sind intelligent. (Its husbands are intelligent.)

Unsre Männer sind intelligent. (Our husbands are intelligent.)
Eure Männer sind intelligent. (Your husbands are intelligent.)
Ihre Männer sind intelligent. (Their husbands are intelligent.)

Meine Katze ist klein. (My cat is small.)
Deine Katze ist klein. (Your cat is small.)
Seine Katze ist klein. (His cat is small.)
Ihre Katze ist klein. (Her cat is small.)
Seine Katze ist klein. (Its cat is small.)

Unsre Katze ist klein. (Our cat is small.)
Eure Katze ist klein. (Your cat is small.)
Ihre Katze ist klein. (Their cat is small.)

Meine Katzen sind klein. (My cats are small.)
Deine Katzen sind klein. (Your cats are small.)
Seine Katzen sind klein. (His cats are small.)
Ihre Katzen sind klein. (Her cats are small.)
Seine Katzen sind klein. (Its cats are small.)

Unsre Katzen sind klein. (Our cats are small.)
Eure Katzen sind klein. (Your cats arc small.)
Ihre Katzen sind klein. (Their cats are small.)

Meine Zauberin ist attraktiv. (My sorceress is attractive.)
Deine Zauberin ist attraktiv. (Your sorceress is attractive.)

Unsre Zauberin ist attraktiv. (Our sorceress is attractive.)
Eure Zauberin ist attraktiv. (Your sorceress is attractive.)

Seine Zauberin ist attraktiv. (His sorceress is attractive.)

Ihre Zauberin ist attraktiv. (Her sorceress is attractive.)

Seine Zauberin ist attraktiv. (Its sorceress is attractive.)

Ihre Zauberin ist attraktiv. (Their sorceress is attractive.)

Meine Zauberinnen sind attraktiv. (My sorceresses are attractive.)

Deine Zauberinnen sind attraktiv. (Your sorceresses are attractive.)

Seine Zauberinnen sind attraktiv. (His sorceresses are attractive.)

Ihre Zauberinnen sind attraktiv. (Her sorceresses are attractive.)

Seine Zauberinnen sind attraktiv. (Its sorceresses are attractive.)

Unsre Zauberinnen sind attraktiv. (Our sorceresses are attractive.)

Eure Zauberinnen sind attraktiv. (Your sorceresses are attractive.)

Ihre Zauberinnen sind attraktiv. (Their sorceresses are attractive.)

Mein Kind ist nett. (My child is nice.)
Dein Kind ist nett. (Your child is nice.)
Sein Kind ist nett. (His child is nice.)
Ihr Kind ist nett. (Her child is nice.)
Sein Kind ist nett. (Its child is nice.)

Unser Kind ist nett. (Our child is nice.)
Euer Kind ist nett. (Your child is nice.)
Ihr Kind ist nett. (Their child is nice.)

Meine Kinder sind nett. (My children are nice.)
Deine Kinder sind nett. (Your children are nice.)
Seine Kinder sind nett. (His children are nice.)
Ihre Kinder sind nett. (Her children are nice.)
Seine Kinder sind nett. (Its children are nice.)

Unsre Kinder sind nett. (Our children are nice.)
Eure Kinder sind nett. (Your children are nice.)
Ihre Kinder sind nett. (Their children are nice.)

Mein Raumschiff ist schön.
(My spaceship is beautiful.)
Dein Raumschiff ist schön.
(Your spaceship is beautiful.)
Sein Raumschiff ist schön.
(His spaceship is beautiful.)
Ihr Raumschiff ist schön.
(Her spaceship is beautiful.)
Sein Raumschiff ist schön.
(Its spaceship is beautiful.)

Unser Raumschiff ist schön. (Our spaceship is beautiful.)

Euer Raumschiff ist schön. (Your spaceship is beautiful.)

Ihr Raumschiff ist schön. (Their spaceship is beautiful.)

Meine Raumschiffe sind schön.
(My spaceships are beautiful.)
Deine Raumschiffe sind schön.
(Your spaceships are beautiful.)
Seine Raumschiffe sind schön.
(His spaceships are beautiful.)
Ihre Raumschiffe sind schön.
(Her spaceships are beautiful.)
Seine Raumschiffe sind schön.
(Its spaceships are beautiful.)

Unsre Raumschiffe sind schön. (Our spaceships are beautiful.)

Eure Raumschiffe sind schön. (Your spaceships are beautiful.)

Ihre Raumschiffe sind schön. (Their spaceships are beautiful.)

D   Each of the sentences in C has been transformed into an *es gibt* statement using the correct form of *ein*.

Es gibt ein Einhorn.	There is a unicorn.
Es gibt Einhörner.	There are unicorns.
Es gibt eine Frau.	There is a woman.
Es gibt Frauen.	There are women.
Es gibt einen Hund.	There is a dog.
Es gibt Hunde.	There are dogs.
Es gibt einen Drachen.	There is a dragon. (masculine N-noun)
Es gibt Drachen.	There are dragons.
Es gibt einen Mann.	There is a man.
Es gibt Männer.	There are men.
Es gibt eine Katze.	There are cats.
Es gibt Katzen.	There is a cat.
Es gibt eine Zauberin	There is a sorceress.
Es gibt Zauberinnen.	There are sorceresses.
Es gibt ein Kind.	There is a child.
Es gibt Kinder.	There are children.
Es gibt ein Raumschiff.	There is a spaceship.
Es gibt Raumschiffe.	There are spaceships.

E   Using the singular and plural forms of the nouns in E and the correct form of *kein*, it has been stated that there is not a and are not any of these things *in diesem Zimmer*.

In diesem Zimmer gibt es kein Einhorn.	There is not a unicorn in this room.
In diesem Zimmer gibt es keine Einhörner.	There are not any unicorns in this room.
In diesem Zimmer gibt es keine Frau.	There is not a woman in this room.
In diesem Zimmer gibt es keine Frauen.	There are not any women in this room.
In diesem Zimmer gibt es keinen Hund.	There is not a dog in this room.
In diesem Zimmer gibt es keine Hunde.	There are not any dogs in this room.
In diesem Zimmer gibt es keinen Drachen.	There is not a dragon in this room. (masculine N-noun)
In diesem Zimmer gibt es keine Drachen.	There are no dragons in this room.
In diesem Zimmer gibt es keinen Mann.	There is not a man in this room.
In diesem Zimmer gibt es keine Männer.	There are not any men in this room.
In diesem Zimmer gibt es keine Katze.	There is not a cat in this room.
In diesem Zimmer gibt es keine Katzen.	There are no cats in this room.
In diesem Zimmer gibt es keine Zauberin	There is not a sorceress in this room.
In diesem Zimmer gibt es keine Zauberinnen.	There are no sorceresses in this room.
In diesem Zimmer gibt es kein Kind.	There is no child in this room.
In diesem Zimmer gibt es keine Kinder.	There are no children in this room.
In diesem Zimmer gibt es kein Raumschiff.	There is not a spaceship in this room.
In diesem Zimmer gibt es keine Raumschiffe.	There are not any spaceships in this room.

Seriously, there are no spaceships in this room. Hopefully you have noticed that with the singular nouns, *es gibt kein/e/en* means both "there is not a" and "there is no". With the plural nouns *es gibt keine* means "there are not any" and "there are no".

F   You have told Lola that you see her nouns.

Ich sehe dein Einhorn.	I see your unicorn.
Ich sehe deine Frau.	I see your wife.
Ich sehe deinen Hund.	I see your dog.
Ich sehe deinen Drachen.	I see your dragon.
Ich sehe deinen Mann.	I see your husband.
Ich sehe deine Katze.	I see your cat.
Ich sehe deine Zauberin.	I see your sorceress.
Ich sehe dein Kind.	I see your child.
Ich sehe dein Raumschiff.	I see your spaceship.

G   You have told me that you see Lola's nouns.

Ich sehe ihr Einhorn.	I see her unicorn.
Ich sehe ihre Frau.	I see her wife.
Ich sehe ihren Hund.	I see her dog.
Ich sehe ihren Drachen.	I see her dragon.
Ich sehe ihren Mann.	I see her husband.
Ich sehe ihre Katze.	I see her cat.
Ich sehe ihre Zauberin.	I see her sorceress.
Ich sehe ihr Kind.	I see her child.
Ich sehe ihr Raumschiff.	I see her spaceship.

H   You have asked Lola how her nouns are doing.

Wie geht es deinem Einhorn?	How is your unicorn?
Wie geht es deiner Frau?	How is your wife?
Wie geht es deinem Hund?	How is your dog?
Wie geht es deinem Drachen?	How is your dragon?
Wie geht es deinem Mann?	How is your husband?
Wie geht es deiner Katze?	How is your cat?
Wie geht es deiner Zauberin?	How is your sorceress?
Wie geht es deinem Kind?	How is your child?
Wie geht es deinem Raumschiff?	How is your spaceship?

I   And you, pretending to be Lola, have answered.

Meinem Einhorn geht es gut, danke.	My unicorn is doing well, thanks.
Meiner Frau geht es gut, danke.	My wife is doing well, thanks.
Meinem Hund geht es gut, danke.	My dog is doing well, thanks.
Meinem Drachen geht es gut, danke.	My dragon is doing well, thanks.
Meinem Mann geht es gut, danke.	My husband is doing well, thanks.
Meiner Katze geht es gut, danke.	My cat is doing well, thanks.
Meiner Zauberin geht es gut, danke.	My sorceress is doing well, thanks.
Meinem Kind geht es gut, danke.	My child is doing well, thanks.
Meinem Raumschiff geht es gut, danke.	My spaceship is doing well, thanks.

J   You have asked about his nouns.

Wie geht es seinem Einhorn?	How is his unicorn?
Wie geht es seiner Frau?	How is his wife?
Wie geht es seinem Hund?	How is his dog?
Wie geht es seinem Drachen?	How is his dragon?
Wie geht es seinem Mann?	How is his husband?
Wie geht es seiner Katze?	How is his cat?
Wie geht es seiner Zauberin?	How is his sorceress?
Wie geht es seinem Kind?	How is his child?
Wie geht es seinem Raumschiff?	How is his spaceship?

K   To really test your understanding, how would the answers change if Lola had identified as a man in G and a woman in J? *Ich sehe sein Einhorn. Wie geht es ihrem Einhorn?*

L   Even more than eggnog, giving your local count a Porsche is in the spirit of the winter holidays.

Ich gebe seiner Schwester ein Buch. (I am giving his sister a book.)	Ich gebe ihrem Vater einen Hut. (I am giving her father a hat.)	Ich gebe ihrem Kind einen Hund. (I am giving their child a dog.)
Ich gebe seinen Großeltern eine Katze. (I am giving his grandparents a cat.)	Ich gebe unsren Brüdern Uhren. (I am giving our brothers watches.)	Ich gebe ihren Brüdern Batterien. (I am giving her brothers batteries.)
Ich gebe meinem Mann einen Ring. (I am giving my husband a ring.)	Ich gebe meiner Frau einen Audi. (I am giving my wife an Audi.)	Ich gebe unsrem Grafen einen Porsche. (I am giving our count a Porsche.)

Hopefully, you remembered that *Graf* is a masculine N-noun.

M   Questions and answers for each sentence in L have been written and translated.

Ich gebe seiner Schwester ein Buch.	I am giving his sister a book.
Was gibst du seiner Schwester?	What are you giving to his sister?
Ein Buch. Ein Buch gebe ich ihr.	A book. I am giving her a book.
Wem gibst du ein Buch?	To whom are you giving a book?
Seiner Schwester. Seiner Schwester gebe ich es.	To his sister. I am giving it to his sister.
Wer gibt seiner Schwester ein Buch?	Who is giving his sister a book?
Ich. Ich gebe es ihr.	I (am). I am giving it to her.

Ich gebe ihrem Vater einen Hut.	I am giving her father a hat.
Was gibst du ihrem Vater?	What are you giving to her father?
Einen Hut. Einen Hut gebe ich ihm.	A hat. I am giving him a hat.
Wem gibst du einen Hut?	To whom are you giving a hat?
Ihrem Vater. Ihrem Vater gebe ich ihn.	To her father. I am giving it to her father.
Wer gibt ihrem Vater einen Hut?	Who is giving her father a hat?
Ich. Ich gebe ihn ihm.	I (am). I am giving it to him.

Ich gebe ihrem Kind einen Hund.	I am giving their child a dog.
Was gibst du ihrem Kind?	What are you giving to their child?
Einen Hund. Einen Hund gebe ich ihm.	A dog. I am giving them a dog.
Wem gibst du einen Hund?	To whom are you giving a dog?
Ihrem Kind. Ihrem Kind gebe ich ihn.	To their child. I am giving it to their child.
Wer gibt ihrem Kind einen Hund?	Who is giving their child a dog?
Ich. Ich gebe ihn ihm.	I (am). I am giving it to them.

I used "them" rather than "it" in the translation since we don't refer to human beings as "it" in English and since *Kind* is gender neutral. If the plural "them" bothers you, use "him" or "her" if you know the gender of the child; otherwise, avoid pronouns and use "their child".

Ich gebe seinen Großeltern eine Katze.	I am giving his grandparents a cat.
Was gibst du seinen Großeltern?	What are you giving to his grandparents?
Eine Katze. Eine Katze gebe ich ihnen.	A cat. I'm giving them a cat.
Wem gibst du eine Katze?	To whom are you giving a cat?
Seinen Großeltern. Seinen Großeltern gebe ich sie.	To his grandparents. I am giving it to his grandparents.
Wer gibt seinen Großeltern eine Katze?	Who is giving his grandparents a cat?
Ich. Ich gebe sie ihnen.	I (am). I am giving it to them.

Ich gebe unsren Brüdern Uhren.	I am giving our brothers watches.
Was gibst du unsren Brüdern?	What are you giving to our brothers?
Uhren. Uhren gebe ich ihnen.	Watches. I am giving them watches.
Wem gibst du Uhren?	To whom are you giving watches?
Unsren Brüdern. Unsren Brüdern gebe ich sie.	To our brothers. I am giving them to our brothers.
Wer gibt unsren Brüdern Uhren?	Who is giving our brothers watches?
Ich. Ich gebe sie ihnen.	I (am). I am giving them to them.

Ich gebe ihren Brüdern Batterien.	I am giving her brothers batteries.
Was gibst du ihren Brüdern?	What are you giving to her brothers?
Batterien. Batterien gebe ich ihnen.	Batteries. I am giving them batteries.
Wem gibst du Batterien?	To whom are you giving batteries?
Ihren Brüdern. Ihren Brüdern gebe ich sie.	To her brothers. I am giving them to her brothers.
Wer gibt ihren Brüdern Batterien?	Who is giving her brothers batteries?
Ich. Ich gebe sie ihnen.	I (am). I am giving them to them.

Ich gebe meinem Mann einen Ring.	I am giving my husband a ring.
Was gibst du deinem Mann?	What are you giving to your husband?
Einen Ring. Einen Ring gebe ich ihm.	A ring. I am giving him a ring.
Wem gibst du einen Ring?	To whom are you giving a ring?
Meinem Mann. Meinem Mann gebe ich ihn.	To my husband. I am giving it to my husband.
Wer gibt deinem Mann einen Ring?	Who is giving your husband a ring?
Ich. Ich gebe es ihm.	I (am). I am giving it to him.

Did you remember to change *meinem* to *deinem* when you asked the questions?

Ich gebe meiner Frau einen Audi.	I am giving my wife an Audi.
Was gibst du deiner Frau?	What are you giving to your wife?
Einen Audi. Einen Audi gebe ich ihr.	An Audi. I am giving her an Audi.
Wem gibst du einen Audi?	To whom are you giving an Audi?
Meiner Frau. Meiner Frau gebe ich ihn.	To my wife. I am giving it to my wife.
Wer gibt deiner Frau einen Audi?	Who is giving your wife an Audi?
Ich. Ich gebe ihn ihr.	I (am). I am giving it to her.

Each of the car brands is masculine.

Ich gebe unsrem Grafen einen Porsche.	I am giving our count a Porsche.
Was gibst du unsrem Grafen?	What are you giving to our count?
Einen Porsche. Einen Porsche gebe ich ihm.	A Porsche. I am giving him a Porsche.
Wem gibst du einen Porsche?	To whom are you giving a Porsche?
Unsrem Grafen. Unsrem Grafen gebe ich ihn.	To our count. I am giving it to our count.
Wer gibt unsrem Grafen einen Porsche?	Who is giving our count a Porsche?
Ich. Ich gebe ihn ihm.	I (am). I am giving it to him.

N   The problems have been solved by using verbs, some of which are reflexive.

Dein Auto ist dreckig. (Your car is filthy.)	Dein Körper ist dreckig. (Your body is filthy.)	Dein Gesicht ist dreckig. (Your face is filthy.)
Deine Haare sind dreckig. (Your hair is filthy).	Deine Zähne sind dreckig. (Your teeth are filthy.)	Du willst kein nacktes Blumenkind sein. (You do not want to be a naked flower child.)
Dir ist kalt, aber du hast einen Pullover. (You are cold, but you have a sweater.)	Dein Kind ist ein nacktes Blumenkind. (Your child is a naked flower child.)	Deinem Kind ist kalt, aber du hast einen Pullover. (Your child is cold, but you have a sweater.)

Before checking your answer, think about it once more. In the first problem, the car is dirty. Would washing yourself make the car cleaner? Obviously not. The first answer is not reflexive. The subject performs the washing on the car, not on itself. In the second problem, the body in question is the subject's body. Here we need a reflexive verb. If you don't understand, ask yourself: if you need a shower, would it help you to power wash the deck? No, you must wash yourself.

Ich wasche mein Auto. (I wash my car.)	Obviously not reflexive. Subject not identical with direct object.
Ich wasche mich. (I wash myself.)	Obviously reflexive. Subject identical with direct object.
Ich wasche mir das Gesicht. (I wash my face.)	Reflexive, perhaps less obviously. The direct object is a part of the subject. Do Germans sometimes simply say *Ich wasche mein Gesicht?* Yes, of course. But that doesn't help you understand the reflexive way of saying it.
Ich wasche mir die Haare. (I wash my hair.)	Reflexive, perhaps more obviously after reading the previous explanation.
Ich putze mir die Zähne.	Reflexive, perhaps obvious after reading the last two examples.

Ich ziehe mich an.	Obviously reflexive.
Ich ziehe mir den Pullover an. (I put on the sweater.)	Reflexive. You are dressing a part of yourself with the sweater, just like you wash a part of yourself (your face).
Ich ziehe mein Kind an.	Obviously not reflexive.
Ich ziehe ihm den Pullover an.	Obviously not reflexive, but it shows how the dative works with the child.

Now, become like a more capable version of the child and put the sweater on yourself – that's the Graf von Anderson Advantage!

Chapter 4

A   The following sentences have been translated into German.

Sie kommt aus der Schweiz.	She is from Switzerland.
Sie wohnt mit ihrem Sohn hier um die Ecke.	She lives with her son around the corner from here.
Wir fliegen nach Paris.	We are flying to Paris.
Der Wein ist ein Geschenk von ihr.	The wine is a gift from her.
Ich arbeite bei einer Bank.	I work at a bank.
Fährst du durch die Stadt? Fahrt ihr durch die Stadt? Fahren Sie durch die Stadt?	Are you driving through the city?
Ich stehe um 7.00 Uhr auf.	I get up at 7:00.
Die Blumen sind für meine Mutter.	The flowers are for my mother.
Ich gehe zum Supermarkt.	I am going to the supermarket
Star Wars ist seit dem Jahr 1977 mein Lieblingsfilm.	*Star Wars* is my favorite film since the year 1977.
Bist du gegen die Todesstrafe? Seid ihr gegen die Todesstrafe? Sind Sie gegen die Todesstrafe?	Are you against the death penalty?
Wir haben bis 15.00 Uhr Deutsch.	We have German until 3:00.

B   The questions have been answered.

Die Guten kämpfen gegen die Bösen.	The good fight against the evil.
Mit Freunden verbringe ich am liebsten meine Freizeit.	I prefer to spend my free time with friends.
Zum Tomorrowland gehen wir nächsten Sommer!	We are going to Tomorrowland next summer!
Aus Hamburg komme ich.	I am from Hamburg.
Seit 2012 wohne ich in Luxemburg.	I have been living in Luxembourg since 2012.
Für meine Mutter kaufe ich jedes Jahr ein Geschenk.	I buy a gift for my mother every year.
Von meinen Eltern bekomme ich jedes Jahr ein Geschenk.	I receive a gift from my parents every year.
Die Post kommt jeden Tag außer Sonntag.	The mail comes every day except Sunday.
Gegen 11.00 Uhr abends gehe ich normalerweise ins Bett.	I normally go to bed around 11:00.
Um 7.00 Uhr morgens öffnet die Universitätsbibliothek.	The university library opens at 7:00 a.m.
Durch das Fenster kommt Sonnenlicht in das Klassenzimmer.	Sunlight comes into the classroom through the window.

Bis 6.00 Uhr abends bleibe ich mittwochs auf dem Campus.	I stay on campus on Wednesdays until 6:00.
Ohne einen Zauberring kann man nicht unsichtbar werden.	Without a magic ring one cannot become invisible.

C   Translated!

Der Eisball rollt (von woanders) zwischen die Kekse und die Kuchen.
Der Eisball schmilzt zwischen den Keksen und den Kuchen.
Ein Raumschiff fliegt über den Wolkenkratzern.
Der Athlet springt über die Wolkenkratzer.
Der Schildkröte geht über die Brücke.
Der Schildkröte steht auf der Brücke und winkt.
Stell die Teller auf den Tisch! Stellt die Teller auf den Tisch! Stellen Sie die Teller auf den Tisch!
Der Hund geht unter den Tisch.
Der Hund schläft unter dem Tisch.
Die Katze geht an das Fenster.
Die Katze sitzt am Fenster.
Vor dem Haus steht ein Baum.
Die Katze schleicht sich an den Baum.
Ein Vogel singt im Baum.
Fahre mich sofort vor das Haus! Fahren Sie mich sofort vor das Haus!
Der Graf bringt die Musiker in das Schloss.
Der Graf wohnt in dem Schloss.
Der Fahrer fährt neben den Porsche auf der Autobahn.
Der Fahrer sitzt neben dem Beifaher im Porsche.
Sie fahren den Porsche ans Meer.
Sie fahren den Porsche nicht ins Meer.
Sie gehen zum Strand.
Wir wohnen am Strand.

D   A question has been crafted using either a *wo*-compound or a preposition and a question word.

Wonach riecht es in der Küche?	What does it smell of in the kitchen? Garlic and tomatoes.
Woran arbeitet er?	What is he working on? His novel.
Wovor haben wir Angst? Wovor habt ihr Angst?	What are we afraid of? What are you afraid of? Surveillance capitalism.
Worüber redet ihr gern?	What do you like to talk about? Politics.
Worauf hoffen wir?	What are we hoping for? A better future.
Woran erinnert ihn alles?	What does everything remind him of? His past.
Womit beginnt er?	With what does he begin? His childhood.
Für wen war das eine sehr gute Zeit?	For whom was that a very good time? For him.
Woraus besteht Wasser?	What does water consist of? Hydrogen and oxygen.

E   The questions have been rewritten using the genitive instead of the dative for the bolded phrase.

Ist das das Schloss **des Grafen**?	Is that the Graf's castle?
Ist das nicht die Nichte **der Professorin**?	Isn't that the professor's niece?
Siehst du das Schicksal **meiner Freundin**?	Do you see my girlfriend's destiny?
Siehst du das Schicksal **meines Freundes**?	Do you see my boyfriend's destiny?
Siehst du das Schicksal **meines Kindes**?	Do you see my child's destiny?
Siehst du das Schicksal **meiner Kinder**?	Do you see my children's destiny?
Welche Musik **der 80er Jahre** findest du besonders cool?	Which 80s music do you find especially cool?

F   What the first sentence means has been "figured out", and a logically related second sentence has been formed from the words in brackets.

Die Sache liegt jenseits meines Verständnisses.	The thing lies beyond my comprehension.
Ihre Wohnung liegt außerhalb der Stadt.	Her apartment is outside the city.
Wir spielen drinnen wegen des Regens.	We play inside on account of the rain.
Wir spielen draußen trotz des Wetters.	We play outside despite the weather.
Sie sollen eine Ferienwohnung anstatt eines Hotelzimmers mieten.	They should rent a vacation apartment instead of a hotel room.
Sie machen eine Reise innerhalb Italiens.	They are taking a trip within Italy.
Bobfried ist während meiner Abwesenheit der Chef.	Bobfried is the boss during my absence.

Chapter 5

A   The following sentences have been translated and rewritten in the future tense.

Ich sehe dich!	I see you!
Du sprichst mit deinem Vater.	You speak with your father.
Sie isst mit ihrer Tochter.	She eats with her daughter.
Wir lernen viel Deutsch!	We learn a lot of German!
Ihr fliegt nach Amsterdam.	You fly to Amsterdam.
Sie lieben einander.	They love each other.

Ich werde dich sehen!	I will see you!
Du wirst mit deinem Vater sprechen.	You will speak with your father.
Sie wird mit ihrer Tochter essen.	She will eat with her daughter.
Wir werden viel Deutsch lernen!	We will learn a lot of German!
Ihr werdet nach Amsterdam fliegen.	You will fly to Amsterdam.
Sie werden einander lieben.	They will love each other.

Each of the original sentences has been rewritten with each of the modal verbs.

Ich will dich sehen!	I want to see you!
Du willst mit deinem Vater sprechen.	You want to speak with your father.
Sie will mit ihrer Tochter essen.	She wants to eat with her daughter.
Wir wollen viel Deutsch lernen!	We want to learn a lot of German!
Ihr wollt nach Amsterdam fliegen.	You want to fly to Amsterdam.
Sie wollen einander lieben.	They want to love each other.

Ich kann dich sehen!	I am able to see you!
Du kannst mit deinem Vater sprechen.	You are able to speak with your father.
Sie kann mit ihrer Tochter essen.	She is able to eat with her daughter.
Wir können viel Deutsch lernen!	We are able to learn a lot of German!
Ihr könnt nach Amsterdam fliegen.	You are able to fly to Amsterdam.
Sie können einander lieben.	They are able to love each other.

Ich muss dich sehen!	I have to see you!
Du musst mit deinem Vater sprechen.	You have to speak with your father.
Sie muss mit ihrer Tochter essen.	She has to eat with her daughter.
Wir müssen viel Deutsch lernen!	We have to learn a lot of German!
Ihr müsst nach Amsterdam fliegen.	You have to fly to Amsterdam.
Sie müssen einander lieben.	They have to love each other.

Ich soll dich sehen!	I should see you!
Du sollst mit deinem Vater sprechen.	You should speak with your father.
Sie soll mit ihrer Tochter essen.	She should eat with her daughter.
Wir sollen viel Deutsch lernen!	We should learn a lot of German!
Ihr sollt nach Amsterdam fliegen.	You should fly to Amsterdam.
Sie sollen einander lieben.	They should love each other.

Ich darf dich sehen!	I am allowed to see you!
Du darfst mit deinem Vater sprechen.	You are allowed to speak with your father.
Sie darf mit ihrer Tochter essen.	She is allowed to eat with her daughter.
Wir dürfen viel Deutsch lernen!	We are allowed to learn a lot of German!
Ihr dürft nach Amsterdam fliegen.	You are allowed to fly to Amsterdam.
Sie dürfen einander lieben.	They are allowed to love each other.

Ich möchte dich sehen!	I would like to see you!
Du möchtest mit deinem Vater sprechen.	You would like to speak with your father.
Sie möchte mit ihrer Tochter essen.	She would like to eat with her daughter.
Wir möchten viel Deutsch lernen!	We would like to learn a lot of German!
Ihr möchtet nach Amsterdam fliegen.	You would like to fly to Amsterdam.
Sie möchten einander lieben.	They would like to love each other.

We all wonder what's holding them back.

B   The following sentences have been translated.

Friedrich lernt Deutsch.	Friedrich is learning German.
Esst ihr noch Fleisch?	Do you still eat meat?
Ich spiele gern Gitarre.	I like playing the guitar.
Wann kommt der Zug in Wien an?	When does the train arrive in Vienna?
Die Kinder werden müde.	The children are becoming tired.
Um wieviel Uhr fliegst du nach Berlin?	At what time do you fly to Berlin?
Sie arbeitet bei der Deutschen Bank.	She works for Deutsche Bank.
Wann wachen wir auf?	When do we wake up?
Wann müssen wir aufwachen?	When do we have to wake up?
Wir lesen *Das Glasperlenspiel* von Hermann Hesse.	We are reading *The Glass Bead Game* by Hermann Hesse.
Das Kind ist mein Sohn.	The child is my son.
Die Frau hat einen Porsche.	The woman has a Porsche.

They have been rewritten in the future tense.

Friedrich wird Deutsch lernen.	Friedrich will learn German.
Werdet ihr noch Fleisch essen?	Will you still eat meat?
Ich werde gern Gitarre spielen.	I will happily play the guitar.
Wann wird der Zug in Wien ankommen?	When will the train arrive in Vienna?
Die Kinder werden müde werden.	The children will become tired.
Um wieviel Uhr wirst du nach Berlin fliegen?	At what time will you fly to Berlin?
Sie wird bei der Deutschen Bank arbeiten.	She will work for Deutsche Bank.
Wann werden wir aufwachen?	When will we wake up?
Wann werden wir aufwachen müssen?	When will we have to wake up?
Wir werden *Das Glasperlenspiel* von Hermann Hesse lesen.	We will read *The Glass Bead Game* by Hermann Hesse.
Das Kind wird mein Sohn sein.	The child will be my son.
Die Frau wird einen Porsche haben.	The woman will have a Porsche.

They have been rewritten in each past tense.

Friedrich hat Deutsch gelernt.	Friedrich learned German.
Habt ihr noch Fleisch gegessen?	Did you still eat meat?
Ich habe gern Gitarre gespielt.	I liked playing the guitar.
Wann ist der Zug in Wien angekommen?	When did the train arrive in Vienna?
Die Kinder sind müde geworden.	The children became tired.
Um wieviel Uhr bist du nach Berlin geflogen?	At what time did you fly to Berlin?
Sie hat bei der Deutschen Bank gearbeitet.	She worked for Deutsche Bank.
Wann sind wir aufgewacht?	When did we wake up?
Wann haben wir aufwachen müssen?	When did we have to wake up?
Wir haben *Das Glasperlenspiel* von Hermann Hesse gelesen.	We read *The Glass Bead Game* by Hermann Hesse.
Das Kind ist mein Sohn gewesen.	The child was my son.
Die Frau hat einen Porsche gehabt.	The woman had a Porsche.

Friedrich lernte Deutsch.	Friedrich learned German.
Aß ihr noch Fleisch?	Did you still eat meat?
Ich spielte gern Gitarre.	I liked playing the guitar.
Wann kam der Zug in Wien an?	When did the train arrive in Vienna?
Die Kinder wurden müde.	The children became tired.
Um wieviel Uhr flogst du nach Berlin?	At what time did you fly to Berlin?
Sie arbeitete bei der Deutschen Bank.	She worked for Deutsche Bank.
Wann wachten wir auf?	When did we wake up?
Wann mussten wir aufwachen?	When did we have to wake up?
Wir lasen *Das Glasperlenspiel* von Hermann Hesse.	We read *The Glass Bead Game* by Hermann Hesse.
Das Kind war mein Sohn.	The child was my son.
Die Frau hatte einen Porsche.	The woman will have a Porsche.

C   The following sentences have been translated and written in the present, future, and each past tense.

Ich bin ein Mensch.	**I am a human being.**
Ich werde ein Mensch sein.	I will be a human being.
Ich bin ein Mensch gewesen.	I was a human being.
Ich war ein Mensch.	I was a human being.

Ich werde klüger und kräftiger.	**I am becoming smarter and more powerful.**
Ich werde klüger und kräftiger werden.	I will become smarter and more powerful.
Ich bin klüger und kräftiger geworden.	I became smarter and more powerful.
Ich wurde klüger und kräftiger.	I became smarter and more powerful.

Ich habe eine Zukunft.	**I have a future.**
Ich werde eine Zukunft haben.	I will have a future.
Ich habe eine Zukunft gehabt.	I had a future.
Ich hatte eine Zukunft.	I had a future.

Of course you have a future – that's the Graf von Anderson Advantage!

Ich studiere Chemie.	**I am studying chemistry.**
Ich werde Chemie studieren.	I will study chemistry.
Ich habe Chemie studiert.	I studied chemistry.
Ich studierte Chemie.	I studied chemistry.

Ich fahre mit Freunden nach Frankfurt.	**I drive with friends to Frankfurt.**
Ich werde mit Freunden nach Frankfurt fahren.	I will drive with friends to Frankfurt.
Ich bin mit Freunden nach Frankfurt gefahren.	I drove with friends to Frankfurt.
Ich fuhr mit Freunden nach Frankfurt.	I drove with friends to Frankfurt.

Ich bringe Kekse zur Party.	**I bring cookies to the party.**
Ich werde Kekse zur Party bringen.	I will bring cookies to the party.
Ich habe Kekse zur Party gebracht.	I brought cookies to the party.
Ich brachte Kekse zur Party.	I brought cookies to the party.

Ich zeige meinen Freunden die Stadt.	**I show my friends the city.**
Ich werde meinen Freunden die Stadt zeigen.	I will show my friends the city.
Ich habe meinen Freunden die Stadt gezeigt.	I showed my friends the city.
Ich zeigte meinen Freunden die Stadt.	I showed my friends the city.

Ich kann fliegen!	**I am able to fly!**
Ich werde fliegen können!	I will be able to fly!
Ich habe fliegen können!	I was able to fly!
Ich konnte fliegen!	I was able to fly!

Ich will mein Deutsch verbessern.	**I want to improve my German.**
Ich werde mein Deutsch verbessern wollen.	I will want to improve my German.
Ich habe mein Deutsch verbessern wollen.	I wanted to improve my German.
Ich wollte mein Deutsch verbessern.	I wanted to improve my German.

D   The following sentences have been rewritten in the passive voice, using *von* to indicate agency.

Bobfried backt feines Vollkornbrot.	Bobfried bakes high-quality whole grain bread.
Feines Vollkornbrot wird von Bobfried gebacken.	High-quality whole grain bread is baked by Bobfried.
Im Park spielt ein Streichquartett schöne Musik.	In the park a string quartet is playing beautiful music.
Schöne Musik wird von einem Streichquartett im Park gespielt.	Beautiful music is being played by a string quartet in the park.
Viele Personen lesen Zeitungen im Cafe.	Many people are reading newspapers in the cafe.
Zeitungen werden von vielen Personen im Cafe gelesen.	Newspapers are being read by many people in the cafe.
In der Kneipe trinken die Leute Bier.	In the pub the people are drinking beer.
Bier wird von den Leuten in der Kneipe getrunken.	Beer is drunk by the people in the pub.
Im Büro erledigen die Angestellten alltägliche Aufgaben.	In the office the workers complete everyday tasks.
Alltägliche Aufgaben werden von den Angestellten im Büro erledigt.	Everyday tasks are completed by the workers in the office.
Die Mitarbeiter feiern am Freitagnachmittag.	The coworkers party on Friday afternoon.
Es wird am Freitagnachmittag von den Mitarbeitern gefeiert.	It is partied on Friday afternoon by the coworkers.

To hear that last one properly, say it in English with a thick German accent. Now, use the same accent to repeat it in German. Do you hear the magic of the passive voice? If the use of "party" as a verb offends you, replace it with "celebrate" or "make merry" or "pursue lusty passions", as you wish.

Each sentence has been rewritten in the future tense.

Bobfried wird feines Vollkornbrot backen.	Bobfried will bake high-quality whole grain bread.
Feines Vollkornbrot wird von Bobfried gebacken werden.	High-quality whole grain bread will be baked by Bobfried.
Im Park wird ein Streichquartett schöne Musik spielen.	In the park a string quartet will play beautiful music.
Schöne Musik wird von einem Streichquartett im Park gespielt werden.	Beautiful music will be played by a string quartet in the park.
Viele Personen werden Zeitungen im Cafe lesen.	Many people will read newspapers in the cafe.
Zeitungen werden von vielen Leuten im Cafe gelesen werden.	Newspapers will be read by many people in the cafe.
In der Kneipe werden die Leute Bier trinken.	In the pub the people will drink beer.
Bier wird von den Leuten in der Kneipe getrunken werden.	Beer will be drunk by the people in the pub.
Im Büro werden die Angestellten alltägliche Aufgaben erledigen.	In the office the workers will complete everyday tasks.
Alltägliche Aufgaben werden von den Angestellten im Büro erledigt werden.	Everyday tasks will be completed by the workers in the office.
Die Mitarbeiter werden am Freitagnachmittag feiern.	The coworkers will party on Friday afternoon.
Es wird am Freitagnachmittag von den Mitarbeitern gefeiert werden.	It will be partied on Friday afternoon by the coworkers.

Each sentence has been rewritten in each past tense, first in the *Perfekt* . . .

Bobfried hat feines Vollkornbrot gebacken.	Bobfried baked high-quality whole grain bread.
Feines Vollkornbrot ist von Bobfried gebacken worden.	High-quality whole grain bread was baked by Bobfried.
Im Park hat ein Streichquartett schöne Musik gespielt.	In the park a string quartet played beautiful music.
Schöne Musik ist von einem Streichquartett im Park gespielt worden.	Beautiful music was played by a string quartet in the park.
Viele Personen haben Zeitungen im Cafe gelesen.	Many people read newspapers in the cafe.
Zeitungen sind von vielen Leuten im Cafe gelesen worden.	Newspapers were read by many people in the cafe.
In der Kneipe haben die Leute Bier getrunken.	In the pub the people drank beer.
Bier ist von den Leuten in der Kneipe getrunken worden.	Beer was drunk by the people in the pub.
Im Büro haben die Angestellten alltägliche Aufgaben erledigt.	In the office the workers completed everyday tasks.
Alltägliche Aufgaben sind von den Angestellten im Büro erledigt worden.	Everyday tasks were completed by the workers in the office.
Die Mitarbeiter haben am Freitagnachmittag gefeiert.	The coworkers partied on Friday afternoon.
Es ist am Freitagnachmittag von den Mitarbeitern gefeiert worden.	It was partied on Friday afternoon by the coworkers.

. . . and the in the *Präteritum*.

Bobfried backte feines Vollkornbrot.	Bobfried baked high-quality whole grain bread.
Feines Vollkornbrot wurde von Bobfried gebacken.	High-quality whole grain bread was baked by Bobfried.
Im Park spielte ein Streichquartett schöne Musik.	In the park a string quartet played beautiful music.
Schöne Musik wurde von einem Streichquartett im Park gespielt.	Beautiful music was played by a string quartet in the park.
Viele Personen lasen Zeitungen im Cafe.	Many people read newspapers in the cafe.
Zeitungen wurden von vielen Leuten im Cafe gelesen.	Newspapers were read by many people in the cafe.
In der Kneipe tranken die Leute Bier.	In the pub the people drank beer.
Bier wurde von den Leuten in der Kneipe getrunken.	Beer was drunk by the people in the pub.
Im Büro erledigten die Angestellten alltägliche Aufgaben.	In the office the workers completed everyday tasks.
Alltägliche Aufgaben wurden von den Angestellten im Büro erledigt.	Everyday tasks were completed by the workers in the office.
Die Mitarbeiter feierten am Freitagnachmittag.	The coworkers partied on Friday afternoon.
Es wurde am Freitagnachmittag von den Mitarbeitern gefeiert.	It was partied on Friday afternoon by the coworkers.

We're all *Mitarbeiter*, and it's always *Freitagnachmittag* somewhere – that's the Graf von Anderson Advantage!

Chapter 6

A   The following sentences have been created by combining the shorter sentences with the specified conjunctions.

Es regnet und wir bleiben im Klassenzimmer.	It is raining and we are staying in the classroom.
Wir bleiben im Klassenzimmer, denn es regnet.	We are staying in the classroom because it is raining.
Weil es regnet, bleiben wir im Klassenzimmer.	Because it is raining, we are staying in the classroom.

The first three should have been fairly easy, unless you thought that it was raining because you remained in the classroom. In that case, you have larger problems than learning German.

Du darfst nicht mit den anderen Kindern Fußball spielen, bevor du deine Hausaufgaben machst.	You are not allowed to play soccer with the other children before you have done your homework.
Ich weiß, dass ich nicht mit den anderen Kindern spielen darf, bevor ich meine Hausaufgaben gemacht habe.	I know that I am not allowed to play soccer with the other children before I have done my homework.

Du darfst mit den anderen Kindern Fußball spielen, nachdem du deine Hausaufgaben gemacht hast.	You are allowed to play soccer with the other children after you have done your homework.
Gegen 20.00 Uhr darfst du mit deiner Freundin in Goa sprechen, aber nach zwanzig Minuten musst du den Hörer auflegen.	Around 8:00 you are allowed to speak with your girlfriend in Goa, but after twenty minutes you have to hang up the phone.
Weil Ferngespräche teuer sind, musst du nach zwanzig Minuten den Hörer auflegen.	Because long-distance calls are expensive, you have to hang up the phone after twenty minutes.
Obwohl Ferngespräche teuer sind, darfst du deine Freundin in Goa anrufen.	Even though long-distance calls are expensive, you are allowed to call your girlfriend in Goa.

We will always be grateful to the boarding school for allowing those long-distance calls, and for arranging our field trips to Goa.

B   The following sentences have been created using subordinate clauses constructed from question words.

Ich weiß nicht, wo Bobfried wohnt.	I do not know where Bobfried lives.
Kannst du für mich herausfinden, welche Farbe seine Lieblingsfarbe ist?	Can you find out for me which color is his favorite color?

What happened to the *es* before *nicht* in the first problem and before *herausfinden* in the second problem? The second clause takes the place of it. That will happen again in the next problem, and again in other problems, and in life. The second clause is the *es*.

Er hat mir nicht sagen wollen, mit wem er nach München gefahren ist.	He did not want to tell me with whom he drove to Munich.
Wir müssen den Schaffner fragen, wann der Zug in München ankommt.	We have to ask the conductor when the train arrives in Munich.
Er hat die Verkäuferin gefragt, wieviel der Pullover kostet.	He asked the saleswoman how much the sweater cost.
Seine Begleiterin konnte nicht verstehen, wieso der Pullover so viel kostet.	His companion could not understand why the sweater cost so much.
Die Verkäuferin hat ihnen nicht erklären können, warum der Preis so hoch ist.	The saleswoman could not explain to them why the price is so high.
Dem Taxifahrer sagte er, zu welchem Hotel er fahren wollte.	He told the taxi driver to which hotel he wanted to go.
Er gab auf dem Zimmerservice-Formular an, was sie zum Frühstück essen wollten.	He indicated on the room service form what they wanted to eat for breakfast.

C   The following sentences have been created using relative clauses.

Ich habe einen Bruder, der in Budapest wohnt.	I have a brother who lives in Budapest.
Ich habe in Budapest einen Bruder, den ich besuche.	I have a brother in Budapest whom I visit.
Ich habe zwei Tanten, die in Antwerpen wohnen.	I have two aunts who live in Antwerp.
Ich habe in Antwerpen zwei Tanten, die ich besuche.	I have two aunts in Antwerp whom I visit.

Ich sehe ein Gespenst, dessen Gesicht im Mondlicht leuchtet.	I see a phantom whose face glows in the moonlight.
Mein bester Freund, mit dem ich gern Gitarre spiele, wohnt in Berlin.	My best friend, with whom I like to play guitar, lives in Berlin.
Ich habe auch neue Freunde, mit denen ich eine Band forme.	I also have new friends, with whom I am forming a band.
Wir spielen psychedelische elektronische Tanzmusik, die unsre Lieblingsmusik ist.	We play psychedelic electronic dance music, which is our favorite music.
Wir sollten einen Hund adoptieren, dessen Charakter zu uns passt.	We should adopt a dog whose character suits us.

D The following sentences have been created using the *Konjunktiv II* and the subordinating conjunction *wenn*.

Wenn wir Hunger hätten, würden wir essen.	If we were hungry, we would eat.
Wenn die Sonne scheinen würde, würden wir eine Sonnenbrille tragen.	If the sun were shining, we would wear sunglasses.
Wenn wir allwissend wären, würden wir alles wissen.	If we were omniscient, we would know everything.
Wenn sie ein Auto hätte, würde sie zu dir fahren.	If she had a car, she would drive to you.
Wenn er Geld hätte, würde er ein Taxi nehmen.	If he had money, he would take a taxi.
Wenn wir klüger wären, gäbe es mehr Umweltschutz.	If we were smarter, there would be more environmental protection.
Wenn wir intelligenter gewesen wären, hätte es in den letzten vierzig Jahren mehr Umweltschutz gegeben.	If we had been more intelligent, there would have been more environmental protection in the last forty years.
Wenn wir vernünftiger sein wollten, würden wir mehr Umweltschutz verlangen.	If we wanted to be more sensible, we would demand more environmental protection.
Wenn es einen anderen bewohnbaren Planeten in der Nähe gäbe, wäre die bevorstehende Umweltkatastrophe immer noch echt tragisch.	If there were another habitable planet nearby, the impending environmental catastrophe would still be really tragic.

Chapter 7

A In each of the following sentences, the adjective *gut* has been inserted in front of *Lehrer*, *intelligent* in front of *Frau*, and *nett* in front of any other nouns.

Der gute Lehrer ist ein netter Mann.	The good teacher is a nice man.
Seine intelligente Frau liebt unsren guten Lehrer.	His intelligent wife loves our good teacher.
Unser guter Lehrer kocht mit seiner intelligenten Frau ein nettes Abendessen.	Our good teacher cooks with his intelligent wife a nice dinner.
Seine intelligente Frau kocht mit unsrem guten Lehrer das nette Abendessen.	His intelligent wife cooks with our good teacher the nice dinner.
Ein guter Lehrer soll einen netten Volvo Kombiwagen haben.	A good teacher should have a nice Volvo station wagon.
Die intelligente Frau eines guten Lehrers sollte immer die Farbe des netten Volvos wählen.	The intelligent wife of a good teacher should always choose the color of the nice Volvo.

B   Each of the following blocks of sentences have been constructed based on the model.

Das Haus ist groß.	The house is large.
Das ist ein großes Haus.	That is a large house.
Das ist sogar das größte Haus der Welt.	That is even the largest house in the world.
Ich sehe ein großes Haus.	I see a large house.
Ich sehe das größte Haus der Welt.	I see the largest house in the world.

Die Professorin ist intelligent.	The professor is intelligent.
Das ist eine intelligente Professorin.	That is an intelligent professor.
Das ist sogar die intelligenteste Professorin der Welt.	That is even the most intelligent professor in the world.
Ich sehe eine intelligente Professorin.	I see an intelligent professor.
Ich sehe die intelligenteste Professorin der Welt.	I see the most intelligent professor in the world.

Der Hund ist freundlich.	The dog is friendly.
Das ist ein freundlicher Hund.	That is a friendly dog.
Das ist sogar der freundlichste Hund der Welt.	That is even the friendliest dog in the world.
Ich sehe einen freundlichen Hund.	I see a friendly dog.
Ich sehe den freundlichsten Hund der Welt.	I see the friendliest dog in the world.

Die Kinder sind nett.	The children are nice.
Das sind nette Kinder.	Those are nice children.
Das sind sogar die nettesten Kinder der Welt.	Those are even the nicest children in the world.
Ich sehe nette Kinder.	I see nice children.
Ich sehe die nettesten Kinder der Welt.	I see the nicest children in the world.

Die Katze ist alt.	The cat is old.
Das ist eine alte Katze.	That is an old cat.
Das ist sogar die älteste Katze der Welt.	That is even the oldest cat in the world.
Ich sehe eine alte Katze.	I see an old cat.
Ich sehe die älteste Katze der Welt.	I see the oldest cat in the world.

Die Studenten sind arm.	The students are poor.
Das sind arme Studenten.	Those are poor students.
Das sind sogar die ärmsten Studenten der Welt.	Those are even the poorest students in the world.
Ich sehe arme Studenten.	I see poor students.
Ich sehe die ärmsten Studenten der Welt.	I see the poorest students in the world.

Das Fenster ist schön.	The window is beautiful.
Das ist ein schönes Fenster.	That is a beautiful window.
Das ist sogar das schönste Fenster der Welt.	That is even the most beautiful window in the world.
Ich sehe ein schönes Fenster.	I see a beautiful window.
Ich sehe das schönste Fenster der Welt.	I see the most beautiful window in the world.

Der Audi ist technisch fortschrittlich.	The Audi is technically advanced.
Das ist ein technisch fortschrittlicher Audi.	That is a technically advanced Audi.
Das ist sogar der technisch fortschrittlichste Audi.	That is even the most technically advanced Audi.
Ich sehe einen technisch fortschrittlichen Audi.	I see a technically advanced Audi.
Ich sehe den technisch fortschrittlichsten Audi.	I see the most technically advanced Audi.

Der Prinz ist weit gereist.	The prince is well traveled.
Das is ein weit gereister Prinz.	That is a well-traveled prince.
Das ist sogar der am weitesten gereiste Prinz der Welt.	That is even the most well-traveled prince in the world.
Ich sehe einen weit gereisten Prinzen.	I see a well-traveled prince.
Ich sehe den am weitesten gereisten Prinzen der Welt.	I see the most well-traveled prince in the world.

C   Each of the following blocks of sentences have been constructed based on the model.

Das Dorf ist klein und freundlich.	The village is small and friendly.
Es gibt ein kleines freundliches Dorf.	There is a small, friendly village.
Ich wohne in einem kleinen freundlichen Dorf.	I live in a small, friendly village.

Das Land ist interessant und tolerant.	The country is interesting and tolerant.
Es gibt ein interessantes tolerantes Land.	There is an interesting, tolerant country.
Ich wohne in einem interessanten toleranten Land.	I live in an interesting, tolerant country.

Die Burg ist schneebedeckt.	The castle is covered in snow.
Es gibt eine schneebedeckte Burg.	There is a snow-covered castle.
Ich wohne in einer schneebedeckten Burg.	I live in a snow-covered castle.

Der Turm ist hoch.	The tower is high.
Es gibt einen hohen Turm.	There is a high tower.
Ich wohne in einem hohen Turm.	I live in a high tower.

Das Schloss ist elegant.	The palace is elegant.
Es gibt ein elegantes Schloss.	There is an elegant palace.
Ich wohne in einem eleganten Schloss.	I live in an elegant palace.

Die Wohnung ist klein aber hell.	The apartment is small but bright.
Es gibt eine kleine aber helle Wohnung.	There is a small but bright apartment.
Ich wohne in einer kleinen aber hellen Wohnung.	I live in a small but bright apartment.

Der Keller ist dunkel.	The cellar is dark.
Es gibt einen dunklen Keller.	There is a dark cellar.
Ich wohne in einem dunklen Keller.	I live in a dark cellar.

Das Hotel ist fein und teuer.	The hotel is fine and expensive.
Es gibt ein feines teueres Hotel.	There is a fine, expensive hotel.
Ich wohne in einem feinen teueren Hotel.	I live in a fine, expensive hotel.

Das Gasthaus ist gemütlich	The inn is cozy.
Es gibt ein gemütliches Gasthaus.	There is a cozy inn.
Ich wohne in einem gemütlichen Gasthaus.	I live in a cozy inn.

D   Each of the following blocks of sentences have been constructed based on the model.

Der Student ist jung.	The student is young.
Hallo! Junger Student! Achtung!	Hello! Young Student! Attention!
Ich frage den jungen Studenten.	I ask the young student.
Ich spreche mit dem jungen Studenten.	I speak with the young student.
Ich schreibe die E-Mail-Addresse des jungen Studenten auf.	I write down the email address of the young student.

Die Studentin sieht athletisch aus.	The student appears to be athletic.
Hallo! Athletisch aussehende Studentin! Achtung!	Hello! Athletic-looking student! Attention!
Ich frage die athletisch aussehende Studentin.	I ask the athletic-looking student.
Ich spreche mit der athletisch aussehenden Studentin.	I speak with the athletic-looking student.
Ich schreibe die E-Mail-Addresse der athletisch aussehenden Studentin auf.	I write down the email address of the athletic-looking student.

Die StudentInnen sind fleißig.	The students are hardworking.
Hallo! Fleißige Studenten! Achtung!	Hello! Hardworking students! Attention!
Ich frage die fleißigen Studenten und Studentinnen.	I ask the hardworking students.
Ich spreche mit den fleißigen Studentinnen und Studenten.	I speak with the hardworking students.
Ich schreibe die E-Mail-Adressen der fleißigen StudentInnen auf.	I write down the email addresses of the hardworking students.

Given those choices, *StudentInnen* seems to maximize representation and efficiency.

Die Professorin ist weltberühmt.	The professor is world famous.
Hallo! Weltberühmte Professorin! Achtung!	Hello! World-famous professor! Attention!
Ich frage die weltberühmte Professorin.	I ask the world-famous professor.
Ich spreche mit der weltberühmten Professorin.	I speak with the world-famous professor.
Ich schreibe die E-Mail-Adresse der weltberühmten Professorin auf.	I write down the email address of the world-famous professor.

Der Professor singt.	The professor is singing.
Hallo! Singender Professor! Achtung!	Hello! Singing professor! Attention!
Ich frage den singenden Professor.	I ask the singing professor.
Ich spreche mit dem singenden Professor.	I speak with the singing professor.
Ich schreibe die E-Mail-Adresse des singenden Professors auf.	I write down the email address of the singing professor.

Die ProfessorInnen lesen.	The professors are reading.
Hallo! Lesende ProfessorInnen! Achtung!	Hello! Professors who are reading! Attention!
Ich frage die lesenden ProfessorInnen.	I ask the professors who are reading.
Ich spreche mit den lesenden ProfessorInnen.	I speak with the professors who are reading.
Ich schreibe die E-Mail-Addressen der lesenden ProfessorInnen auf.	I write down the email addresses of the professors who are reading.

Der Graf ist edel.	The count is noble.
Hallo! Edler Graf! Achtung!	Hello! Noble count! Attention!
Ich frage den edlen Grafen.	I ask the noble count.
Ich spreche mit dem edlen Grafen.	I speak with the noble count.
Ich schreibe die E-Mail-Adresse des edlen Grafen auf.	I write down the email address of the noble count.

Die Gräfin ist gnädig.	The countess is gracious.
Hallo! Gnädige Gräfin! Achtung!	Hello! Gracious countess! Attention!
Ich frage die gnädige Gräfin.	I ask the gracious countess.
Ich spreche mit der gnädigen Gräfin.	I speak with the gracious countess.
Ich schreibe die E-Mail-Adresse der gnädige Gräfin auf.	I write down the email address of the gracious countess.

Die Grafen und Gräfinnen werden von allen geliebt.	The counts and countesses are loved by all.
Hallo! Von allen geliebte Grafen und Gräfinnen! Achtung!	Hello! Counts and countesses (who are) loved by all! Attention!
Ich frage die von allen geliebten Grafen und Gräfinnen.	I ask the counts and countesses (who are) loved by all.
Ich spreche mit den von allen geliebten Grafen und Gräfinnen.	I speak with the counts and countesses (who are) loved by all.
Ich schreibe die E-Mail-Addressen der von allen geliebten Grafen und Gräfinnen auf.	I write down the email addresses of the counts and countesses (who are) loved by all.

Someday everyone will be loved by all – that's the Graf von Anderson Advantage!

Index